I0657190

Thomas Thellusson Carter

The doctrine of confession in the Church of England

Thomas Thellusson Carter

The doctrine of confession in the Church of England

ISBN/EAN: 9783337262020

Printed in Europe, USA, Canada, Australia, Japan

Cover: Foto ©Lupo / pixelio.de

More available books at **www.hansebooks.com**

THE DOCTRINE OF CONFESSION

IN THE

CHURCH OF ENGLAND.

THE

DOCTRINE OF CONFESSION

IN THE

CHURCH OF ENGLAND.

BY THE

REV. T. T. CARTER, M.A.,

RECTOR OF CLEWER, BERKS.

LONDON:
JOSEPH MASTERS, ALDERSGATE STREET,
AND NEW BOND STREET.
MDCCCLXV.

LONDON :
JOSEPH MASTERS AND SON, PRINTERS,
ALDERSGATE STREET.

TO THOSE,

WHETHER LIVING OR DEPARTED,

INTO WHOSE LABOURS WE HAVE ENTERED,

WHO THROUGH EVIL REPORT AND GOOD REPORT,

HAVE WON BACK THIS LOST PORTION OF OUR INHERITANCE,

WHICH EVIL DAYS HAD FORFEITED,

SO BLESSED TO MANY WHO HAVE NEEDED AND HAVE FOUND

ITS HEALING VIRTUE,

THIS VOLUME

IS WITH RESPECTFUL AFFECTION

DEDICATED.

CONTENTS.

THE DOCTRINE OF CONFESSION
IN THE CHURCH OF ENGLAND.

PRELIMINARY CHAPTER.

NO question affecting the Church of England can be fairly considered, except by connecting together its earlier and its later history, as presenting different phases of one living body, holding in substance the same truth. It was not the purpose of the English Reformation to ignore the traditions of the past, the changes which then took place being avowedly grounded on an appeal to an earlier standard. Its object, as the oft-repeated declarations of its leaders abundantly testify, was to correct abuses, and remove novelties of doctrine or practice, which had grown up during the middle ages at variance with primitive revelation.

It is but one instance of this fundamental principle, that our existing formularies are framed upon the ancient service books of the Catholic Church. They profess to be, and are, at least in their essential features, a reconstruction of its traditionary system; and only on this ground they claim our allegiance.

The following declarations selected from the authoritative documents of the period, are sufficiently con-

B

clusive on this point, and, having special reference to the changes made in the Order for the Administration of Sacraments, they bear with peculiar force on our immediate subject. In the Preamble to the Act of Edward VI., "for the Uniformity of Prayer and Administration of Sacraments," it is stated that "the Archbishop of Canterbury, with several others of the most learned Bishops and Divines, commissioned to draw up an Office for all the parts of the Divine Service, were charged that in doing this they were to have a regard to the direction of Holy Scripture and the usage of the Primitive Church."[1] The same principle is embodied in the reply given, A.D. 1551, to a letter soliciting of the king and council, on behalf of the Princess Mary, the free exercise of her religion: "We use the ceremonies, observations, and sacraments of our religion, as the Apostles and first Fathers of the Primitive Church did."[2] Queen Elizabeth gave the same assurance to the Emperor and foreign princes, who interfered in favour of the ejected Bishops: "There was no new faith propagated in England; no religion set up, but that which was commanded by our SAVIOUR, practised by the Primitive Church, and unanimously approved by the Fathers of the best antiquity."[3]

This principle, adopted as the basis of our formularies, must of necessity also be taken as the rule of their interpretation. It would have been schismatical to esta-

---

[1] Collier, vol. ii. p. 263, fol. edit., or vol. v. p. 306, 8vo. edit.

[2] Wheatley, Common Prayer, Appendix to Introduction.

[3] Collier, vol. ii. p. 436, fol. edit., or vol. vi. pp. 263—264, 8vo. edit. See a catena of similar passages in Mr. Heathcote's "Documentary Illustrations of the Principles to be kept in view in the interpretation of the Thirty-nine Articles."

blish a new system of belief or worship; for the Church of England, as a branch of the Church Catholic, could not—the Church Catholic itself cannot—construct new ordinances of grace, or alter the essential features of those originally constituted. It were no less schismatical, while retaining the ancient forms, to force on them a new meaning, for it is in effect the same thing, to invent new forms, or to use the old in a new sense.

It follows from these premises, that in our present inquiry, reference must needs be made to the earlier usages of the Church. And such reference will bear on two points; (1) the interpretation of doubtful passages, if such there be, occurring in our formularies; and (2) the supplying answers to questions which may arise where the Church of the Reformation period is silent.

In the quickenings of a deeper life which it has pleased GOD mercifully to awaken in us, a revived desire has been felt for the restoration of "godly discipline," an answer we may trust to the solemn "wish" uttered by our Church year by year continually;[1] and many among us stirred by a keener sense of sin, have been drawn to seek "the benefit of absolution," and spiritual guidance, offered at all times by our Church in her public offices, though suffered for many years to fall into disuse in practice.

These quickenings have led to a revived study of sacramental[2] Confession, with special anxious searchings

[1] "In the Primitive Church there was a Godly discipline" . . . . "instead whereof, until the said discipline may be restored again, which is much to be wished," &c. Commin. Service.

[2] "Sacramental confession" means "confession made to a Priest," as distinguished from confession made direct to GOD; so named, because

B 2

of heart on the part of those who desire, in their views regarding it, to adhere loyally to the teaching and spirit of our Church. Such anxiety has been the occasion of the inquiry, the results of which are embodied in the following pages.

On such a momentous question, no apology, the writer trusts, is needed for adding yet one more to the many treatises which have already appeared. The present work does not profess to contain any fresh matter or novel interpretations. It is simply an attempt to arrange in order, and present as a connected whole, facts and arguments more or less familiar to every one who has studied the questions at issue. Little indeed that is new can be added to the mass of materials, bearing on the subject, which have, from time to time, been brought forward in explanation of the mind of the Church of England in this matter, and only through the aid thus provided could the writer have ventured to undertake this work. He is most grateful to those whose previous labours have accumulated references and quotations of the utmost value, which constant pressure of active duty would have prevented his obtaining without such assistance. In availing himself of such aid his earnest desire has been to regulate his conclusions by the consensus of authorities to which we have been accustomed to look, as the truest exponents of the Church side in the doctrinal controversies of the last three centuries, and he would wish to retract by anticipation any opinion here expressed

of the grace promised to accompany the act of the Priesthood in the remission of sins. The term is so interpreted by Bishop Cosin in a passage subsequently quoted.

which can be proved to be at variance with their collec-
tive judgment. If in dealing with this much vexed
question he has advanced anything which needlessly
disturbs or tends to strife, he would most truly deplore
such a result. A question touching so closely the finer
elements and keener sensibilities of the secret life of
devout souls, if not tenderly and considerately handled,
must itself suffer, as well as cause sorest woundings
where one would most desire to promote peace. Such
an inquiry need not of itself involve such a result. A
clear understanding of the true bearings of the questions at issue, of the principles by which they must be
determined, and their relation to other questions of
practical religion, would naturally tend rather to quietness and confidence, if not by the removal of ungrounded
apprehensions and suspicions, at least by shewing the
honesty of purpose with which the disputed doctrine
or practice is vindicated.

It will be a ground of deepest thankfulness, if any of
the explanations or arguments here advanced serve in
any degree to save those who use confession from the
charge of undutifulness and disloyalty to the rule of the
communion to which they owe obedience, or to guard
them against the temptation to disparage such as are
seeking to live to God, perhaps with equal devotion, only
by other means. Both they who use and they who do
not use confession, may find within the Church of England ample assistance and encouragement for their respective spiritual needs, and thus may strive together
in love for their common hope in the Gospel. For
while we cannot too earnestly desire that all who have
sinned grievously against grace, so as to hinder peaceful

communion with their LORD, should be led, according to all true ancient precedent, to ensure their restoration by Confession and the grace of Absolution, we may trust that, for others who have not so sinned, the freedom of choice allowed among us may be helpful, whether Confession be used or not,—the recommendation of its use tending to promote self-distrust in those who use it not, by the constant suggestion of its possible need, and, on the other hand, the encouragement given to the soul's secret intercourse with GOD alone, acting as a warning to those who use Confession against its possible abuse in the loss of the consciousness of personal responsibility, and of the need of personal effort.

Further, the writer would rejoice, if in days when such a strong tendency exists to distrust the Church of England's power to provide for the inner needs of the soul, and to disparage her rule and principles in contrast with the powerful system pressing upon her so closely, from which nevertheless she is unhappily at present constrained to stand apart,—if at such a time he should succeed in convincing any thus in doubt, that there were at the time of the Reformation overwhelming reasons for a change in the penitential discipline which then prevailed in England; and moreover, that after making all fair allowance for the difficulties unavoidably attending any attempts to rule and systematise matters so closely touching the inner life, where liberty is most forcibly claimed, and can be most effectually asserted by every man within the fence of his own conscience,—the Church of England has nevertheless, through GOD's blessing, held her way wisely and considerately amidst most perplexed, entangled controversies, while yet she

has carefully secured adequate means alike for release
from guilt, and for the promotion of a manly piety, insisting on the use of Confession as far as is consistent
with the purest traditions of antiquity, and withholding
a more absolute rule only because experience has sufficiently proved, that in the present temper of men's
minds, occasioned in no small degree by the very enforcement of a more authoritative system during the ages preceding the Reformation, such a course would but provoke
a re-action more detrimental to piety than the present
abeyance of the Church's legitimate discipline, sad as
its consequences unquestionably are; and the more so,
because such discipline, where it is attempted, can be
upheld only by motives and doctrines having, as we think,
no warrant whatever in the Divine revelation " once
delivered" to us, for which the Church was charged by
the Apostles to " contend earnestly."

CHAPTER I.

THE TESTIMONY OF HOLY SCRIPTURE.

THE relief of a burdened conscience by the open acknowledgment of its guilt, is an instinct of natural piety. The recorded dealings of Almighty God with the first penitents of our race, implied it.[1] His appearing to Adam and Eve in visible Form, and by questioning leading them to open declaration of their transgression, and again to Cain with the same object in view, involves the principle of Confession in its simplest rudiments. The same original use is proved by the fact, that there is no express enactment establishing Confession in the Mosaic law; there are only regulations which manifestly imply a previously existing practice. Confession resembles in this respect many other ordinances in use among the Israelites, which, taking their rise in an unknown antiquity, were adopted and sealed with a new authority in the Law. Thus, e.g., sacrifice, insti-

---

[1] "The LORD GOD called unto Adam, and said unto him, Where art thou? . . . Who told thee that thou wast naked? Hast thou eaten of the tree, &c.? . . . And the LORD GOD said unto the woman, What is this that thou hast done? . . . And the LORD said unto Cain, Where is Abel thy brother? . . . What hast thou done?"—Gen. iii. 9—13; iv. 9, 10. In each case, the acknowledgment of the transgression, though already clearly marked by the all-seeing Eye of GOD, must be drawn forth from the lips of the transgressor, thus condemning himself.

tuted as soon as sin was committed,[1] was afterwards reduced to an elaborate system in the detailed appointments of the Levitical ritual. Confession was always closely connected with sacrifice in the provisions of the Law, and is in like manner traceable to the beginning, coeval with the first penitential act of fallen humanity.

Hooker thus briefly explains the practice of Confession according to the regulations of the Mosaic Covenant. " The law imposed upon them (the Israelites) that special Confession which they in their books called confession of that particular fault, for which we namely seek pardon at GOD's hands. The words of the Law concerning Confession in this kind are as followeth ; ' When a man or woman shall commit any sin that men commit, and transgress against the LORD, their sin which they have done,' (that is to say, the very deed itself in particular,) ' they shall acknowledge,' (Numb. v. 6.) In Leviticus, after certain transgressions there mentioned, we read the like ; ' When a man hath sinned in any one of these things, he shall then confess how in that thing he hath offended,' (Lev. v. 5.) For such kind of special sins they had also special sacrifices, wherein their manner was, that the offender should lay his hand on the head of the sacrifice which he brought, and should there make confession to GOD, saying, ' Now, O LORD, that I have offended, committed sin, and done wickedly in Thy sight, this and this being my fault ; behold, I repent me, and am utterly ashamed of my

[1] For the full confirmation of this truth, see Magee on the " Atonement," and Mr. Freeman's " Principles of Divine Service," Vol. II., passim.

B 3

doings; my purpose is never to return more to the same crime.' Finally, there was no man amongst them at any time, either condemned to suffer death, or corrected, or chastised with stripes, nor even sick and near his end, but they called upon him to repent and confess his sins. Of malefactors convicted by witnesses, and thereupon adjudged to die, or otherwise chastised, their custom was to exact, as Joshua did of Achan, open confession; 'My son, give glory to the LORD GOD of Israel, confess unto Him, and declare unto me what thou hast committed, conceal it not from me.' "[1]

The Levitical law is most express as to the necessity for special cleansing after special sins. The law could indeed provide no remedy for sins of a deadly character, and of these therefore there is no mention; but of such as fell within its limited scope, the enumeration is sufficiently full to show the universal application of these remedial provisions. They applied both to the clergy and people alike, and to people of the highest equally as to those of a lower social grade. Be it observed, moreover, that neither the solemn paschal offering, nor the annual day of atonement, nor the regular morning and evening oblations, sufficed for the cleansing of these special sins of individuals. Each separate offender, however faithfully he might join in the regular oblations in union with the congregation, must nevertheless seek his own special cure through sacrifices of atonement applied to his particular case.

Thus, " if the priest that is anointed do sin according to the sin of the people; then let him bring for his sin which he hath sinned a young bullock without blemish

---

[1] Eccles. Pol., l. vi., c. iv. 4, or Vol. III. part 1, p. 23, (Keble's Edit.)

unto the LORD for a sin-offering,"[1] &c.   " When a ruler hath sinned, and done somewhat through ignorance against any of the commandments of the LORD his GOD, . . . and is guilty; or if his sin, wherein he hath sinned, come to his knowledge, he shall bring his offering,"[2] &c. " And if any one of the common people sin through ignorance, while he doeth somewhat against any of the commandments of the LORD . . . . and be guilty; or if his sin, which he hath sinned, come to his knowledge : then he shall bring his offering,"[3] &c.   " If a soul sin, and hear the voice of swearing . . . . if he do not utter it," &c.; " if a soul touch any unclean thing," &c.; " or if a soul swear, pronouncing with his lips to do evil, or to do good," &c.; . . . " and it shall be, when he shall be guilty in one of these things, that he shall confess that he hath sinned in that thing, and he shall bring his trespass offering unto the LORD for his sin,"[4] &c.

The special personal cleansing through special personally applied sacrifices must thus, in each case, be superadded to the regular ordinances in which the penitent might join together with the assembled congregation.   No doubt these special sacrificial rites had their bearing on the need of individual souls preserving their personal hold continually, each man for himself, on the One true Atonement, his being an integral portion of the Congregation of Israel not being enough to ensure his personal interest in the benefits of the Atonement, without an individual application also of its virtues; nevertheless, the fact remains with its typical bearing on the Gospel life, which the law foreshadowed, that individual

---

[1] Lev. iv. 3, &c.   [2] Lev. iv. 22, &c.
[3] Lev. iv. 27, &c.   [4] Lev. v. 1—10

sacrifices accompanied by confession of the fault were required as the means ordained for the personal application of the promised grace.

Confession bears to the Christian system precisely the same relation that it bore to the Mosaic Covenant. No express enactment appointed it. It is not mentioned among the new ordinances of the Spirit. It appears at the very opening of the Gospel, as a practice already existing, a fixed universal law, a feeling, the natural expression of penitence, which taken up into the Christian life was thus again stamped with a new Divine authority.[1] The commission[2] of the Christian Priesthood, "Whosoever sins ye remit," &c., did not institute, but in itself implicitly involved, the practice of Confession; for, having been required throughout the Mosaic dispensation as a necessary condition, at least in certain cases, for the remission of sins, its continuance in a similar connexion with the corresponding ministry of reconciliation under the new dispensation, would consequently be understood to be implied, unless expressly excluded. And again for a more convincing and more vital reason. Such a commission could not possibly be exercised in its direct personal application to individual souls, with assurance to them of such application, unless

---

[1] Thus, e.g., we read;—"John did baptise in the wilderness, and preach the baptism of repentance for the remission of sins. And there went out unto him all the land of Judæa, and they of Jerusalem, and were all baptised of him in the river of Jordan, confessing their sins." —S. Mark i. 4, 5.

[2] The Council of Trent grounds the absolute necessity of Confession on this commission, but for a very different reason. See chap. iii., where this difference is explained.

their secret state were sufficiently known to the Priest to enable him to form a judgment as to their fitness, and such knowledge could not ordinarily be had without confession.

On this ground Bishop Cosin, commenting on the first Exhortation in the Communion Office, observes that " confession of sins must necessarily be made to them to whom the dispensation of the mysteries of GOD is committed," and quotes S. Basil adducing New Testament authority for the statement : " For so they which in former times repented among the saints are said to have done. It is written in the Gospel that they confessed their sins unto S. John Baptist.[1] (S. Matt. iii. 6.) In the Acts they all confessed their sins unto the Apostles, of whom they were baptized. (Acts xix. 18.)" Cosin adds S. Augustine's application of a passage of S. Paul: " He that willingly judgeth himself, lest against his will he be judged of the LORD, let him come to the priests, by whom the keys are ministered unto him in the Church, and receive of them that have the oversight of the Sacraments, the manner of his satisfaction."[2]

[1] S. John Baptist, not being a priest, yet receiving confessions, was not an exception to a general rule, but, according to Jewish custom, the special case of a prophet gathering disciples devoting themselves to a new and advanced form of life. Lange says : " It was his mission to restore the community as members of the old economy, in order to present them pure and set apart for the transition into the kingdom of heaven. What he required of the people was in perfect accordance with that mission. Each individual was to purify himself as an Israelite, to change his mind in earnest repentance, and in consequence to put away the evil of his life," &c. Lange's Life of CHRIST. Part iii., sec. 11. (John the Baptist.) Clark: Edinburgh.

[2] Notes on the Book of Common Prayer, Cosin's works, vol. v. p. 9. Library of Anglo-Catholic Divines.

The cardinal text, however, which of all others in the New Testament bears most fully on the subject, is that of S. James : "Is any sick among you? let him call for the elders of the Church, and let them pray over him, anointing him with oil in the Name of the LORD; and the prayer of faith shall save the sick, and the LORD shall raise him up; and if he have committed sins, they shall be forgiven him. Confess your faults one to another, and pray one for another, that ye may be healed. The effectual fervent prayer of a righteous man availeth much."[1]

It has been urged, that this injunction, expressed as it is only in general terms, refers but to the acknowledgment of faults by one man to another under any circumstances, and is therefore irrespective of a priestly ministry. That the passage includes all modes of confession, may readily be granted, but it can scarcely be questioned, that its primary and special reference is to the exercise of an appointed ministry. The injunction to confess, is given in intimate connection with the order to "call for the elders of the Church." The penitent's being "healed," the consequence of confession and prayer, is represented as identical with his "sins being forgiven him" in the preceding verse. Accordingly our best ritualists have understood sacerdotal absolution to be here intended. "Absolution," says Dean Comber, "seems to be positively enjoined by S. James to be given to the sick penitent by the priest that comes to pray over him; for the Apostle adds, 'and if he have committed sins, remission or absolution shall be given him,' which is the right

[1] S. James v. 13—16.

translation of the impersonal word used in the original, and the practice of the primitive Church (the
best of commentaries) confirms this exposition, they
being always wont to grant absolution to all sorts of
penitents lying in danger of death."[1] · Comber, moreover, is of opinion, that the expression, "a righteous
man," is used by S. James in this passage as synonymous with "a minister of GOD." The phrase, one
to another, he adds, "may seem to allow us to confess
to any, yet the use of those words elsewhere assures us
that they are to be limited according to the preceding
matter; so 'be subject one to another' is meant only
of inferiors to superiors, and 'use hospitality one to
another,' is meant only of the rich to the poor, even as
here 'confess one to another' is the people to 'the
elders of the Church,' for to them only CHRIST committed the power of binding and loosing, and 'when a
man is overtaken in a fault, he that is spiritual must restore him;' and this was so received a doctrine in the
primitive times, that the confession of sins to a priest, in
the case of a troubled conscience, was esteemed an
Apostolical constitution."[2] Bishop Wilson takes the
same view of the passage, grounding his interpretation
on the authority of Hammond: "If we have committed sins against GOD, these are to be confessed to
the elders of the Church, and ἀφεθήσεται αὐτῷ, he shall be
absolved, or absolution shall be given him (Hammond),
i.e., upon his confession."[3] Marshall also confirms this

[1] Fol. 750. Quoted by Stretton, "Guide to the Infirm, &c."
[2] On the Offices, pp. 309, 310.
[3] Notes on the Holy Scripture, Bishop Wilson's Works. Anglo-
Cath. Lib., vol. v. 667.

interpretation, referring to the system of clinical confession, i.e., confession of the sick, in the primitive Church, with which in his judgment this passage closely corresponds. "Considering the known usage of the penitential confession, which was indeed a confession to one another, i.e., a confession in the face of the Church, I cannot help understanding S. James as having here in his view the process of clinical penance." . . . . "According to S. James the course was this: some elder of the Church was to be called for, and was to offer up the prayer of the persons then present on the behalf of the sick, who, for his own part was exhorted to confess his sins in the presence of that elder, and of the other bystanders, and thus all in their turns were to confess their faults to each other, whenever this occasion shall call them to it. These passages are all apparently connected, and have a mutual relation; and the whole process of this affair, as here represented, was exactly agreeable to the practice which afterwards succeeded. Nor is there anything extraordinary in the passage of S. James, which was not afterwards adopted into the standing usages of the Church, except only what related to the miraculous cure of the distemper."[1]

Bingham[2] indeed quotes S. Augustine, to prove that the Apostle's injunction refers to confession of a fault by one Christian man to another. But it does not follow, because the passage admits this wide interpretation, that it may not also include confession to a Priest. Jeremy Taylor takes this same wide view of the passage as gene-

[1] Marshall, Penitential Discipline of the Primitive Church, p. 81. Library of Anglo-Cath. Theol.

[2] Orig. Eccl. 1. xviii., ch. iii., sec. v.

rally applicable to all kinds of confession, and yet considers it to have a specific bearing on confession to a
Priest. " S. James," he says, " gives an express precept, that we Christians should confess our sins to each
other, that is, Christian to Christian, brother to brother,
the people to their minister, and then he makes a spe-
cification of that duty which a sick man is to do when
he hath sent for the elders of the Church."[1]

Holy Scripture therefore leaves the question of Confession in the most general terms, affirming its principle, and its Divine origin, but defining nothing as to
the occasions, the extent, or the details of its practice.
Whether it should be public only, or both public and

---

[1] Holy Dying. Exhortation to move a sick man to confession, s. 20.
Roman divines generally deny the application of this passage to sacramental confession. An obvious motive tends to produce this bias ; for
ordinary Roman teaching assumes, that private Confession, as now practised, is the original institution ordained by our LORD, the public penance
a later introduction, resting only on Church authority. If the passage
of S. James applies at all to confession to a Priest, it must be to the
public penance, because the presence of many joining in the intercession
for the sick penitent is described. It would follow from hence, that the
public system is meant, and if so, this must be the original institution.
Hooker quotes Cajetan, as " denying that any other confession is meant
than only that which seeketh either association of prayers, or reconciliation, and pardon of wrongs ;" and he adds, that " the greatest
part" of Roman divines consider it "uncertain" whether sacramental
confession is meant. Yet Bellarmine takes the opposite view, and uses
the passage in support of Confession. De Pœnit. C. iii. c. 4, referred to
by Hooker. Hooker himself sets the text aside as arguing nothing in
favour of sacramental Confession, so far coinciding with the majority of
Roman divines, but being in this at variance with the stream of authority among our own, of whom some noted instances are given in the
text. Eccl. Pol. L. vi. ch. iv. 5.

private, and in what cases, under what conditions, and within what limits, it should be practised, and what are its due results,—all such questions are left undetermined. For the solution of them we must refer to the usages of the Church, the ground and principle of the ordinance being embodied in the Divine law, but its application entrusted to the decision of Ecclesiastical Councils, and the wisdom and experience of those to whom from age to age the cure of souls has been committed.

CHAPTER II.

THE penitential discipline, or as it was technically termed, the "Exomologesis,"[1] of the primitive Church is thus briefly described by Hooker. "There was," he says, " first the offender's intimation of those crimes to some one Presbyter, for which imposition of penance was sought; secondly, the undertaking of penance imposed by the Bishop; thirdly, after the same performed and ended, open confession to GOD in the hearing of the whole Church; whereupon ensued the prayer of the whole Church, then the Bishop's imposition of hands, and so the party's reconciliation, or restitution to his former right in the holy Sacraments."[2] Bingham quotes S. Cyprian to show that the reconciliation of penitents on a death-bed was administered in the same manner, only the accustomed penance was dispensed,[3] on condition, however, that it should be afterwards performed in case of recovery.

Hooker's account shows that the public penance in-

[1] The term means literally, "confession" or "open declaration;" but it was generally used to include the whole course of public penance. Etymologically it implies public, rather than private, confession. ἐξομολογέω, confiteor, Mark i., Matt. iii. Item palam profiteor et prædico, Esai. xlv., Psal. xviii. Item spondeo, i.e., dico me facturum, polliceor, Luc. xxii. Scap. Lex.

[2] Eccles. Pol. l. vi. ch. iv., sect. 13.   [3] Eccles. Ant. l. xix. ch. v. sec. iv.

volved previous private confession, made either for the purpose of determining whether public penance was necessary, or to obtain advice for its due performance. And this private confession was therefore necessarily, as Marshall observes, full and minute. "The party who thus confessed his private offences, must have opened them at large, or else the penitentiary" (or confessor) "could not judge of them, whether they needed such a cure or no."[1] Marshall moreover makes the important assertion, that in the earliest times there was no private confession, except in connexion with the public discipline. It was made, as he shows, either because the sin committed needed public penance, or else to relieve the mind of the penitent from the fear of having committed such sin. "It is true that all who mention the confession of secret sins, do it still with some eye of reference to public discipline. This Origen, Tertullian, and S. Cyprian, do all, as far as I can judge, agree in."[2] Morinus, who, of all theologians of the Latin Church,

---

[1] Marshall's Penit. Discipline, p. 39. Lib. Ang. Cath. Theol.

[2] Perrone, indeed, assumes a contrary view, asserting in opposition to the Jansenists, that private, or "sacramental," penance is to be distinguished from the public discipline as to their respective origin, the former alone, according to him, being appointed by our LORD, and so necessary, the latter by the Church in the course of the third century. But Perrone, be it noted, gives no proof whatever of such a distinction, nor does he refer to any ancient authority in support of his statement. He assumes a different historical order of events, indeed the very reverse of that which is here proved to have been the real order, supposing private to have preceded public penance, and represents the changes which the practice of Confession underwent in the course of time, as marks of a difference in kind. His bias is evident, to lower public and canonical penance, in order to exalt, and show the divine necessity of, the private ministry in contrast to the former. Tract. de Pœnit, c. iv., sec. 218—219.

has the most fully treated the whole subject of Confession, also supports this view. He shows in his elaborate exposition of the subject that there was in the beginning but one tribunal of penance, and that this only gradually after many centuries branched off into two courts, —the "forum externum," the court of Ecclesiastical discipline, and the "forum internum," the secret confession to a Priest, as they exist in the present practice of the Church. Morinus further asserts it to be a fact, "clear as the midday light," that the many exhortations to penance occurring in the writings of the Fathers relate always to the public canonical discipline.[1] Among various authorities for this assertion, he quotes S. Augustine to prove that, in his day, public penance being allowed once only in a life-time, if this failed to effect its object, the relapsed person was left to the mercy of God, no allusion being made to any separate private tribunal of penance as still open to him,[2] and implying therefore that no such alternative then existed. The question relates to the more grievous sins which needed the exomologesis, because, as will afterwards be seen, lesser sins

[1] Hæc omnia luce meridiana fulgentius ostendunt S. Ambrosium cæterosque patres, quum toties pœnitentiæ actiones urgent, ad solemnem vel saltem canonicam respexisse. L. iv., c. vii. xi.

[2] Fatetur quoque Augustinus semel tantum humilem illam pœnitentiam concedi . . . . An recurrit Augustinus ad solvendam Macedonii objectionem ad iteratam sed privatim pœnitentiam, quæ erat propositio, si ex usu fuisset, ad objectionis dissolutionem expeditissime? Longa est Epistola (Epis. 54); varia in ea tractantur, et retractantur, sed de hac re ne verbum quidem. Ad Dei misericordiam confugit semper. . . . . Unicum remedium post actam publice pœnitentiam proponit, ad hoc amplectandum criminis Pœnitentes tantum exhortantur. Ad secundam vero pœnitentiam privatim aut publice ab Ecclesia propositam, nunquam. L. v. cxxx., s. iv.

might be dealt with in private confession without such discipline, but in this case, without being followed by the formal absolution of the Church; for Morinus adds the important circumstance that in primitive times absolution was not given except in public,[1] a fact indeed necessarily involved in the former, because absolution, being the reconciliation of the penitent following upon the due performance of penance, if the one were only publicly administered, so neither could be the other, at least in the case of the whole, special provision being always made, as has been already shown, for the dying.

Dr. Pusey maintains the same position with an overwhelming mass of evidence, proving, moreover, the momentous point in the questions pending between us and Rome, that the main stress laid by the Fathers was on "the act of public penance," not on "mere confession."

Dr. Pusey defines the "exomologesis" to be "a course of public penance, whereby the penitent humbles himself before God." "Confession," he adds, "is rather incidentally involved in it (in that such a course could not be entered upon without it), than an integral part of it, or required for its own sake." "The point at issue," as he observes, "between the Romanists and ourselves as to Confession, relates (as themselves admit) not to its general advantage, or its necessity in particular cases, or its use as a means of discipline, or the desirableness of public confession before the whole Church, or the great difficulty of true penitence often without it, or the duty of individuals to comply with it, if the Church require it; but it is whether confession to men

[1] Nam si Pœnitentia negatur, multo magis absolutio, cum Pœnitentia tantum imperetur, ut absolutionem impetret. Ib. s. ix.

THE TESTIMONY OF ANTIQUITY.

be so essential to absolution that the benefit of absolution cannot be had without it." "Public penitence implied confession before man, in part also to the priest,
who had to decide whether certain cases required a course
of public penitence or no; it implied that the penitent
at the close of his public penitence, and before his re-
admission to communion, should bewail his sins before
the priest in presence of the congregation, and receive
absolution from him; since also this was the prescribed
discipline of the Church, one who withdrew himself
from it, for fear of the public shame, had reason to fear
that he shrunk also from the necessary discipline of
humiliation. Again, the penitent by shrinking from
public penitence, lost the continual intercessions of the
congregation." . . . . "The Roman theologians insist
on private confession as essential, on the authority of
the Fathers, when these are insisting on public humiliation, or on private, with a view to public, confession,
and this of flagrant overt sins of a more deadly nature."

Dr. Pusey thus sums up the objects of Confession, as
held of old: "In all the places in which the Fathers
speak of the necessity of confession, they have regard
to it, (1) as the door to a course of public penance
which humbled the penitent, subjected him to a healthful
discipline (which, privately, it was to be feared, few
would practise,) and kept him for a while from the Holy
Communion which might be hurtful to him; (2) as
obtaining for individuals spiritual counsel for the specific
case of each; (3) as gaining the intercession of the
Church and so of CHRIST."[1]

---

[1] Notes L. and M. on Tertullian, Vol. i. pp. 377—380. Library of the
Fathers. These most valuable disquisitions, on the term "exomologesis,"

Two facts therefore may be considered to be established, (1) that the original penitential system, the only one known to the Church of the primitive ages, was the public discipline; (2) that private confession was then in frequent use, but only in connexion with the public discipline, and not as a means of obtaining private absolution.

Nothing is intended to be implied in what has been said, as to the comparative frequency of public or private confession. The only point insisted on is the dependence of the private on the public system, and therefore its subordination to it. Private confession must necessarily have been the more frequent of the two, if only from the fact that private confession might be made, and no public penance follow. Of the amount of frequency no judgment can be formed, except by estimating the influences tending to promote it, and the encouragement given to it by the clergy. Hooker says, " Private and voluntary repentance (under which term he includes confession) was of far more general use, whereas public was incident unto few, and not oftener than once incident to any."[1] A well known passage of S. Jerome proves, that private confession was encouraged whenever the mind was disturbed with the fear of deadly sin, but still only with reference to the possible need of public penance. " Consider," he says,

and on the " absolute necessity of Confession," ought to be carefully studied by any one desirous of understanding with accuracy the detailed view of the teaching of the Fathers, and the precise meaning of the terms they were accustomed to use on these vexed points of primitive practice.

[1] Eccl. Pol. l. vi., c. iv., s. 11; or vol. iii., pt. 1, p. 52. Keble's Edit. Some are of opinion that public penance might be repeated, but *not for the same sin*, or an offence of the same kind. (See Marshall, p. 23.)

"what the Holy Scripture teaches us, that we ought
not to conceal our sin within our own breast. For perhaps, as they who are inwardly oppressed with the
humour or phlegm of undigested meat, which lies heavy
upon the stomach, if they vomit it up, are relieved; so
they who have sinned, if they hide and conceal their
sin within themselves, are inwardly oppressed and
almost suffocated with the phlegm and humour of sin;
but if any become his own accuser, and confess his sin,
in so doing, he, as it were, vomits up his sin, or rejects
and removes the cause of his distemper. Try first the
physician to whom thou art to reveal the cause of thy
distemper, and see that he be one who knows how to be
weak with him that is weak, and to weep with him that
weeps; one who understands the discipline of condoling
and compassionating; that so at length if he shall say
anything who hath first showed himself to be both a
skilful and a merciful physician, and give thee any
counsel, thou mayest cleave and follow it. If he discern and foresee thy distemper to be such as will need
to be declared and cured in the full assembly of the
Church, whereby others perhaps may be edified, and
thou thyself healed; this is to be done with great de-
liberation and the prudent advice of such a physician."[1]
Bingham refers to S. Gregory of Nyssa, S. Basil, &c.,
for similar teaching.[2]

2. Further, whatever may have been the amount of
frequency with which private Confession was practised,

[1] Homil. ii. on Ps. xxxvii., quoted by Bingham. Eccl. Ant. l. xviii.
ch. iii. sec. 8.
[2] Ibid. l. xviii. ch. iii. sec. 7.

C

it is clear that, with the exception at least of overt and grievous sins, to which the public discipline properly applied, it was strictly voluntary. The public discipline could be enforced according to the canons, on pain of excommunication. Sins for which it was due, if notorious, might be charged on the offender by the Priest acting on his own knowledge, or on the information of others; and such sins would consequently become the subject matter of Confession, as part of the enforced discipline, and so far necessary; but secret or unknown sins, and sins of thought, were confessed, or not, at the will of the offender.

It is unnecessary to multiply evidence on this point after the full array of quotations adduced by Dr. Pusey. A few instances will suffice to show the weight of proof bearing upon it. Dr. Pusey quotes, among other Fathers, Origen, who " distinguishes sins into two classes, one for which public penitence was done, and there was public excommunication; the other, (mental sins) came under the cognizance of God only, and the sinner is by Him excommunicated by the withdrawal of His HOLY SPIRIT," (Hom. 2, in Jud. § 5,)—S. Augustine who distinguishes from the sins figured by the death of Lazarus, "a grievous wound, deadly, mortal," sins of concupiscence, of those "who have the sin within, in the heart, not as yet in deed," and these having sinned within, are he says, "like Jairus's daughter, raised within. This resurrection of the soul takes place within, in the secret places of the conscience," (Serm. 98, in Luc. vii. § 5,) healed, i.e., without Confession, within the soul by CHRIST Himself;—S. Cyprian (de Laps. civ.) who "praised those who did penance for, and therewith confessed, the thought of denying the faith, implying that they were not ecclesiastically bound so to do ;" S. Chrysostom exhorting thus, " But now it is not even necessary to confess before witnesses. Be the examination of transgression in the thoughts of conscience, be the judgment seat unwitnessed, let GOD alone see thee confessing, GOD Who upbraideth not sins, but remitteth sins on confession,"—passages which, as Dr. Pusey observes, are altogether inconsistent with any law or custom of compulsory confession.[1]

3. According to the ancient penitential system sins were classified under three heads. The two-fold division into mortal and venial sins belonged to a later period. The earlier classification was into sins grievous, sins most grievous, and sins less grievous.[1] Idolatry, adultery and homicide were generally held to form the most grievous class.[2] Sins considered to be of less magnitude, which yet would be included under the general and indefinite term, deadly, were placed in the second class. Faults, the incursions of which are felt more or less by all, constituted the third, or less grie-

[1] See Note M. on "the Absolute Necessity of Confession," passim, specially p. 379.

[2] Antiqui Christiani, quantum legendo et conjiciendo possumus assequi, peccata in tres tantum classes distinguebant, levia, gravia, et gravissima, quibus purgandis, et castigandis tria tantum constituerunt pœnarum, sive alexipharmacarum, genera. Mori. l. iv. c. ii.

[3] The first class, or most grievous sins, were also called " capital," sometimes " mortal," sometimes " canonical," as being specially the subject matter of canonical discipline. Ibid. l. v. c. i. ii. There were certain variations in different places, or ages. E.g., S. Cyprian reckons as the three, " adultery, fraud, homicide," (de Pat. c. 9,) ; S. Augustine, " murders, thefts, adulteries" (iv. 12 in Joann.). Note M. in Tertul.

c 2

vous, class. Corresponding with these three classes of
sins, there were three different modes of spiritual healing. The first class alone were by the canons necessarily subject to the public discipline, although penance
was often voluntarily undergone for sins of the second
class. Morinus quotes S. Augustine (de fide et operibus,
ad fin.) thus briefly distinguishing the ordinary modes
of dealing with the three classes of sin. "The first is
chastised (plectitur,) by penance, the second by bro-
therly correction; the third and lightest, without which
this life cannot be passed" . . . "the daily prayer of
the faithful reconciles (satisfacit)."[1] Morinus also quotes
S. Pacian, as to the different remedies for the first and
second classes of sin. "First, there are three deadly
or capital sins, for which canonical and public penance
is undergone, to which forgiveness is imparted only with
great difficulty, after many labours have been borne.
Secondly, other sins in their own nature deadly, i.e.,
deserving hell and everlasting death, but not specified
in the canons, and for which, therefore, that same laborious penance was not imposed, were healed by the

---

[1] L. iv. c. vii. 4. S. Augustine's words, quoted by Morinus, are, as
to the *first* class of sins : Est pœnitentia gravior, et luctuosior, in qua
proprie vocantur in Ecclesiâ pœnitentes, etiam remoti a sacramento al-
taris participando, ne accipiendo indignè judicium sibi manducent et
bibant . . . Adulterium forte commissum est, forte homicidium, forte aliquid sacrilegium. Gravis res, grave vulnus, lethale, mortiferum, sed
omnipotens medicina . . . Of the *second* class : Item si essent quædam,
non eâ humilitate pœnitentiæ sananda, qualis in Ecclesiâ datur eis qui
proprie pœnitentes vocantur, sed quibusdam correctionum medica-
mentis. Of the *third* class of sins : De quotidianis autem brevibus, levi-
busque peccatis, sine quibus hæc vita non ducitur, quotidiana oratio
fidelium satisfacit. Delet omnino hæc oratio minima et quotidiana
peccata.

counteraction (compensatione,) of the opposite virtues. Not but that this same healing was required in case of the three greater sins, but the Fathers held that, besides the remedies common to them with all other deadly sins, they needed other more efficacious, more laborious and more solemn modes of cure, known as the Penance."[1]   He also quotes S. Augustine, speaking more fully of the remedies of the third class of sins; "Sins which are not mortal, every one easily cures for himself by the recitation of the LORD's Prayer, and other good works,"[2] which in another place he specifies as "smiting the breast, giving of alms, a good disposition of heart towards GOD, and like actions."[3]

4. Penance always preceded absolution, the direct reverse of the later and modern use. It was imposed as a means of deepening repentance, and a test of its genuineness—a curative or remedial process for chastening and correcting the life. Its publicity formed a large part of its severity, and therefore of its value in humbling the penitent. Penance was not considered to be essential for the remission of sins,—in clinical repentance it was dispensed,—but as a discipline, partly for the correction of the penitent, partly for the sake of warning and example to others. "The Church for this reason instituted the stations of penitence, and exercised penitents with various labours and inflictions, not merely as punishments, but also in order that the wounds of the soul caused by sin might be healed by them, as by medicines, and that it might be judged by the fulfil-

[1] L. v. c. xxxi. sec. 8.   [2] Ibid. sec. 9.
[3] L. v. c. i. sec. 2.

ment of these external actions, how far the sin was healed."[1] Morinus shows by accumulated evidence that this principle obtained, and the rule ordinarily was observed, throughout the first seven centuries, exceptions being allowed only in special cases.[2] Thus, e.g., as he notes, after the Montanist and Novatian heresies had extended their influence, and the Church was forced by their stern criticism and rivalry to impose severer and longer penances, it was not uncommon, as a merciful mitigation of the newly added rules, to give absolution, while some portion of the penance yet remained to be fulfilled. Or, on the other hand, the fear of precipitating a penitent, too weak to bear the Penance, into schism, might lead the Priest altogether to dispense with it. Moreover, as the private system of dealing with penitents gradually superseded the public, a change to be hereafter more fully spoken of, then if the Priest were satisfied of the sincerity of the penitent, he might be disposed to absolve at once, the effect of penance as an example to others having ceased with the cessation of its publicity, and when its influence on the penitent alone needed to be considered. These, however, were manifestly exceptions to the general rule, and were allowed only as dispensations, on the belief that the repentance was sincere, the principle, equally as before, holding good, that penance was remedial, counteracting the effects of sin, and preparing the soul for a perfect reconciliation with GOD.

From this view of Penance, " the Fathers," as Morinus remarks, " much more frequently employed the term ' medici,' than ' judices,' in reference to Priests,

---

[1] Lib. ix. o. v. ec. 18.   [2] L. ix. c. iii. 1.

and spoke of penitential labours as medicines, imposed for the health of the soul, rather than as punishments."[1]   He quotes Maldonatus, allowing that "the
ancient Fathers very sparingly and seldom mention
punishment, as the object of penance; and that whenever they speak of satisfaction, it is not for punishment
(pro pœnâ), but for sin (pro culpâ").[2]   The importance
of marking this, the patristic, view of the object of Penance will be evident when we come to consider the
mediæval system.

5. The term "satisfaction" frequently occurs in the
writings of the Fathers, in connexion with penance.
But it is most important to note, that the Fathers did
not employ the term in the sense which it acquired in
the theology and popular use of later centuries.   Dr.
Pusey says; "The words 'satisfacere,' 'satisfactio,' when
used of works of repentance, have not in the Fathers
any technical sense, as in recent Romish theology, as
though the sinner anyhow made satisfaction to the
Divine justice; they simply mean 'make amends,' and
are used of such outward acts of contrition, as being
opposed to the former sins, serve to express and deepen
the repentance for them, and thereby turn away the
Divine wrath" . . . "It is used by the Fathers in connexion with all those habits of mind or actions, which
express contrition, without having in themselves any-

[1] L. iii. c. xii. sec. 24.

[2] Maldonatus proceeds to account strangely enough for this absence
of the mention of punishment.   Non quidem quod ignorarint hanc sa-
tisfactionem pro pœna, sed quod cum egissent tam accuratè de satisfactione pro culpa, quæ difficilior esset, *non putarint esse opus* agere de altera
satisfactione.   Mal. tom. 2, De Sacramentis, quoted L. iii. c. xi. sec. 14.

thing punitive, much less any payment to the Divine justice." The term as Dr. Pusey shows, was used, e.g. by Tertullian, of a " defiled dress," as the garb of " satisfaction," joining to it, "prostrating, humbling oneself;" by S. Cyprian, as connected with "holding fast humility," "prayer," "tears," "alms;" by S. Augustine, in referring to "the LORD's Prayer," and generally " of all acts of penitence, whether punitive or no;" by S. Ambrose, "as equivalent to verbal confession," "tears and groans," "turning to GOD;" by S. Gregory the Great, as equivalent to "revenge and its effects, solely with reference to its effect on the penitent,"— expressions which, as Dr. Pusey remarks, are strictly in accordance with the original sense of the word as pointed out by Heraldus (Dig. v. ii. 4,) i.e., " making amends by acknowledging a fault, when any one besought him whom he had offended, and confessed his fault in such wise, as to signify he was exceedingly sorry for it, and wished it had not been done." . . . In the same sense satisfaction was said to be given to the Church, when grieved and injured by the offence. In the technical language of Theology, the difference between the ancient and modern (Roman) doctrine, is represented by the terms, "satisfactio pro culpâ," and "satisfactio pro pœnâ," satisfaction for the fault, and satisfaction for the punishment due for it to the Divine justice. The former is the sense in which alone the term was known to the Fathers.

At the same time, as Dr. Pusey adds, "it is equally plain, that self-affliction in token of displeasure at one's sins, or as a means of keeping up that displeasure, was held by the ancient Church to be acceptable to GOD, and to turn away His wrath; and this truth they de-

rived from S. Paul's mention of 'revenge,' as a part
of penitence, (2 Cor. vii. 11.)"[1]

6. The opinion of the Fathers as to the value of Penance, and of the superior value of the public, in comparison with the private, dealing with penitents, is so
well known—their exhortations to its use so constant
and so urgent, — that it is unnecessary to adduce
testimony on this point. " That public and canonical
penance is most useful, and has the greatest efficacy in
obtaining from GOD the remission of sins, was immove-
ably fixed in the minds of the holy Fathers. They
often speak of its benefit and virtue as so essential, that
they seem to imply the impossibility of the worst sins
being healed without it. Unless the same opinion had
possessed generally the mind of the people, men would
not have sought, nay, demanded, to be admitted to
penance with so great ardour." . . . Again, " public canonical penance must have been esteemed of far greater
efficacy than private, for had both been attended with
equal results, who would have desired the public discipline ? Who would not have preferred the light yoke
of private penance to the severe bondage of the public
discipline ?"[2]   Moreover, the recommendation by the

---

[1] Note K. p. 369, on Tertull. passim.
[2] Morinus, l. v. c. vi. This view of the patristic belief of the superior value of public penance, at least of public confession, is not held
by all Roman divines. It has indeed been even questioned, whether
it is not of the essence of "sacramental confession" that it should be
" secret and auricular ;" so great has been the tendency to disparage
the public system of dealing with penitents in comparison with the
later use. However Estius, Suarez, Coninck, Townely, Berti, &c., take
the affirmative, arguing that confession, whether public or private,

Fathers of the confession even of secret sins, with the view of undergoing Penance, is clear and constant. Thus "Tertullian set himself to debate the point with such as through a false modesty endeavoured to conceal their crimes; and recommends penitence even for sins which as yet lurked only in the will, and were never ripened into action." "S. Cyprian commends the practice, even when there was no direct offence in the fact, but only a purpose of it; he imputes it to a liveliness and vigour of faith, and to an extraordinary degree of the fear of GOD."[1]

But however great the value which the Fathers set upon Penance, they regarded it, Morinus observes, only as a most effectual aid, not as a channel of grace so necessary that forgiveness could not be had without it. "It would be untrue, and absolutely contrary to the mind of all the Fathers, to conclude that salvation could not be obtained without the exercise of penance. They held in the fullest and most absolute sense the efficacy of true internal contrition. Their strong language in urging penance only implied, that the grace of contrition was far more likely to be obtained through its use than without it, and with less probability and increased difficulty, if it were deferred till the last days of life."[2]

equally avails. Billuart on the Summa S. Thomæ notes the question and gives the references. Vol. ix. Dissert. v. Art. 1. Billuart, however, asserts that the public confession of secret sins was never enjoined as a command, but that the private confession of them was so enjoined both by Divine and ecclesiastical law. Ibid. He gives instances from the Fathers (s. 2) of exhortations to the use of private confession of secret sins, such as are adduced in the text, but no further proof of his position as to the Divine injunction of secret confession.

[1] Marshall, Pen. Disc., c. ii. sec. 1.   [2] L. v. c. vi. xiii.

Morinus speaks of it as an axiom in theology, that "true contrition cannot fail to obtain the instant forgiveness of sin."[1] "It is, and always was, certain,

[1] Apud (Deum) nullas patitur moras vera conversio. L. ix. c. v. s. 5. Roman divines sometimes speak as though this principle could not be admitted, and that confession is as essential as contrition, or rather that no contrition is true which does not contain at least the will to confess. This will appear more fully in the next chapter in considering the Mediæval systems. Billuart (Summa S. Thomæ, Vol. ix. Dissert. v. Art. iii. s. 1) thus argues the case: "Neque refert remissionem peccatorum habere posse per contritionem ; quia primo ipsa confessio præcepta est a Christo, et quidem est medium necessarium ad hoc ; unde non est vera contritio quæ non includit votum confessionis." Yet this can hardly be meant to be taken absolutely; for the Catechism of the Council of Trent (Question xxxiv.) says: "Contrition itself can certainly never be otherwise than grateful and acceptable to GOD, according to the words of the Prophet, *A contrite and humble heart, O God, Thou wilt not despise.* Nay, more, that no sooner do we conceive this contrition in our hearts, than our sins are forgiven us by GOD, the same prophet elsewhere declares in these words : *I said, I will confess against myself my transgressions unto the Lord, and Thou forgavest the iniquity of my sin.* Of this we observe a figure in the ten lepers, who when sent by our LORD to the priests, were cured of their leprosy before they reached them ; giving us to understand, that such is the efficacy of true contrition, that by virtue thereof we obtain from the LORD the immediate pardon of all our sins." It is indeed added in Question xxxvi., "Granting, that by contrition sins are blotted out, who is ignorant that (to effect this) it must be so vehement, so intense, so ardent, as that the bitterness of our sorrow may be compared with and bear a proportion to the magnitude of our crimes ? But as this is a degree of contrition to which very few could reach, the consequence also was, that very few could have hoped thereby to obtain the pardon of their sins." The next question shows how confession was instituted in order to make contrition perfect—a doctrine of which more will be said in the succeeding chapter. (Buckley's translation.) It becomes therefore a question merely of degrees. True contrition is affirmed to be in itself alone sufficient to obtain the pardon of sins, but whether such contrition be possible, is doubted.

and even now is most frequently asserted (decantatissi-
mum) among the schoolmen, that so great may be the
contrition of a penitent even in a moment of time (tan-
tam esse posse uno momento Pœnitentis contritionem)
that it may avail to obtain the remission, not only of
the sin, but also of all the punishment." . . . . At the
same time this principle is affirmed only as a possible or
abstract truth, irrespective of the ordinary working of
grace in converting and healing sinners. "No one denies
the possibility of the instantaneous perfect conversion of
the most sinful, though all agree that such an occurrence
is most rare and extraordinary, and to be regarded as a
miracle, the ordinary law being, that sinners are con-
verted and return to GOD gradually, being slowly freed
from the power of sin, and that only after long and vehement conflicts between grace and evil desire, GOD reigns
in the heart, and the soul is justified; therefore, although
speaking with refined metaphysical subtlety, instantaneous justification may be said to be possible, it really
requires a long period, and many precedent preparatory
actions, the progress of grace varying in different persons, in some, it may be, the work of a few days, in
others, of many years."[1]

It appears, then, that according to ancient belief and
practice, the remission of sins after baptism, at least
those of the gravest kind, was ordinarily to be obtained
only through Penance, preferably through public Penance, and consequently with .the use of Confession,
as part of Penance, true repentance being held to be
always necessary as a condition of its profitable use.

[1] L. ix. c. v. sec. 2.

Holy Baptism was not supposed of itself by any pro-
spective or implied gifts to remedy its own losses in the
case of the excommunicate. Nor was the Blessed Sacrament of the Eucharist, though applying the full benefits of the Atonement, to be approached by those who
had thus fallen, without a previous cleansing. Penance
was held to be a distinct ordinance, having its own
proper place and efficacy, renewing the pure baptismal
position, and removing the hindrance which deadly sin
causes to the vivifying and spiritual reception of the
LORD's Blessèd Body and Blood.

Yet at the same time the unquestionable fact, that
Penance, and with it Confession, were not regarded
as absolutely obligatory, even in the case of the most
deadly sin, and that secret sins, though of a deadly
character, did not necessarily fall within the scope of
the canonical discipline, and further, a fact to be
afterwards considered, the suspension of the office of
Penitentiaries at Constantinople and in the East, in
the 5th century,—sufficiently prove that the remission of sin might, in the judgment of the Fathers,
be obtained without the use of such means. The
availing power of true contrition alone, through the
merits of CHRIST, was ever believed to be such that,
even in case of sins for which the law of the Church
properly required the Penance, grace overflowed its
ordinary channels in response to its appeal, through
direct and secret intercourse of the soul with GOD,
though the safer course, and that which reverent and
careful minds would ever follow, was through the ordained ministry of the commissioned Priesthood.

No difficulty was felt by the Fathers in the co-existence of these apparently conflicting principles. They acted and reacted mutually on each other, perfect trust being reposed on each revelation of the will of GOD, and truth resulting from the balance of their separate forces. The principle on which this view rests, is not confined to the question immediately before us. It extends through various dispensations of GOD towards His creatures. Two or more modes of the Divine actions, or truths, are revealed, apparently inconsistent, but equally binding on us, depending, it may be, for their mutual harmonious action on a common relation to some higher law, not as yet to be discerned by us, and intended by their mutual counteraction to modify each other. "In almost all cases in which a mysterious truth is propounded by Almighty GOD for our acceptance, it is in reality to a twofold or compound, and not to a single or simple article of belief, that our assent is required. The peculiar task which our faculty of belief is set in such cases, is no other than this,—to hold in conjunction, simply and without reserve, some *two* divinely affirmed matters or positions, either of which we should probably make no difficulty of accepting by itself, but whose *compatibility*, or *possible co-existence*, we are unable to perceive."[1] Mr. Freeman applies the principle to the co-existence of the natural and supernatural substances in the Holy Eucharist, and adduces as similar cases the union of the two natures in the One Person of CHRIST, the co-existence of GOD's foreknowledge and our free-will, and again that of Divine inspiration and human composition in the Scriptures.

[1] Freeman's "Principles of Divine Service." Introduction, Part II. pp. 14, 15.

This same law was believed by the Fathers to obtain in respect of the benefit of absolution, and the
inherent acceptableness of contrition. It was no uncertainty of belief in the promises attached to the
priestly ministry, no lack of definiteness of view, which
occasioned the variations in the statements of the Fathers, sometimes representing the grace of remission, as
shed forth within the soul directly through GOD's own
secret workings, sometimes as flowing only through the
ordained ministry, but rather a profound consciousness
of the living energy and love of the HOLY SPIRIT, and
the closeness of communion between the elect soul and
the Divine indwelling Presence. They affirmed without
question and in the strongest terms the grace of sacerdotal absolution, while yet they scrupled not to ascribe
an absolute value, irrespective of all outward means of
grace, to the living force of true contrition, at the same
time not supposing that the acceptance of contrition
superseded the use or value of a subsequent absolution.
They affirmed both principles, and left them to be held
equally and in common.

Morinus sums up the views of the Fathers on the
subject of absolution, which prevailed, as he affirms,
for eleven centuries, reconciling their apparent differences, which are in fact only statements of two co-
existent and harmonious truths. "The proper effect
of priestly absolution is the renewed assistance of the
HOLY SPIRIT, by which the soul is justified, the guilt
of sin removed, its bonds broken, and the true and actual remission of sins bestowed, CHRIST through the
virtue of His Spirit co-operating with the act of His
minister, approving and confirming in Heaven, what he

on earth according to the Church's law has granted;"
"but if through the fervour of repentance, (ob pietatis
vehementiam,) the Divine has anticipated the sacerdotal
absolution, then the sacerdotal sets a further seal on
the Divine absolution, and is the means of imparting a
larger grace of the HOLY SPIRIT, with increased joy and
more abundant fruits."[1]   Thus GOD was believed to accompany or precede the ministerial act, working either
through or independently of it, according to the secret
purpose of His own will, while at the same time a true
promise and spiritual grace were ever believed to attach
to the ministry, and a true relation still to exist between
the inward and the outward act.

Hooker thus expresses the primitive belief of the
concordant action of the two principles, allowing to each
its own separate claim, as alike operative within its own
sphere, yet each in harmony with the other in the fulfilment of the merciful designs of GOD.   "It is true
that our SAVIOUR by these words, 'Whose sins ye remit
they are remitted,' did ordain judges over sinful souls,
give them authority to absolve from sin, and promise to
ratify in heaven whatsoever they do in earth in execution of this their office; to the end that hereby as well
His ministers might take encouragement to do their
duty with all faithfulness, as also His people admonition,
gladly with all reverence to be ordered by them; both
parts knowing that the functions of the one towards the
other have His perpetual assistance and approbation.
Howbeit, all this with two restraints which every jurisdiction in the world hath; the one, that the practice
thereof proceed in due order, the other, that it do not

[1] L. viii. cap. ii. sec. 1, 2.

extend itself beyond due bounds, which bounds or limits have so confined penitential jurisdiction, that although there be given unto it power of remitting sin, yet no such sovereignty of power, that no sin should be pardonable in man without it."[1]

[1] Eccl. Pol. l. vi. cap. vi. 3.

CHAPTER III.

THE ancient discipline declined when the Roman empire became Christian. That momentous crisis in the fortunes of the Church tended powerfully to occasion the decline. There was less urgent need to enforce discipline, when the power of paganism was overcome, and the danger of apostasy had ceased. The difficulty of maintaining it was also greatly aggravated by the sudden and great increase of converts, many of a doubtful character, and many also of the more powerful and wealthier classes. The spread of heresy was acting in the same direction, through breaking down the barriers of spiritual authority. Moreover, the mutual action of the ecclesiastical and civil courts furthered this tendency, all the more when they became friendly, from fear of subjecting the penitent to civil penalties, which would follow the crime, if divulged.

S. Augustine, even though, as previous references to his writings show, feeling most strongly the value and necessity of the public Penance, yet alludes specially to this last hindrance, and expresses his sense of its influence in deterring the clergy from recommending it, when the case nevertheless clearly fell within its intended scope. "We ought," he says, "to correct secret sins in secret, lest if we publicly reprove them, we betray the man.

We would reprove and correct him; but what if an enemy lies upon the catch, to hear something for which he may punish him? A Bishop, put the case, perhaps knows a man to be a murderer, and besides himself no one knows it; I would publicly rebuke the man, but then you would seek to take the law upon him. In this case, I neither betray the man nor neglect him; I reprove him in secret; I set before his face the judgment of GOD; I terrify his bloody conscience, and persuade him to repentance."[1]

Independently of such special causes, the natural shrinking from the public exposure of secret sins, the desire to obviate the sufferings which a disclosure would occasion the relatives of the penitent, and the dread of the scandals likely to arise, casting reproach even upon the Church itself,—would be certain in the course of time to operate with the same result. Even so early as the commencement of the third century, Tertullian complained of the neglect of penance.[2] In the middle of the fourth century Pacian lamented the case of those who when " they had opened their grievances to their spiritual physician, yet neglected afterwards to pursue his advice, and to go through the course prescribed for them."[3] At a somewhat later period S. Jerome expressed his astonishment at a " lady of rank submitting to public penance,"[4] as though it were then an unusual act of humiliation. Marshall states as the result of his

[1] Serm. xvi., quoted by Bingham, l. xviii. ch. iii. sect. 9.
[2] See Marshall, Pen. Disc., p. 101.
[3] Pacian in Parænes. ad Pœnit. sec. 9, quoted by Marshall, Penit. Disc. Lib. of Anglo-Cath. Theol., p. 102.
[4] Marshall, Pen. Disc., p. 103.

researches, that "the clergy did with much ado sustain and keep alive this discipline during the four first centuries."[1] Hooker is more precise in his statement : "The public penance continued in the East not much above two hundred years, in the West almost four hundred."[2]

The first step towards systematising private confession was the appointment of Penitentiaries, an institution which arose in, and was limited to, the East. They were select confessors, to whom the guidance of penitents was specially entrusted, and under whose direction they performed in secret the penance imposed upon them.[3] Hooker quotes Sozomen's explanation of the institution : "Whereas men openly craving pardon at God's hands, it could not be avoided, but they must withal confess what their offences were ; this in the opinion of their prelates, seemed from the first beginning (as we may probably think) to be somewhat burdensome, that men whose crimes were unknown should blare their own faults, as it were upon a stage, acquainting all the people with whatsoever they had done amiss ; and therefore to remedy this inconvenience, they laid the charge upon one only Priest, chosen out of such as were of best conversation, a silent and discreet man, to whom they which had offended might resort and lay open their lives. He, according to the quality of every man's transgression, appointed what they should do or suffer, and left them to execute it upon themselves."[4]

In the West, a letter of S. Leo to the Bishops of Cam-

---

[1] Marshall, p. 102.   [2] Eccl. Pol. l. vi. ch. iv. sec. 13.
[3] See Bingham. Eccl. Ant. l. xviii. ch. iii. sec. 11, 12.
[4] Eccl. Pol. vi. c. iv. 11.

pania, A.D. 441, marks a similar tendency to organise private confession separately from the public discipline. The special object of the letter was simply to prevent the continuance of an innovation which was causing scandal to the Church, and needless distress to penitents; but at the same time it asserted principles which could hardly fail to develop into a systematic use of private, in the place of public, penance. "They were," he said, "to discontinue the usage which then obtained, of publishing out of a paper the nature of such crimes as had been privately confessed, and that because private confession to the priest was sufficient to the expiation of guilt (cum reatus conscientiarum sufficiat solis sacerdotibus indicari confessione secretâ). And although it might seem to argue the power of their faith, when their fear of GOD surmounted all apprehension of shame from man, yet in regard that the sins of all men which, however, did demand expiation by penance, were not of a nature fit to be published, therefore he judged it proper to remove such an inconvenient custom, for fear of driving many from the advantages of penance, who might either be afraid or ashamed of letting their enemies into the knowledge of their guilt, and of exposing themselves thereby to the edge of the laws, inasmuch as that confession did suffice, to all intents and purposes, which was made at first to GOD, and next to the priest, who is appointed to intercede with GOD on behalf of penitents; and that then, in all likelihood, greater numbers would be prevailed with to submit to penance, if the secrets of their consciences should not be made public."[1]

[1] Leo. Epis. No. 136, ad Epis. Camp., as quoted by Marshall, p. 104.

The highest authorities came gradually to recommend this more private ministry, as a permission rendered advisable by the altered circumstances of the times. Marshall quotes as an instance, the advice given by S. Augustine; " It is allowed that in the time of Augustine the public discipline was declining, and had much ado to maintain itself; and therefore this same Father, in his Epistle to Amelius, recommended the softer way of treating sins, which had multitudes to countenance them."[1] Morinus concludes, that about A.D. 700, public and private penance had become distinct and separate systems, the former being reserved for public and notorious, the latter for secret, sins. The mode of reconciling penitents in the private ministry, was formed upon the model of the public discipline, thus showing its derived character and later use.[2] The administration of the public penance as coming more under the jurisdiction of the canon law, was still left, as at the beginning, in the hands of the Bishop; that of private penance was committed to Priests.[3]

Dr. Pusey agrees with Morinus as to the period when the distinction became fixed between public and private penance. He adds the date at which public penance al-

---

[1] Marshall, p. 116.

[2] This of course is not admitted by the school of Roman divines represented e.g. by Billuart, who asserts the direct contrary. Constat e dictis publicam, tum pœnitentiam, cum confessionem a secretâ derivari, et hanc fuisse publicæ normam et regulam. But the proofs to which he refers for this assertion, are simply such passages as have been quoted from the Fathers in the text as to the difficulty or inconvenience of continuing the public system. Summa S. Thomæ, l. i. Dissert. v. Art 1, digressio historica.

[3] Morinus, l. vii. ch. i. sec. 1, 8.

together ceased to be practised, and private penance alone remained in use, a change strikingly marked, as he observes, in the altered language of the Church. In an elaborate argument proving that the modern practice of private penance was unknown to the ancients, he says; " Another and unquestionable ground of proof has been furnished by the different use of the word, ' penitents,' at different periods. In the early Church, it signified in itself public penitents (as above Conc. Carth. p. 390, S. Augustine, p. 398. Conc. Tolet., A. 400, canon 2); from the 8th to the 13th century the nature of the penitence is distinguished by the addition, ' public' or ' private;' then, ' public' penitence being wholly disused, the terms again ceased to be distinguished by any addition, and, as in the first period, when used alone, it signified ' public,' so now, ' private penitence,' or ' penitent.' "[1]

The progressive changes in the penitential discipline of the Church thus seem to be clear. At first it was administered, as confession was made, in public. Even sins only privately confessed were remitted after penance performed in public. Afterwards secret sins were followed by secret penance; only notorious guilt, being the subject-matter of canonical jurisdiction, and special cases of voluntary self-abasement, were still atoned by public penance. Lastly, even these latter cases came to be dealt with more and more in private, the public exposure of penitents being more and more rare, and reserved for extraordinary instances of flagrant transgression.

Thus far the changes, which had taken place, were the

[1] Notes. M. de Pœnit. Tertullian.

unavoidable result of altered social circumstances. The first material innovation on the practice of antiquity, purposely introduced, and the one fraught with the most eventful and enduring consequences, was the decree of the Fourth Lateran Council, A.D. 1215, under Innocent III., which established the absolute necessity of Confession under all circumstances as a condition of Communion. It declared, that "all the faithful, men and women, should confess their sins at least once a year to their pastors." This decree was enforced by severe penalties—excommunication, and the denial of Christian burial—which were renewed with repeated enactments in the succeeding century, as though resistance had arisen, and required to be met by the most stringent measures. In 1378, it was enjoined in England; "Let Confessions be heard thrice in the year, and let men be admonished to communicate as often, namely, at Easter, Pentecost, and Christmas. But whoever does not confess to his proper Priest once in the year at least, and receive the Sacrament of the Eucharist at Easter (unless he think he ought to abstain by the advice of the Priest), let him be forbidden entrance into the Church while he is alive, and be deprived of Christian burial when dead. And let them be often told of this."[1]

The object of this decree of compulsory Confession was no doubt to uphold the failing discipline of the Church at a period of general and increasing laxity of morals. As public penance had gradually fallen into disuse, so there was probably a growing tendency to escape the pressure of the private ministry, and the

---

[1] Archbishop Sudbury's Constitutions, made at Lambeth, A.D. 1378. Johnson's English Canons.

rulers of the Church sought to maintain by moral force what was universally allowed to be necessary in its season, and in better times had been sought, when needed, with comparative readiness, or even with forward zeal. This compulsory law, when first established, was only a matter of discipline; but by degrees it became associated with doctrines, which about the same period began to be taught, and which were supposed to prove this necessity as part of the Divine law. Thus it arose, that what was at first merely a canonical enactment, became a dogma of the faith, so that to question it was made thenceforth throughout the West to be a heresy. By this new rule Confession became obligatory, not merely when the conscience was burdened, and in the case of the more grievous sins, but as a necessary habit, as a law of life, even for the most blameless.

There is a remarkable similarity between the changes which took place in the ministry of Penance, and the more eventful developments affecting the Holy Eucharist. In both cases alike the transition was gradual, and at first almost imperceptible. In both, change of practice preceded change of doctrine, and mainly occasioned it.[1] It might seem as though the desire of upholding the novel practice by an absolute rule, quickened the invention, and then promoted the elaboration of doctrine, in order to form a more authoritative basis, on which the new use could be maintained as a truth of the revelation of GOD. As the withdrawal of the consecrated Cup had partially at least commenced, before the doctrine of concomitance was introduced, and then, sustained by this doctrine, its entire withdrawal from the

---

[1] See Freeman's Introduction, 2nd vol. pp. 50—53.

laity followed,[1] so Confession to a Priest was made
necessary as a rule of discipline, before it was taught to
be essential as a matter of faith and Divine revelation.

2. It is not meant that one uniform teaching prevailed
in the schools.   Morinus says: " As soon as the scholastic theology arose, this subject (of Penance) was most
keenly debated."   He represents the theologians of the
middle ages being led into various and contrary opinions; and "even yet," he adds, " the contest is not at
an end."[2]   He enumerates nine different schemes of
doctrine, which during the middle ages prevailed in
turn, each in succession superseding its predecessor.
There was indeed a constant agreement in the schools
as to the necessity of confession, or at least of the purpose to confess; but the ground on which this necessity
was supposed to rest, continually shifted.   Thus some of
the earlier schoolmen taught, that " contrition, confession, and satisfaction by works, must precede absolution,
and on absolution being given, GOD forgave the sins;"
others, that " absolution was only conditional, the
Priest absolving dependently on the imposed penance
being afterwards completed, and that then, not at the
time of absolution, the forgiveness of the sin followed."
Others, again, " distinguished between internal, and external, confession and satisfaction, and taught that sins
were remitted on contrition accompanied with the purpose of external confession and satisfaction, and therefore before the reception of priestly absolution, but that

---

[1] Freeman's Introduction, 2nd vol. p. 79.   See also note to p. 79.

[2] Lib. viii. cap. xi.   Morinus composed his treatise about the middle
of the sixteenth century.

afterwards it was necessary to confess in order to have penance imposed, on which being completed, the penitent was admitted to communion, the absolution according to this idea being held to be simply declaratory." Another " opinion which was most approved by the earliest Canonists, distinguished between open and secret sins, and ruled that the former were remitted only after public and canonical penance and absolution, the latter before outward confession and satisfaction, solely on contrition and inward confession and satisfaction before GOD."

But the theory which was finally adopted by the most celebrated theologians of the middle ages, supposed a threefold bond or debt to arise from sin—the inward stain or fault, the temporal, and the eternal, punishment. They held that the first was removed by GOD alone on contrition: the third by GOD conditionally on confession and absolution; the second, the temporal and purgatorial punishment, remaining to be worked out by the penitent, either in this or the next world, but the punishment also could be remitted by the Priest conditionally on the imposed penance being fulfilled. Yet another opinion had its day, according to which it was supposed, that on contrition GOD of Himself alone remitted the fault, and changed the eternal into a temporal punishment, which itself, being greater than the penitent could bear, might be commuted through confession and priestly absolution into one more tolerable; and this again, through satisfaction imposed by the Priest, might be altogether removed. Amid all the varieties which mark these several theories, they still agree in the one point of the absolute necessity either of confession or the purpose to confess.

3. Fresh complications of the theory of Penance arose out of the abstruse questions discussed in the schools concerning the infusion of grace. It was conceived, that grace is infused into the soul, as "a Divine spiritual quality," distinct from virtue or any specific power of goodness in operation, such power or virtue being an effect of it, flowing out from it; and that this new quality, thus secretly become part of the soul, and latent within it, renders it well-pleasing to God, and forms its first justification.[1] When this opinion was applied to the doctrine of Penance, it was held,—Morinus shows that all the later theories of the schoolmen involved the assertion,—that habitual grace, as this infused quality was technically called, was imparted in the very act of confession, the precise moment of its bestowal being undetermined, whether during the act of confession, or on the prayer of the Priest preceding absolution.

A most eventful change in the whole view of Penance resulted from the introduction of this new ele-

---

[1] This first infusion was known in scholastic language as *gratia gratum faciens*, or *gratia habitualis*, because forming as was supposed an abiding possession or habit. Mr. Keble in his note to Hooker's Serm. ii. 5, vol. iii. pt. 3, p. 605, quotes S. T. Aquinas' definition of the doctrine. (Tho. Aquin. Summa Theol. 11, par. 1, quæst. 100.) " Gratia gratum faciens, i.e. justificans, est in animâ quiddam reale et positivum ; qualitas quædam supernaturalis, non eadem cum virtute infusâ, ut magister, sed aliquid præter infusas virtutes, fidem, spem, charitatem, habitudo quædam quæ præsupponitur in virtutibus istis, sicut earum principium et radix ; essentiam animæ tanquam subjectum occupat, non potentiâ, sed ab ipsâ." The term "habitual" was used in this connection, not in its present ordinary sense of a " fixed growth resulting from long use," but, as its etymology simply implies, " of an actual possession."

ment. Hence sprang the idea, that through this secretly infused grace given in recompense for the outward act, inward dispositions might be formed capable of supplying any defect which otherwise would render the act invalid. Thus, so it was argued, attrition, or repentance grounded on a servile fear of punishment, might through the very act of confession be transformed into contrition, or repentance grounded on love and a true, keen sense of sin. It was on this principle taught, that an imperfect repentance accompanied with confession, through reception of this secret quality bestowed in confession, might become perfect, the mere act itself entitling the penitent to the further grace. It followed that an imperfect faith and a merely servile fear were a sufficient preparation for a true confession, because what was wanting to perfect fitness for entire reconciliation with GOD, was supplied in the act. This opinion finally prevailed, and fixed its firm hold on the theology of the Latin Church, being at length confirmed by the Council of Trent.[1]

That penitence may, and often does, deepen in the act of confession, grace working at the time increased and tenderer convictions of sin, and opening the soul to new or larger impressions of the love of GOD,—is a matter of experience which may have conduced to the introduction of this theory, or given to it an apparent confirmation. The attitude of the soul confessing its sins especially under the guidance of one experienced in receiving confessions, is no doubt favourable to the reception of such deepened feelings of repentance. Con-

---

[1] The present general belief among Roman theologians, as stated by Perrone, is that attrition becomes contrition through confession.

fession may thus become the occasion of obtaining further grace, or it may not be so. The injury done to primitive belief was in systematising an occasional and incidental consequence, making such possible super-added convictions or impressions part of the necessary sacramental benefit, a sure covenanted consequence of the outward act; and then constituting this theory to be the basis of further consequences, bearing intimately on the whole practical life.

Perrone observes, that it became all but a matter of faith (ad fidem proxime accedit), at least after the Council of Trent, that "true contrition with love is not necessary for the right reception of the sacrament of penance."[1]   He at the same time scruples not to acknowledge the novelty of the opinion, while accounting for the motives which led the Council to sanction it.   "We are fully aware," he says, "it was everywhere firmly held by all the schoolmen before the Council of Trent, at least up to the time of S. Thomas Aquinas, that true contrition is necessary to the right reception of the sacrament of penance.   But in the Council of Trent that opinion was seriously questioned, because of its close resemblance to the errors of the Protestants, namely, that sins were not really remitted by the

---

[1] The Jansenists were condemned for holding the opposite opinion. The subsequent history of the discussion is remarkable. Two parties continued to exist after the Council of Trent, one called the "attritionistæ," the other the "contritionistæ." Alexander VII., in a decree dated 5 Mar., 1667, forbad under pain of excommunication either party to censure the other, adding—"The opinion which denies the necessity of any love of GOD in attrition, appears at the present day to be the more commonly held in the schools." Perrone, Tract. de Pœnit. cap. ii. contrit. sec. 38, note (1).

words of priestly absolution, but only declared to be remitted. Yet the Tridentine fathers did not censure that opinion, lest they should fix blame on the ancients. Nevertheless, if we except the Jansenists, who made that obsolete opinion their own, and a very few theologians besides, all Catholics have renounced it."[1] Morinus observes, that this theory concerning attrition reached its climax among the later schoolmen, when it was taught by very many, and those of great weight and celebrity (viri graves et celebres permulti), that it is "possible for a penitent to be reconciled to God, even after the commission of manifold sins, without an act of contrition and love to God, if only the sacrament of penance be received;" nay, even—a statement painful to record, though it legitimately follows

[1] Tract. de Pœn., cap. ii. sec. 90. By the term, Protestant, in this and similar statements, the foreign Protestants who rejected all sacramental views, are intended. It is to be carefully noted that the anathemas of the Council of Trent, like Moehler's Symbolism, are aimed at a directly unsacramental theory, and do not properly apply to a system such as our formularies represent. The Canon of the Council of Trent, "De contritione" (Sess. xiv. Can. iv.), decrees (1) that contrition without the sacrament of Penance, or the desire of it, does not suffice for the forgiveness of sin—" Docet, etsi contritionem hanc aliquando charitate perfectam esse contingat, hominemque Deo reconciliare, priusquam hoc sacramentum actu suscipiatur, ipsam nihilominus reconciliationem ipsi contritioni, sine sacramenti voto, quod in illâ includitur, non esse adscribendum ;" and (2) that attrition, together with the sacrament, or the desire of it, suffices for justification ; " Quamvis sine sacramento pœnitentiæ (contritio imperfecta, quæ attritio dicitur,) per se ad justificationem perducere peccatorem nequeat, tamen eum ad Dei gratiam in sacramento pœnitentiæ impetrandam disponit."

Again, in (Sess. vi. Can. vi.) the passage quoted by Perrone, the Council decreed, that " the wicked are prepared for justification *even through the act*, by which they begin to love God as the Fountain of all righteousness."

from the foregoing premises,—that "the superiority and special prerogative of the evangelical sacraments in comparison with those of the old law, consists in this—that the former release us from the heavy yoke of the exercise of contrition and the love of GOD (gravissimo contritionis et dilectionis Dei jugo nos liberarent), CHRIST having taught the necessity of confession, in order that the sinner should no more be weighed down by the too great burden, substituting instead of the necessity of Divine love the habit or quality of loving (i.e., the infused latent grace, spoken of above), which is bestowed in the sacrament."[1]

The maze of intricate and perplexed subtleties involved in these and similar theories, apparently arose out of the felt difficulty of reconciling two conflicting and incongruous propositions, namely, the later view of the absolute necessity and meritoriousness of confession, and the earlier belief, which yet was not, and could not be denied, that true contrition is itself a sufficient condition for the reconciliation of a penitent soul with GOD.

4. A yet further change in the doctrine of confession,

---

[1] Lib. viii. c. iv. sec. 2, 26. Even the Council of Trent, contrasting the case of the unbaptized with that of the baptized, implies that less is required of the latter than of the former, the access to the sacrament of penance making a lower degree of repentance sufficient for acceptance. The Canon, which after saying that contrition was at all times before baptism necessary to obtain pardon of sins, at its close rules that attrition, though without the sacrament of Penance it cannot bring a sinner to justification, yet disposes him to obtain it in the sacrament. See the preceding note where the passage is quoted. Sess. xiv. Can. iv. The proposition seems only a less startling statement of the view detailed in the text.

and one, like the former, of a most eventful character, resulted from the new opinions concerning satisfaction, which grew up during the same period. The need of satisfaction viewed as a corrective discipline, was shown in the last chapter to have been held from the beginning, but this, the primitive, view of the subject was gradually superseded by what may be called the punitive theory. Penances originally imposed for the purpose of satisfying the requirements of Church discipline, and for deepening repentance in the soul, came to be regarded as a means of satisfying the demands of Divine Justice. The opinion grew, that besides the eternal punishment due for sin, which is wholly remitted through the merits of CHRIST, there yet remained temporal penalties to be borne by the absolved penitent. As the doctrine of the meritoriousness of human actions gained acceptance, this also fell in with the new theory. It was believed, that penitential acts imposed by the Priest might by their merit compensate for penalties due to GOD. Moreover, the custom which had grown of allowing penances to be performed after absolution in trust on the penitent's faithfulness in fulfilling them, and because they were held to be a discipline of the after life, as well as a preparation for forgiveness of sin,—this practice again, especially when viewed in connection with the new doctrines, seemed to favour the idea that such acts had relation to the consequences following sin though pardoned. These concurring views gradually acquired consistency, and were shaped into laws, ruling the practice of the Church, till at length they were permanently fixed by the decrees of the Council of Trent.

Perrone thus explains the modern and authorised

theory of Satisfaction. "Satisfaction is the compensation of the injury done to GOD by our sins. In all at
least grievous sin a twofold property (proprietas) is found
to exist, viz., the guilt (reatus) of the fault and its eternal
punishment, which are removed as soon as the sinner
returns to the grace and favour of GOD, and, secondly,
the guilt of temporal punishment, which for the most
part (plerumque) remains after the forgiveness of the
sin; and, in order to expiate this latter consequence, the
penitent is bound to pay to GOD alms, prayers and fasts,
as the Council of Trent teaches (Sess. vi. cap. 14), and
other pious works or punishments to be patiently endured, when either voluntarily undertaken or enjoined
by the priest, so that according to his ability he may
compensate for the injury done to GOD by his sins, and
satisfy His justice."[1]

It is not to be understood as though this new theory
implied human satisfaction to be in itself available before
GOD for the remission of punishment. Perrone, referring to the decrees of Trent (Sess. xiv., c. viii.), guards
against this supposition, and explains that "our satisfactions derive all their force or virtue (totam vim) from
CHRIST's merits, and that His satisfaction and our own
are thus reconciled together." But notwithstanding
this disclaimer, the idea of the efficacy of human acts
of penance for the remission of Divine punishment,
though derived and dependent, still remained, and became so prominent a characteristic of the modern Roman theory of Confession, that it was accounted by the
Tridentine Divines to be the one reason for its absolute
necessity, Priests being declared to be judges especially

[1] Tract. Pœn., cap. iv. sec. 183.

in this sense, that they are GOD's commissioned agents
to determine and impose the exact amount of satisfaction due to Him, in order to expiate the amount of sin
committed against Him, and for this reason require
to know the sins committed with all their circumstances, inasmuch as without such knowledge they
could not estimate the due amount of satisfaction.
Perrone thus explains the belief as affirmed at Trent :—
" It is evident from these words (' Whosesoever sins ye
remit,' &c., 'Whosesoever sins ye retain,' &c.), that
Priests ordained by CHRIST are judges, invested with
the power of binding and loosing, remitting and retaining, sins; but, as the Council of Trent says (sess. xiv.
cap. v.), it is certain that Priests cannot exercise such a
judgment without knowing the causes, nor *preserve
equity in apportioning punishments*, unless men declare to
them their sins, not only generally, but also specifically
and in detail." On this ground, assuming a true analogy to exist between the sacrament of penance and
human courts of justice, the conclusion followed, as
a legitimate consequence ; "When therefore CHRIST
erected the tribunal of penance after the likeness of a
civil court of justice, it must necessarily be acknowledged, from the authority of Scripture, that unless
there be confession of every deadly sin, with the circumstances determining its species or kind, sins cannot
be remitted or retained."[1]

[1] Perrone, Tract. c. iii. sec. 106. The words of the Canon of Trent are ;
Dominus noster, Jesus Christus, etiam ascensurus ad cœlos, sacerdotes
sui ipsius vicarios reliquit tamquam præsides et judices, ad quos omnia
mortalia crimina deferantur in quæ Christi fideles ceciderint, quo pro
potestate clavium remissionis aut retentionis peccatorum sententiam
pronuntient. Constat enim, sacerdotes judicium hoc incognitâ causâ

5. To complete our view of the changes of opinion which so greatly affected the whole penitential system of the Western Church, we must moreover trace, however succinctly, the progress of ideas which led to the establishment of Indulgences. It is not difficult to account for the growth of this practice. A canon was passed at the Council of Nice (Can. 12), giving to Bishops a discretionary power of relaxing, or altogether dispensing, penances imposed according to the Church's

exercere non potuisse, neque æquitatem quidem illos in pœnis injungendis servare potuisse, si in genere duntaxat, et non potius in specie ac sigillatim, sua ipsi peccata declarassent. Sess. xiv., cap. v., de Confess. The system of dealing with penitents according to this theory is evidently founded on the analogy of human courts of justice, rather than on the idea of a ministry of grace. Hence, as a criminal is wholly committed to the judge, his cause wholly depending on his sentence, so the forgiveness of the penitent came to be considered as wholly dependent on the sentence of the Priest, and his judgment of the punishment due for the offence.

The hope of Divine forgiveness is thus entirely dependent on confession. Hooker quotes Bellarmine, asserting, "that there is not any promise of forgiveness upon confession made to GOD without the priest." His words when commenting on 1 S. John i. 9, are, "Verba illa, 'Fidelis et est et justus,' &c., referuntur ad promissionem divinam; ideo enim Deus fidelis et justus dicitur, dum peccata confitentibus remittet, quia stat promissis suis, nec fidem fallit." And then follows the momentous statement; "At promissio de remittendis peccatis iis, qui confitentur Deo peccata sua, non videtur ulla exstare in divinis literis; exstat autem promissio apertissima iis qui ad illos accedunt, quibus dictum est Johannis xx. 21. Quorum remiseritis peccata, remittuntur eis." In loc.

It is probable that one cause of the difference between the Roman and English judgment on this point, is to be found in the difference between the Roman and the English mind in respect to objectiveness. The tendency of the Roman mind is to the objective, that of the English to the subjective, aspect of a truth. An excess in dwelling on the outward form, would therefore naturally characterise the one; an excess in regard to the inward action of the soul, the other.

law. The canon is thus paraphrased by Marshall:—
" It entrusted the Bishops with a discretionary power
of relaxing the penitent's sentence, and of shortening
the time he should continue under it, as they should
observe his behaviour to be more or less deserving. If
he contented himself with the common forms of coming
into the church, and of leaving it with other penitents;
if he did not manifest a compunction of heart, as well
as submit to the outward appearances and gestures of
penitential sorrow; he was then to have no abatements,
but was to go completely through the stages and the
time assigned him. Whereas, if either his former
conversation had been exemplary before his lapse, or if
his conduct after it did sufficiently prove the realities of
his inward grief, in such cases his Bishop might contract
the time allotted for his continuance under the penitential discipline, and might restore him to communion
before its expiration."[1]

The various theories of Penance which have passed
under our review, necessarily affected the character of
a dispensation. When regarded in connexion with
them, a dispensation became virtually a release from
the pains and penalties due to the Divine justice; and
as these penalties were believed to extend beyond the
grave, a dispensation would embrace the sufferings of
another world. Moreover, from the supposed meritoriousness of human actions, it followed, as a possible
inference, that some more distinguished Saints, doing
more than was of necessity required, could merit more
than was needed for themselves; and these superabundant acts, added to our LORD's merits, might form a

[1] Marshall, Pen. Disc., p. 127.

store or treasure to be applied by the Church, as part of the ministry of reconciliation. Further, the idea obtained, as a supposed consequence of the doctrine of the "Communion of Saints," that by virtue of the mystical fellowship uniting together the members of the One Body, the merits of one person might be transferred to another—those who possessed an excess supplementing others who were deficient.[1]

[1] Dr. Ulmann, "Reformers before the Reformation," thus traces the growth of the theory of Indulgences, (Vol. I., p. 238, 240.) "As in early times, the penances of the excommunicated were frequently mitigated, so in the course of the Middle Ages, an analogous mitigation was introduced with reference to the works of penance, to which delinquents were subjected. Permission was given to exchange a more severe for a gentler kind of penance. Sometimes in the place of doing penance himself, the party was allowed to employ a substitute, and sometimes *in fine*, instead of the actual penance prescribed, some service conducive to the interest of the Church and the glory of GOD, was accepted. This last was the real basis of indulgence. Even here, however, the process was gradual. At first only personal acts for the Church were admitted. Then pecuniary gifts became more and more common, until at last the matter assumed the shape of a mere money speculation. The abuse grew up in practice. Then came Scholasticism, and furnished it with a theoretical substratum; and not until the institution had thus received an ecclesiastical and scientific basis, was a method of practice introduced which overstepped all limits." " Indulgence has that precise amount of efficacy which the Church assigns to it. In order to this six conditions are required, two on the part of him who dispenses it, viz., competent authority and a pious cause, two on the part of the receiver, viz., repentance, and faith in the power of the keys, and two on the part of the Church, viz., the superabundance of the treasure of merits, and a proper appreciation of the deliverance for which indulgence was instituted.

"The whole exposition, both of Alexander of Hales, and of Albert the Great, proceeds on the radical though unexpressed supposition that the Church is properly an indivisible whole, the parts of which are all connected with each other, as a mystical body, in which the acts of the head redound to the advantage of the members, and those of any one

A change had gradually passed over the popular idea
of sanctity. Instead of being viewed as a form of
character having a unity of life, it came to be regarded
as an accumulation of acts, the sum of an appreciable
series, the items of which could be computed and valued.
Even our LORD's acts of obedience and His sufferings were thus regarded as divisible into individual
details, each having its own separate value. As but
one drop of His Precious Blood was believed to suffice
for the redemption of the world, there would remain an
indefinite treasure over and above what was necessarily
required for our salvation, to be applied as the ground
of additional dispensations from the temporal consequences of sin. According to the same principle every
sin was supposed to have its fixed measure of temporal
punishment, which could be remitted only by some
adequate penance. This might be borne either by the
sinner, or by another on his behalf. Out of the stock
of superabundant merits there could be drawn at will
an endless amount of dispensations, which, originally
standing in the stead of the canonical penances, availed
equally, as was supposed, for the remission of the temporal penalties judged to be due. Morinus[1] quotes,
among others, Alexander Hales, Albertus Magnus, and
his greater pupil, S. Thomas Aquinas, as expositors of
this theory of works of supererogation, and their application to Indulgences, and then adds:—"Following
these chiefs of the scholastic theology, all the later

member to that of all the others ; so that in consequence of their mutual connexion as members one of another, the merits of each are trans-
ferable to any of the rest."
   [1] Morinus, l. x. cap. xx. sec. 3.

schoolmen not only took for granted this treasure of the Church, but also taught that it was the ground on which Indulgences were granted."[1]

Morinus distinguishes three successive developments of this doctrine, before it reached the climax of abuse, which led directly to the outbreak of the first Reformation movement in Germany. Its first application, as he describes it, was the redemption of penances by money payments, to be disposed of for charitable uses. Days or years of penance might be redeemed by alms according to a fixed and authorized scale, graduated to meet the pecuniary circumstances of the penitent.[2] It was, as has been observed, the principle of the *wereguild* applied to the laws of the spiritual life. There was, no doubt, a seeming harmlessness and plausibility in such a permission which might be construed to be a mere modification of the self-sacrifice which constitutes the essence of acts of penance. But when such a rule of barter could be formally and authoritatively established, it is evident, that penance had ceased to be regarded as a discipline of the inner life, and had practically become a matter of external value. The principle of redemption thus far admitted, was capable of an indefinite extension. For if money were an adequate substitute for penance, why not also any act of charity or holy zeal? Morinus notes, as the second stage of development, the use of Indulgences in mustering armies to wage war

---

[1] L. x. c. xxi. sec. 15, and passim.

[2] Some have thought that this practice of money payment was introduced by our Archbishop Theodore. Others, and among the rest Morinus and Marshall, with greater probability suppose that he only reduced an existing practice to rule. His Penitential contains minute details of the practical working of the system.

against the heathen, against heretics or schismatics, and more especially for the defence of the Holy Land. On a gigantic scale Indulgences were granted to those who perilled their lives in the battles of the Church, and absolutions were lavishly bestowed in anticipation of the warrior's possible death. The Crusades were mainly sustained by the power of this supernatural stimulus.[1] Morinus says; " Because the labour was immense, and full of hazard, and the benefit arising from it singularly great, affecting the whole Church, it was judged not undeservedly to be an equivalent for the severest penance." Pilgrimages, visits to holy places, member-ship with religious guilds, &c., &c., were regarded as acts involving the same idea, and so entitled to the same privileges.

A further stage in this downward progress was yet to be reached. Hitherto the objects proposed as the sub-ject matter of Indulgences, had been connected with the interests of religion, or at least of the Church. But if any merely worldly objects were approved by the Clergy, why might not the same authority apply to alms given in its behalf the same benefits? Thus it came to pass that any work, however purely secular, which for any reason the Church authorities desired to carry out, might be urged forward by the same inducement. Not merely were churches generally built, or repaired, by this means, Morinus mentions also the construction of "bridges and highways," as included within the scope of Indulgences.

[1] Ulmann remarks that the first powerful stimulus given to the spread of the principle of Indulgences was through the Crusade movement at the great Council of Clermont, in the year 1096. Vol. i. p. 37.

The exercise of this extraordinary power was at first committed to the Pope, and it was always regulated by his express authority; but it was not limited to him. Bishops generally received authority to give the same privileges at their discretion. "It might happen," observes Morinus, "that several Bishops being together present at the consecration of a church, and each offering indulgences for sale, the same individual might obtain the much desired boon from more than one Bishop, thus indefinitely multiplying immunities from the temporal penalties due by him, whether in this world or the next, to the justice of God."[1]

The pastors of the Church offered commutations of penance under this comprehensive formula: "Whosoever shall have fulfilled this work, or strive with all his might for its fulfilment, shall obtain the remission of all his sins."[2] This was indeed but technical language, and meant originally to imply only the remission of the penalties due to sin. But the popular mind would be always ready to confound the two; for what but fear of the penalty of sin ordinarily causes apprehension at the commission of sin? To remit the one is felt to be, as the ecclesiastical formula literally expressed it, to remit the other.

The least effect of such an application of spiritual power was the dissolution of ecclesiastical discipline. "For," as Morinus observes, "who would be willing to endure such long and hard penances by night and by day, if for one denarius, or even one obolus, paid under the direction of a Bishop, he could satisfy the fourth

[1] Mor. de Pœn. l. x. cap. xx. sec. 11.
[2] L. x. cap. xix. sec. 100.

part of the canonical penance, and by trebling the sum
altogether expunge the whole debt ?" A profounder
wrong, one from which all Western Christendom, equally
with ourselves, still keenly suffers, was the prostitution,
and consequent disparagement, of the grace of absolution, which at such an easy cost, and through such
questionable means, could almost at will be at once
secured.

It is true, that all Indulgences were by the express
tenor of their provisions available only to those who
were penitent, and had confessed their sins. Thus ran
the form of the Indulgence. Thus far professedly at
least the principle of the ancient penitential discipline
was preserved. We cannot doubt but that all possible
care was taken by the more earnest of the Clergy
to preserve the true penitential spirit in the use of the
modern system. But the effort needed to obtain an
Indulgence was so slight, the gain so immense, so incalculable, that every conceivable inducement was held
out to meet the requirements by which it could be obtained at the lowest cost of self-sacrifice. Moreover,
the true value of the conditions which the form of the
Indulgence implied, must be estimated by the view which
with the highest sanction prevailed as to the nature and
degree of the penitence required. The supposed meritoriousness of the mere act of confession must likewise be
taken into account. Morinus puts the case of one who
confesses, and is absolved without any even the lowest
degree of sorrow for his sins—"non est absolutus non
attritus." In the judgment of all it is certain that such
a person has not received grace, that he still remains
in a state of sin. But suppose that while being in a

state of sin, he has executed the task required in order to obtain the Indulgence? What does the Indulgence profit him? Morinus quotes S. Raymund's answer to the question: "Indulgences avail a sinner, if he make an offering from pious devotion, though imperfect, for the sake of attaining grace. For to this end all other alms avail, and every good work."

Albertus Magnus says still more strongly: " Indulgences avail to all, as well to those who are in mortal sin, as to those who are in a state of grace, though after a different manner. To those in a state of grace, they avail for the diminution of expiatory punishment, whether actually imposed, or to be imposed, if the priest should have erred. But to those in mortal sin they avail in two ways; partly in that one man can merit for another the first grace of conversion, if he, the sinner, pray, and fast, and perform other good works according to his ability; for if an individual can affect this, much more can the Church by means of the treasure of common merits which an Indulgence imputes to him : and partly because works good in their kind approximate a person who does them to grace, in that grace passes as a quality to such sinners as are worthy of justification through the merit of congruity, though not being simply worthy."[1]

It is scarcely possible to contemplate the aspect which society and the Church must needs have presented under

---

[1] Quod opera de genere bonorum vicinant hominem gratiæ, eo quod procedit ut quiddam in peccatoribus quibusdam, ut dicit Ambrosius, qui digni sunt justificatione dignitate congruentiæ non dignitatis. L. x. c. xxii. sec. 12. See on the whole subject of Indulgences l. x. cap. xvii. —xxii., passim.

the full influences of such a system, without feeling that
the time was ripe for the reconstruction of the Church's
penitential discipline, and in order to this end a return
to an earlier and purer faith and practice; and further,
that if attempts to reform were continually obstructed
and over-ruled by authority, when earnest minds had
perceived the contrast between the earlier and later
teaching of the Church, and this in a matter touching
so closely the whole question of morals, and the soul's
inmost life and communion with GOD, sooner or later a
rupture within the Church was inevitable.

Before closing this review of the mediæval system,
the main principles at least of which are embodied in
the discipline of the Church of Rome, a caution is
needed, lest an undue charge lie against that great portion of the Catholic Church, especially when our own
manifold defects should make us the more fearful of
condemning others, and defects in this very subject,
not indeed in our principles, as hereafter will be
shown, but in our faithfulness to them.

Reforms have from time to time been made in the
Church of Rome, correcting, or aiming at the correction
of, abuses arising from the principles described. The
Council of Trent e.g. was convened partly with the view
of correcting such abuses. Moreover the pastoral work
and writings of the saints and masters of the spiritual life,
formed within the communion of Rome, must be studied
before any fair opinion can be formed as to what the
application of its penitential discipline is capable of
being made. Their practical counsels and exhortations
must always be reckoned among the most valuable aids
to all who, under any system, would learn the critical

art of guiding souls.[1]   They often speak as the simplest natural piety would dictate, interpreting the decisions of the schools so as to meet the simple wants of the

---

[1] In illustration of the mode in which the principles objected to are, sometimes at least, explained and practically applied in the Roman Communion, let two extracts be considered, one from the writings of a Saint before our time, the other from those of a great teacher but just departed to his rest.   Both extracts relate to the same point, namely, the care to be taken to enforce the need of contrition, notwithstanding the doctrine which teaches the sufficiency of mere attrition.

S. Charles Borromeo thus writes : " Mais ils (prêtres) rechercheront avec beaucoup de soin la préparation intérieure, qui est *nécessaire* à ceux qui se présentent à ce sacrement, laquelle consiste en avoir fait un très-exact et diligent examen de ses péchés, et en avoir conçu une douleur proportionnée à leur énormité, avec une ferme propos et une résolution constante de satisfaire aux péchés qu'on a commis, et de s'amender à l'avenir.   C'est pourquoi les confesseurs s'efforceront de persuader par raison à ceux dans lesquels ils remarqueront que cette préparation n'est pas, de s'en retourner pour se préparer dignement. . .
. . Le confesseur doit prendre garde que quand il voit que les pénitents ont fait de leur côté quelque diligence pour se préparer dignement à la confession, et que néanmoins, ou pour leur incapacité, ou pour quelque autre sujet, il ne leur semble pas qu'ils aient les dispositions *nécessaires*, il doit suppléer à cela, s'efforçant de les exciter à la contrition de leurs péchés . . . et avec cela il les doit porter et les disposer de sorte qu'ils soient pour le moins si attristés de tous et d'un chacun de leurs péchés mortels, qu'il les puisse absoudre avec sureté de conscience."   Quoted by Gaum, Manuel des confesseurs, pp. 229—31.

Again, Père de Ravignan says : " Il y a la pénitence intérieure et la pénitence extérieure.   La pénitence intérieure n'est autre chose que la contrition.   C'est la douleur, le regret de nos péchés, avec la ferme détermination de ne plus les commettre à l'avenir.   Cette pénitence intérieure vous le savez bien est absolument nécessaire pour recevoir la remission des péchés.   C'est une disposition précieuse qu'il faut demander à Dieu, qu'il faut nourir en soi, et qui produit les plus grands resultats ; car c'est cette douleur de nos fautes qui nous fait prendre des généreuses résolutions de ne plus les commettre, avec le secours de la grace divine, qui ne nous manque jamais.   La pénitence

truly penitent. Practically, moreover, points of doctrine such as we have been considering, are for the most part withdrawn from ordinary cognizance, and may have a comparatively slight effect on the religious life. It is also to be borne in mind, that principles are always open to be largely modified in practice. Systems, when acted upon, do not always produce the results, which in theory legitimately flow from them. They must always depend in large measure on their administrators, as well as on the circumstances under which they are administered.

Nevertheless, after all the abatements which ought to be taken into account, before we presume to judge the Roman penitential system, the question must still remain, whether the principles which have been detailed are true, or reconcilable with the Apostolic traditions to which the Church is bound to adhere; and, secondly, whether they are not, in proportion as they operate, detrimental to the growth of true ideas of practical religion.

extérieure est le fruit de la première; elle resulte de la pénitence intérieure. Et en effet si nous sommes contrits, repentants, humiliés devant Dieu au souvenir de nos offences," &c. Entretiens spirituelles. Paris, 1862. La pénitence.

It is evident that these great teachers and guides of souls here speak independently of the systems of the schools. Their own true life superseded the mediæval theory, though they were formally committed to it. They assert the necessity of contrition as a preparation for an acceptable confession, quite as strongly as those who openly reject the doctrine which is at variance with this vital principle.

CHAPTER IV.

THE FOREIGN REFORMERS.

FOR a thousand years and upwards no controversy on the subject of Confession arose. It was, as Mr. Freeman has observed in reference to a similar remarkable fact in the greater instance of the Holy Eucharist, a millennial period, during which the peace of the Church of GOD on this vital question was undisturbed. The Montanists indeed, and with them their greatest disciple Tertullian, and afterwards in the third century the Novatians, denied the power of the keys in the remission of the more deadly sins. But the question in these cases was one rather of discipline than of doctrine; for the Church's power to absolve was fully admitted, only the inexpediency of applying this power in the case of certain heinous sins, was urged on the ground that encouragement might thereby be given to commit such sins. It was argued that persons thus guilty ought to lie under a permanent ban of excommunication, and be committed to the mercy of GOD in another world. This resistance to the Church's penitential system rather proved its spiritual power: for the very efficacy of the Church's absolution was the cause of the desire to restrain its exercise in certain cases. The object was to maintain a high standard of morals; and it was thought that the greater severity would be the

more powerful means of effecting this object.   Moreover these were everywhere condemned heresies.

Nor, again, did the substitution of private in the
place of public penance, provoke opposition.   The new
system was the unavoidable result of the altered circumstances of society, and it involved 'no change in
doctrine.   There was indeed the loss of the intercessions of the people, and of the greater humiliation
which the public exposure involved.   But confession,
penitential discipline and absolution, remained as before;
and these constituted the essence of the ministry.   Its
spiritual form and grace depended neither on its publicity, nor on the intercessions of the congregation, but
on the institution of CHRIST embodied in these special
acts.   Nevertheless, during the latter portion of this
period changes were going on, and gradually established themselves in the practice of the Church, which
prepared the way for, though they did not in themselves involve, the revolution in doctrine which formed
the subject of the preceding chapter.   The law of
compulsory confession in the twelfth century was the
practical turning point of the change of system.   When
associated with the new doctrines, it overset the balance
by which the two contrasted elements of primitive truth
had been maintained.   It exalted the ministerial agency
to the detriment of the soul's own secret communion
with GOD, thus giving an undue preponderance to one
member of the complex system.[1]   The mutual action

---

[1] Perrone, stating the modern Roman belief, shows how the Council
of Trent allows, that " contrition, when perfected by charity, reconciles
many to GOD before the Sacrament of Penance is actually received;"
but he adds, " it further teaches that this reconciliation is not to be
attributed to contrition, (sine sacramenti voto) unless the purpose of

E

of these two elements of the system was disturbed; and as in the material world disorder would arise from an undue impulse given to one of two balanced forces, so in the spiritual world the doctrine of priestly authority set free from the counteracting influences exercised on it by the power of the secret contrition of the heart, introduced confusion into the laws of repentance and reconciliation with God. The theory of the absolute necessity of confession, or its intention, for the remission of sin, combined with the new views of satisfaction and of supererogatory works of merit; and these doctrines, finding their expression in the sale of Indulgences, and aggravated by the abuses attending their promiscuous application,—finally awakened opposition, and provoked throughout Europe the reaction which forms the subject of the present chapter.

confession be included in it." C. ii. s. 37. Thus confession is still represented as an absolute necessity, although the grace of reconciliation is supposed to be obtained before it is fulfilled in act, and therefore really without it. The Jansenists sought to restore the ancient simple belief that perfect contrition with charity reunites a man to God. This proposition was condemned, and Bellarmine even réfutes the opinion, though still held by some Roman Divines, that an exception is to be made in the case of death being imminent (in articulo mortis). The supposition of others, that pardon may in some extreme cases be obtained without such intention,—"raro, in casu nempe necessitatis, ac deficiente confessarii copiâ, non autem ordinarie, neque frequenter, multo minus semper,"—was equally condemned. Tract. cap. ii. 71, &c.

Perrone represents, in the following brief statement, the exact modern Roman view of the Sacrament of Penance: "Contrition and confession constitute the *essence* of the Sacrament, and suffice for (conferunt) the remission of the guilt of eternal punishment. Satisfaction constitutes its *integrity*, and serves for the remission of that part of the temporal punishment, which for the most part remains after the Sacrament, to be borne either in this life or in the life to come." Cap. iv. sec. 183.

" From the thirteenth century, when the system reached its maturity, loud and many were the voices raised by learned theologians, preachers, and poets, in condemnation of the sale of Indulgences, or in endeavours to bring it back to the purity of its origin, and separate it from all that was injurious to morality. The worse the corruption grew, the louder and more powerful became the opposition. In the course of the fifteenth century especially it spread far and wide, and assumed a character of greater determination; and at last, at the commencement of the sixteenth, it gave the watchword of the Reformation in the theses of Luther."[1]

Dr. Ullman has accumulated copious illustrations of the line of attack made by the Reformers still living within the Roman obedience before the crisis of the German Reformation. The two, from whose writings he quotes most largely, John of Wesel and John Wessel, were both born within the century in which the Reformation took place, and had apparently the greatest influence in forming the mind of the succeeding generation; for Luther said of the former, that "he had studied his writings for his degree," and of the latter, that "it might seem as if he received from him all that he knew."[2]

It is important to observe that the attacks of these forerunners of the Reformation were directed, not against the essential principles either of confession or absolution, but against the incidental doctrines, or modes of ministration, which had become associated

---

[1] Ullman's "Reformers before the Reformation" (vol. i. p. 250), translated into English, and published by Clarke, Edinburgh.

[2] Ib., Preface, p. xiii.

with them, and which, as has been already observed,
had so vitally affected their original character.

Wesel embraced the main points of his argument
against the prevailing system of his day, in the seven
following propositions :—

1. On every one who has infringed His law, God, as
Lawgiver, in the exercise of His justice, imposes a
penalty, and this penalty He does not remit, although,
in His mercy, He may forgive the guilt; for, as Augustine says, God is always merciful in ·a way that
leaves free course to His justice.

2. Christian Priests, to whom are committed the
keys of heaven, are the ministers of God in the remission of guilt.

3. The penalty which God has imposed upon a
transgressor no man can forgive; for nothing can resist
the Divine will.

4. The Holy Scriptures nowhere state, that any
Priest, or even the Pope, can grant an indulgence
which shall liberate a man from the penalties denounced against him by God.

5. The Pope, however, has it in his power to absolve
from the penalties which even a positive law has denounced for sin, because the Pope is appointed by the
Church the founder of positive law, in as far as it sub-
serves the Church's edification, and not its destruction.

6. That the penalties, which man or positive law
has denounced, correspond with the awards of God's
penal justice, in such a manner as that when they are
annulled, God's justice is also satisfied, is by no means
certain, unless it has been revealed by God. For the
Divine will (which of· course means, in such particular

cases) is unknown to man, and nothing is said of this in Scripture.

7. The opinion of theological teachers regarding a treasure of the Church, accumulated from the merits of CHRIST, and other supererogatory works of the Saints, and committed to the charge of the Pope, is undoubtedly very pious, but is at the same time an opinion to which certain modest objections may be profitably made. In particular it may be objected, that the Saints have left behind them on earth no such treasure, because the Scripture says, "their works do follow them." So long as the Saints sojourn in this life, their works are by their very nature transitory; and when the Saints cease to labour, their works have no independent existence of their own, but in as far as, through the grace of GOD, they are in any degree meritorious, they follow their authors from the scene of their labours, and enter with them into rest.[1]

Again, Wessel, "by no means rejecting the sacrament of penitence, understood as inward sorrow and outward confession of sin, rather calling earnestly for both," contests the scholastic definition of the constituent parts of Penance, viz. contrition, confession, and satisfaction. He reasserts the ancient belief, that confession is "not absolutely necessary to obtain forgiveness, but is only a guarantee of true repentance." He also argues at length against the prevailing theory of satisfaction, and of the doctrine on which it mainly rested, namely, the Priest's power to judge and apportion by his sentence the due amount of punishment.

[1] " Reformers before the Reformation," vol. i. pp. 260, 1.

" Sacramental confession is, as respects its form, not judicial, so that if a sentence, and that a strict sentence, of a confession be omitted, the act of the party making the confession, and the act of him who administers the absolution, would not be a true sacrament. For it is sufficient for the truth of an efficacious sacrament, that the penitent speak the truth, and that the confessor, after receiving the confession, pronounce absolution without stating a judicial opinion." Again; "They (who affirm satisfaction to form an essential part of penitence) do not recognize the full efficacy of the sacrament, inasmuch as they deny that the pardon of the King suffices for forgiveness. They also falsify the words of the absolution, and after saying, ' I absolve,' yet bind the penitent and dismiss him unabsolved. But what is worst of all, they likewise subject the whole sacrament to danger, because they protract it (i.e., postpone its proper efficacy) until the penance enjoined has been fully paid. Accordingly, if in the meanwhile, and before the sacrament is perfected, the penitent from frailty commit another lapse, he interposes an obstacle in one part, and thereby nullifies the whole of the sacrament. For things which constitute an essential unity are by the nullity of one rendered all null."[1]

Luther held a similar course, maintaining the ancient belief in confession and absolution as to all essential features, with one notable exception. Luther's solifidianism, i.e., his tendency to reduce all operations of grace to exercises or results of faith, entered into his views

[1] " Reformers before the Reformation," vol. ii. pp. 540, 1.

of penance. He regarded all sacraments alike, not as means conveying the grace which they exhibit, but as mere stimulants, which, when presented to the soul, excite faith, and so work on the consciousness. Thus absolution is, in Luther's view, only the exhibition of the promised forgiveness of GOD, which the soul by its own act appropriates to itself.[1]

The Lutheran doctrine is explained in the Augsburg Confession of Faith. The expressions which mark Luther's solifidianism are given in italics.

" First, we teach the necessity of contrition, i.e., of real terror and grief of mind, acknowledging the wrath of GOD, lamenting its sin, and leading to amendment of life. . . . . Faith is to be added, i.e., a sure trust in the mercy promised through CHRIST, a settled belief that sin is remitted freely for His sake. *When in the midst of grief for sin we are raised up by such faith, we*

[1] " Omnia sacramenta ad fidem alendam sunt instituta."—Op. Sen. tom. iii. fol. 266, b. Melancthon also said, in his " Loci Theologici," " Apparet quam nihil sacramenta sunt, nisi fidei exercendæ μνημόσυνα."

The opinions of the later Lutherans however varied on this point, and they at last returned to the full belief of the Catholic Church.

In their " disputes with the Sacramentarians, the Reformers of Wirtemberg," says Moehler, " approximated again to the doctrine of the Church." The " Apology" goes beyond the Augsburg Confession, and attributes to sacraments an actual conveyance of grace. " Sacramentum est ceremonia vel opus, in quo Deus nobis exhibet hoc quod offert annexâ ceremoniæ gratiâ."

Moehler observes that the difference between the Lutherans and the Church, as to the nature of a sacrament, after a time altogether disappeared. " Macheineke," he says, " admits this at least, and says the difference between the two Confessions consists simply in this, that Catholics teach, sacramenta *continere* gratiam; Protestants, on the other hand, inculcate, sacramenta *conferre* gratiam."—Moehler's Symbolism, Robertson's translation, vol. i. pp. 294, 295.

surely obtain the remission of our sins ; and this faith is conceived by the soul by means of the Gospel, and also through absolution which announces and applies the Gospel to the terrified conscience. Therefore we teach that private absolution is to be retained in the Church, and we greatly extol (amplissimis laudibus ornamus) its value and the power of the keys ; because the power of the keys applies the Gospel, not only generally to all, but privately to individuals . . . . and we ought to trust to the voice of the Gospel, conveyed to us by the ministry of the Church in absolution, as to a voice sounding out of heaven. . . . .

" Moreover, since confession gives occasion for administering private absolution, and the rite itself *maintains among the people the knowledge* of the power of the keys, and remission of sins ; and further, because of its great value for the guidance and instruction of men's souls, we therefore carefully retain confession in our Church ; but yet we teach that the numbering of sins is not necessary by the law of GOD, nor that consciences ought to be burdened by such numbering.[1] For there is no precept in the Apostolic

---

[1] The context shows that by "numbering of sins" is not meant the free unburdening of a guilty conscience, but the harassing pressure of a forced examination in detail, coupled with the idea that the hope of forgiveness rested not on the truth of the repentance, but on the exactness of the enumeration. The character of the practice alluded to, is evident from the terms expressive of distress applied to it, as, e.g., in the preface to the Saxon Confession of Faith, where the " numbering of sins" is described as "carnificina conscientiarum, impediens fidem et invocationem."

As the special object of confession, according to the prevailing practice, was not so much to ascertain the truth of the repentance, but rather the amount of sin, in order to apportion the penance, the reason for such " numbering " is evident.

writings requiring this numbering. Moreover, the exact enumeration of all sin is impossible, as is written in the Psalm: 'Who can tell how oft he offendeth?' Also Jeremiah says, 'the heart of man is inscrutable.' And if no sins are remitted, unless they are openly confessed, the conscience can never rest, because the greater number of sins can neither be perceived, nor remembered. For which reason, it is easy to be understood, that the ministry of absolution and remission of sin does not depend on this numbering.

"Lastly, there is the greatest need, that the minds of the devout should be warned on the subject of satisfactions; for these have been more hurtful than the numbering of sins. Satisfactions have obscured the gracious gift of CHRIST, because the unlearned were wont to think that the remission of guilt was obtained through their own works, and, if anything were omitted, they were troubled. Moreover, ceremonies, pilgrimages, and unprofitable works of this kind, were more esteemed than the Divine commandments. And even the learned themselves feigned that eternal death was compensated by these things. Therefore we teach that canonical satisfaction profits not towards the remission of guilt, or of eternal punishment, neither are they necessary. Formerly it was the custom not to receive back the fallen to the peace of the Church, unless certain penalties were enjoined for example's sake. From this custom satisfactions arose; but the ancients, by such example, sought to deter people from sinning, not imagining that the act enjoined was a compensation for sin, or eternal punishment. Unlearned men afterwards thus feigned. But those ancient customs have grown obsolete in the lapse of years. We do not, therefore, load the conscience with satisfactions, but teach that the necessary fruits of repentance,—obedience, fear of God, faith, love, charity, and universal newness of spirit,—ought to grow in us.

"We admonish, also, that sins are often punished by temporal penalties in this life, as David, Manasseh, and many others were punished. And we teach, that these punishments are mitigated by good works and repentance, as Paul teaches, 'If we judge ourselves, we shall not be judged of the Lord.'

"Thus formerly the disputes concerning penance were inextricable, and full of absurd opinions, but now the reformed doctrine is so delivered to the people, as to be intelligible and conducive to piety. We retain and teach the true facts of penance, viz., contrition, faith, absolution, remission of sins, amendment of life, and mitigation of temporal punishment."[1]

Hooker thus describes the Lutheran doctrine and its practical working :—"But concerning confession in private, the Churches of Germany, as well the rest, as the Lutherans, agree all, that all men should at certain times confess their offences to God in the hearing of God's ministers, thereby to show how their sins displease them; to receive instruction for the warier carriage of themselves hereafter, to be soundly resolved if any scruple, or snare of conscience, &c., entangle their minds; and, which is most material, to the end that men may at God's hands seek every one his own particular pardon, through the power of those keys, which

---

[1] The Saxon Confession of Faith entirely agrees in substance with that of Augsburg, in the article of " Penance."

the ministers of God using according to our Blessed Saviour's institution in that case, it is their part to accept the benefit thereof, as God's most merciful ordinance for their good, and without any distrust or doubt, to embrace joyfully His grace so given them, according to the word of our Lord, which hath said, 'Whose sins ye remit, they are remitted.' So that grounding upon this assured belief they are to rest with minds encouraged and persuaded concerning the forgiveness of all their sins as out of Christ's own word and power by the ministry of the keys."[1]

Calvin in this, as in all questions touching sacramental life and ordinances, had the melancholy distinction of being the first to pervert the ancient belief. He scrupled not to overthrow the unvarying traditions of fifteen centuries, and, as far as his teaching and influence extended, to deprive one of the most solemn institutions of Christ, one most intimately bearing on the life and peace of the soul, of its true efficacy and covenanted grace. The deep impression of his powerful mind is vividly manifest to the present day in the total absence of any sacramental conception of confession and absolution, wherever his influence has spread.

Calvin indeed recommended confession, as, e.g., in his Institutes, where he says; "Let every believer remember that it is his duty, if he feels such secret anguish and affliction from a sense of his sins, that he cannot extricate himself without some exterior aid, not to neglect the remedy offered to him by the Lord, which is, that, in order to alleviate his distress, he

---

[1] Eccl. Pol. lib. vi. c. iv. s. 14. See note at the end of this chapter.

should use the private confession with his pastor, and,
to obtain consolation, should privately implore his
assistance, whose office is, both publicly and privately,
to comfort the people of GOD with the doctrine of the
Gospel."[1]   The Swiss confession of faith also upholds
private confession.   But confession, as understood in
the Swiss system, is altogether different from the Lutheran view of it.

The Lutherans were careful to preserve the connexion
between confession and the ministry of the keys, and
absolution as the ordinance in which this ministry is
exercised.   The Swiss Reformers, on the contrary, represent confession to be merely a means of spiritual
discipline or teaching, irrespective of the remission of
sins, such as might be administered by a layman equally
as by an ordained minister of GOD, and absolution as
identical with preaching or expounding the Gospel.   As
Calvin taught a doctrine of the Eucharist, which made
the Sacred Presence to depend on the faith of the receiver, not on the act of consecration, so he invented a
theory of penance which had no reference to an ordained
ministry.   These views are thus expressed in the Swiss
Confession of Faith :—

" It is necessary that we confess our sins to GOD our
FATHER, and be reconciled with our brother, if we have
offended him.   Of which kind of confession James the
Apostle speaking says ; ' Confess your sins one to
another.'   If anyone, moreover, oppressed with the
weight of sin and perplexing temptations, desire privately to seek counsel, instruction, and consolation,
either of a minister of the Church, or *any other brother
learned in the law of God*, we condemn it not.   In like

---

[1] Institutes of the Christian Religion.   l. iii. c. iv. sec. 12.

manner we greatly approve, as accordant with the Scriptures, the general and public confession of sins, wont to
be made in church and in public assemblies.

"Concerning the keys of the kingdom of heaven, delivered by our LORD to His Apostles, many speak marvellous things, and of them forge swords, lances, sceptres,
and crowns, and plenary power against mightiest king-
doms, and against souls and bodies. We, judging simply
by the Word of GOD, affirm that all ministers duly
called have and exercise the keys, when they preach
the Gospel, i.e., instruct the people committed to their
charge, exhort, control, rebuke, and rule with discipline.
For thus they open the kingdom of heaven to the
obedient, and close it against the disobedient. . . . .
*They use the keys, when they lead to faith and repent-
ance. Thus they reconcile to God. Thus they remit sins.
Ministers absolve duly and efficaciously when they preach
the Gospel, and in it the remission of sins promised to individual believers,* testifying, as in the case of baptism,
that it belongs specially to individuals."

Hooker's account of the practice of the French Protestants—and the same applies to all communities
formed, like the French, after the Swiss model— is as
follows :—

"Private confession to the minister alone touching
secret crimes, or absolution thereupon ensuing, as the
one to the other, is neither practised by the French discipline, nor used in any of those churches which have
been cast by the French mould. Open confession to be
made in the face of the whole congregation by notorious
malefactors they hold necessary, howbeit not necessary
towards the remission of sins, but only in some sort to
content the Church, and that one man's sympathy may

seem to strengthen many, which before have been weakened by one man's fall."[1]

The history of the practice of confession in these two Protestant communities, illustrates the essential difference of the principles on which their views are respectively grounded. Among the followers of Calvin confession has altogether ceased. Such a practice could not be expected to live as a mere mode of discipline, without any promise or result as to the forgiveness of sin. Among the Lutherans on the other hand confession is practised at the present day, and, though subject to occasional decline, yet in revivals of spiritual life the desire for its more frequent use revives also.[2] An instance of such a revival occurred so late as May, 1856, when a Conference, representing the Protestants of Saxony, Bavaria, Wurtemburg, and other German states, was held at Dresden, and a resolution was passed, affirming "the necessity of re-establishing the use of regular confession and absolution."[3]

The comparison between these two Protestant communities proves, that where, as in the case of the Lu-

---

[1] Eccl. Pol. l. vi. See the note at the end of this chapter. The writer also begs to refer to some remarks on the character of Calvinistic teaching as regards the Sacraments, in his volume on the "Doctrine of the Priesthood." (Masters.)

[2] Melancthon's striking language, quoted by the late Mr. Newland in a pamphlet, entitled, "Confession as it is in the Church of England," is an instance of the doctrine impressed on the Lutheran mind by the early German Reformers. "Impium esset de ecclesiâ privatam Absolutionem tollere. Neque quid sit remissio peccatorum, aut potestas clavium intelligunt, si qui privatam absolutionem aspernantur."

[3] An account of the Conference was given in the *Guardian* of Nov. 22, 1856, being copied from the *Deutsche Volksblathe*. A form of abso-

therans, Catholic antiquity is respected as a standard of truth, there confession is maintained in connection with the ministry of reconciliation; and only where, as in the case of the Swiss or Calvinistic communities, Catholic antiquity is disregarded, and the Church's primitive traditions set aside, confession and absolution are no longer believed to possess a sacramental virtue, or to have any effect in the reconciliation of the penitent to GOD.

This comparison has an important bearing on the question of Confession in the Church of England, which has uniformly professed to rest its interpretations of doctrine on the judgment of the early Catholic Church. For the fact that the Lutherans, looking in this matter to the same sources of authority, as the standard of truth, with ourselves, have come to the same conclusion, is a strong confirmation of the truth which we claim as the legitimate heritage of the Church of England.

NOTE.

I. The following extracts illustrate the practical working of the rule of confession in the Lutheran communities:—

Extracts from the Evangelical Liturgy, (Evangelische Handagende) Edited by G. C. Dieffenbach and C. Müller. Stuttgart, S. G. Liesching. 1858. Page 325.

"PRIVATE CONFESSION.—First Form.

"How simple (einfältig) folk are to be taught to confess. (From Dr. M. Luther's Small Catechism.)

"What is confession?

"Confession includes two things: *first*, to confess one's sins; se-

lution was then determined on, which is as follows:—"Almighty GOD have mercy upon you, and by the authority of our LORD JESUS CHRIST I absolve you from all your sins, in the Name of the FATHER, and of the SON, and of the HOLY GHOST. Amen. Go in peace. Amen."

condly, to receive the absolution or pardon from the confessor as if from GOD Himself, not doubting, but surely believing, that sin is *thereby* forgiven by GOD Himself in heaven.

"What sins are to be confessed?

"We shall acknowledge all sins before GOD, even those we are not aware of, as we do in the LORD's Prayer. But to the confessor we shall only acknowledge such sins as we are aware of and feel in our hearts.

"Which are these?

"See what your situation in the world is, and what the ten commandments say. Whether you be a father, mother, son, daughter, master, mistress, man or maid servant; whether you have been disobedient, false (lying or unfaithful), lazy, angry, impure, hating; whether you have injured anyone in words or deeds; whether you have stolen, been negligent, careless, or have done any other wrong whatever.

"Dear friend, teach me a short way to confess.

"Say to the Father Confessor:

"Reverend dear Sir, I beg you will hear my confession, and give me Absolution of my sins for GOD's sake.

"I, poor sinful man, confess to GOD and to you that I have greatly sinned against all GOD's laws in thought, word, and deed; that by nature I was conceived and born in sin, and deserving death and GOD's wrath; wherefore I am heartily sorry that I have drawn upon me the wrath of GOD my LORD, and I do heartily pray that GOD may graciously forgive me all my sins for the sake of our LORD JESUS CHRIST, and renew my heart by the HOLY SPIRIT, inasmuch as I do believe in and trust upon His holy Word.

"And insomuch as you have our LORD JESUS CHRIST's command to forgive all penitents their sins, I beseech you for CHRIST's sake to teach and console me with GOD's Word, to pronounce upon me in His Name the pardon of my sins, and to give me the Body and Blood of JESUS CHRIST, to the strengthening of my faith; I will, GOD being my Helper, willingly amend my ways.

"(Here follows the *private* confession.)

"Then the confessor says,

"May GOD be merciful unto thee and strengthen thy faith. Amen.

"Dost thou believe that my absolution (pardon, [Vergebung]) is GOD's absolution?

"Yes, I believe it is.

"As thou hast believed, so be it done unto thee; and I, by command of our LORD JESUS CHRIST, forgive thee all thy sins in the Name of the

FATHER, and of the SON, and of the HOLY GHOST. Amen. Go in peace. Amen."

As a contrast to these specimens of the Lutheran practice, the following extract from a private letter illustrates the present system of so-called confession in Presbyterian communities based on the Calvinistic system. The account relates to the Scotch Kirk, and is written by a friend of the author, one well able to judge by personal experience of the prevailing practice. It was written in answer to an inquiry, how far confession is now known to the Kirk?

"The intending communicant must see his minister. The minister has this opportunity afforded him of rejecting unworthy persons. But supposing the respectability of the applicant to be unimpeachable, all his inquiry is directed to ascertain his religious knowledge and orthodoxy. He performs the duty of repelling those who are not found worthy, not so much as invested with individual ministerial authority, but rather as the chairman of his Kirk Session who cite and hear delinquents, sitting as a kind of committee on morals, and using their own name, coupled with that of the minister, to enforce ecclesiastical censures and decrees. The 15th Article of the Confession of Faith speaks of confession of sins to those whom men may have offended, and the consequent duty of being reconciled and receiving back to love and kindliness : but not a word of sacramental confession.

"Then, again, Article XXX. on Church censures, speaks of Absolution as being merely a freeing from these, and not in any sense what the Church has always understood it to be. And such absolution is to be pronounced by 'Church officers,' a title which includes the elders and Kirk Session, &c.

"In the larger Westminster Catechism (Questions 171—173) the duty of preparation is explained and enforced : but recourse to GOD's ministers, even in a case of doubtfulness, is never recommended. Even the 'ignorant and scandalous' are only to 'receive instruction and manifest reformation.'

"I can find nothing to lead me to suppose that the practice as at -present existing in the Kirk and other Presbyterian bodies, is anything beyond what is thus laid down. The earnest-minded ministers may deal more closely with the conscience, but all inquiry is into the state of the mind, and has regard rather to the intellectual apprehension of truth, than to the practical application of it to the life and conscience. And I am further convinced that any person coming to the best Presbyterian

minister under deep remorse, would receive sympathy indeed and kind-
ness (the men being better Christians than their Calvinistic system), but
that the only ministerial action would be the repetition of Scripture
promises, and the general declaration that GOD forgives sinners for
CHRIST'S sake on their true repentance, and then the offering of prayer
for the penitent, all ended by an expression of personal kind wishes in
the shape of a ' GOD be with you,' or some other form of blessing.

"The Presbyterians, in short, are in practice very faithful to their
theory. And the whole tendency of that theory has been to destroy
the idea of personal and priestly authority, and to substitute for it the
notion that all authority resides in the general body, and is delegated by
them to the officers, who are popularly elected and act as a kind of Committee; and that even this authority does not reach beyond the removal
of open scandal, and the decent ordering of the Visible Church."

CHAPTER V.

RICHARD Hooker, Jeremy Taylor, and Archbishop Usher, are the three of our Divines of chiefest note, who have canvassed the question of Confession most fully with special reference to the differences between us and the Church of Rome. They are therefore the fittest authorities for distinguishing the separate views of Confession, as now held respectively in the two communions.

The fact of Hooker himself practising confession,[1] is enough to prove that his opposition could only be against a certain mode of viewing it, not against the ordinance itself. The following passage, moreover, is inconsistent with any thought of disparagement; "Because the knowledge how to handle our souls is no vulgar and common art, but we either carry towards ourselves for the most part an over soft and gentle hand, fearful of touching too near the quick, or else endeavouring not to be partial, we fall into timorous scrupulosities, and sometimes into those extreme discomforts of mind from which we hardly do ever lift up our heads again; men thought it the safest way to disclose their secret faults, and to crave imposition of Penance from them whom

[1] Life, by Isaac Walton; quoted in a later chapter of this work.

our LORD JESUS CHRIST hath left in His Church to be
spiritual and ghostly physicians, the guides and pastors
of redeemed souls, whose office doth not only consist in
general persuasions unto amendment of life, but also in
the private particular cure of diseased minds.   Howsoever the Novatianists presume to plead against the
Church, saith Salvianus, that 'Every man ought to be
his own penitentiary, and that it is a part of our duty
to exercise, but not of the Church's authority to impose or prescribe repentance,' the truth is otherwise,
the best and strongest of us may need in such cases
direction."[1]

Nor did Hooker demur to the substitution of private
for public confession. He considered this change in the
Church's practice to have been necessary, and traces the
evils which he exposes, not to the secrecy, but to the
forced obligation, of the more modern rule.   " Forasmuch," he says, "as public confession became dangerous, it seemed first unto some, and afterwards generally, that voluntary penitents should surcease from
open confession. When once private and secret confession had taken place with the Latins, it continued as
a profitable ordinance, till the Lateran Council had
decreed that all men once in a year at least should confess themselves to the Priest."

Hooker's opposition was directed primarily against
the assumed necessity of confession.   " We everywhere
find the use of confession, especially public, allowed of
and commended by the Fathers, but that *extreme* and
rigorous necessity of auricular and private confession,
which is at this day so mightily upheld by the Church

[1] Eccl. Pol. vi. ch. iv. 7.

of Rome, we find not." The same point he urges more in detail in the following passage; "It was not then the faith and doctrine of God's Church, as of the Papacy at this present; (1) That the only remedy for sin after Baptism is sacramental penitency. (2) That confession in secret is an essential part thereof. (3) That God Himself cannot now forgive sin without the Priest. (4) That because forgiveness at the hands of the Priest must arise from confession in the offender, therefore to confess unto him is a matter of such necessity, as being not either in deed, or at the least in desire performed, excludeth utterly from all pardon, and must consequently in Scripture be commanded wheresoever any promise of forgiveness is made. No, no; these opinions have youth in their countenance: antiquity knew them not; it never thought nor dreamed of them."

Hooker moreover argues against the threefold definition of the sacrament of Penance. "Contrition" he explains to be "an inward thing which belongeth to the virtue, and not to the sacrament of repentance, which must consist of external parts, if the nature thereof be external." And he urges further, that being a state of mind, a fitness for receiving grace, it cannot from its very nature be part of a sacrament; "for a sacrament by their doctrine must both signify and also confer some special Divine grace."

Moreover Hooker thus explains, while he controverts, the Roman doctrine of satisfaction. "They imagine, beyond all conceit of antiquity, that when God doth remit sin, and the punishment eternal thereunto belonging, He reserveth the torments of hell fire to be nevertheless endured for a time, either shorter or longer, according to the quality of men's crimes, yet so that there is between GOD and man a certain composition (as it were) or contract, by virtue whereof works assigned by the Priest to be done after absolution shall satisfy GOD, as touching the punishment which He otherwise would inflict for sin pardoned and forgiven."

Against this idea he argues: "They cannot assure any man, that if he perform what the Priest appointeth, it shall suffice," . . . "insomuch that the Priest hath no power to determine or define of equivalency between sins and satisfaction."   And, further, striking at one root of the principle on which the Roman theory of satisfaction rests, he urges, that "if GOD be satisfied and do pardon sin, our justification restored, is as perfect as it was at first bestowed;" "that the truth of this doctrine is not to be shifted off by destraining it unto eternal punishment alone;" "that to be subject to revenge for sin, although the punishment of it be but temporal, is to be under the curse of the law;" that "if it please GOD to lay punishment on them whose sins He hath forgiven, yet is not this done for any destructive end of wasting or eating them out, as in plagues inflicted on the impenitent, neither is the punishment of the one or of the other proportioned by the greatness of the sins past, but according to that future purpose whereunto the goodness of GOD referreth it, and wherein there is nothing meant to the sufferer but furtherance of all happiness, now in grace, and hereafter in glory."   Finally he quotes a saying of S. Augustine, which he terms "a general axiom for all such chastisements:" "Before forgiveness they are the punishments of sinners; and after forgiveness, they are exercises and trials of righteous men."

Hooker implies that he was ready to admit confession and absolution as component parts of the sacrament of penance, had Rome been willing thus to limit its definition. " Forasmuch," he says, " as a sacrament is complete, having the matter and form which it ought, what should lead them " (the Roman theologians) " to set down any other part of sacramental repentance, than confession and absolution, as Durandus hath done? Will they draw in contrition with satisfaction which are no parts, and exclude absolution (a principal part), yea, the very complement, form, and perfection of the rest, as themselves account it."[1]

Jeremy Taylor, as will hereafter be shown, in his devotional treatises, recommends confession more strongly than any other Divine in our communion. Even in his controversial treatises on the subject[2] he opens the discussion by an express disclaimer of any intention to disparage the practice. " Whether," he says, " to confess to a priest be an advisable discipline, and a good instance, instrument and ministry to repentance, and may serve many good ends in the Church, and to the souls of needing persons, is no part of the question;" adding, "the Church of England is no way engaged against it, but advises it, practises it." Moreover, in common with Hooker, he expresses his approval of the substitution of private for public penance, while yet regretting the necessity for the change. " The old ecclesiastical discipline having passed into desuetude and indevotion, the Latin Church especially kept up

[1] See the Eccl. Pol. l. vi. ch. iv., v. passim.
[2] " Dissuasive from Popery," Heber's Edit., vol. xi. p. 10.

some little broken planks of it, which so long as charity
and devotion were warm, and secular interest had not
turned religion into art, did in some good measure
supply the want of the old better discipline."

Taylor's main argument is directed against the universally compulsory rule; "Let it be commanded," he
says, "to all, to whom it is needful or profitable; but
let it be free, as to the conscience precisely, and bound
but by the cords of a man, and as other ecclesiastical
laws are, which are capable of restrictions, cautions,
dispensations, rescindings, and abolitions, by the same
authority, or upon greater reasons. *The question is,
whether to confess all our greater sins to a priest, all that
upon strict inquiry we can remember, be necessary to
salvation.*"

Again, "When CHRIST said to His Apostles, 'Whose
sins ye remit, they shall be remitted to them; and whose
sins ye retain, they shall be retained,' He made (says
Bellarmine, and generally the later school of Roman
doctors,) the Apostles, and all priests, judges upon
earth; that without their sentence, no man, that hath
sinned after baptism, can be reconciled. But the
priests, who are judges, can give no right or unerring
sentence, unless they hear all the particulars they are
to judge. Therefore by CHRIST's law they are tied to
tell in confession all their particular sins to a priest.
This is the sum of all that is said in this affair. Other
light skirmishes there are, but the main battle is here."

Taylor, moreover, argues against the principle of
satisfaction. The position he controverts is, "that
priests have power to impose a punishment according
to the quality of every sin."

Taylor argues, on the contrary, that "the judgment the priest is to make, is not of the *sins*, but of the *persons*. It is not said, ' Quæcumque,' but ' Quorum-cumque remiseritis peccata.' And therefore it becomes the minister of souls, to know the state of the penitent, rather than the nature and number of the sins."

Again, " We do not find anything in the words of CHRIST, obliging the priest directly to impose penances on the penitent sinner; he may voluntarily submit himself to them, if he please, and he may do very well, if he do so; but the power of retaining sins, gives no power to punish him, whether he will or no; for the power of retaining is rather to be exercised upon the impenitent than the penitent." Again; " If we con-sider that without true repentance no sin can be par-doned, and with it all sins may, and that no one sin is pardoned as to the state of our souls, but at the same time all are pardoned, it must needs follow, that it is not the number of sins, but the condition of the person, the change of his life, the sorrow of his heart, the truth of his conversion, and his hatred of all sin, that he is to consider."

In a previous passage Taylor assumes that priests in receiving confessions, are judges; but he argues against the idea of a " proper judicial power," i.e., as opposed to one ministerial or dependent, which GOD Himself, as He wills, ratifies. He quotes S. Ambrose in proof of his position; " ' Men give their ministry in the re-mission of sins, but they exercise not the right of any power; neither are sins remitted by them in their own, but in the Name of the FATHER, SON, and HOLY SPI-RIT. Men pray, but it is GOD forgives; it is man's obsequiousness, but the bountiful gift is from GOD. So likewise there is no doubt, sins are forgiven in baptism, but the operation is of the FATHER, SON, and HOLY SPIRIT.' Here S. Ambrose affirms the priest's power of pardoning sins to be wholly ministerial, and optative, or by way of prayer. Just as it is in baptism, so it is in repentance after baptism, sins are pardoned to the truly penitent; but here is no proper[1] judicial power. The Bishop prays, and GOD pardons; the priest does his ministry, and GOD gives the gift." Taylor insists that the sentence of the priest is that of " an ambassador, not of a judge;" that "GOD alone can remit by His own right;" "but yet to this pardon the Church doth co-operate by her ministry."[2]

Usher pursues a similar line of argument in his answer to Fisher the Jesuit. He first expressly guards himself against being supposed to disparage the use whether of private or public confession, while strongly opposing certain details of the Roman practice. " Be it therefore known unto you, that no kind of confession, either public or private, is disallowed by us, that is requisite for the due execution of that ancient power of the keys, which CHRIST has bestowed upon His Church."[3] His first and main attack is directed against the compulsory rule. " The thing which we reject is that new picklock of sacramental confession, obtruded

[1] For the meaning of the term "proper" in English theology, the writer begs to refer to chapter xii. in his "Doctrine of the Priesthood in the Church of England."

[2] "Dissuasive from Popery," Heber's Edit., vol. xi. p. 10, seq. passim.

[3] Usher's Works. Oxford Edit., vol. iii. 91.

upon men's consciences, as a *matter necessary to salvation.*" He argues also against the idea of absolution being more than "ministerial," or, as he explains the term, "operative through the efficacy of prayer and the gift of the HOLY GHOST, which GOD imparts for the remission of sins through the ministry of the priest." "But our new masters," he says, "will not content themselves with such a ministerial power of forgiving sins, as hath been spoken of, unless we yield that they have authority so to do properly, directly, and absolutely." He also opposes the idea of the sinner being thereby, i.e., by absolution, immediately acquitted before GOD, howsoever that sound conversion of heart be wanting in him, which otherwise would be requisite. For a conditional absolution, upon such terms as these, "If thou dost believe and repent as thou oughtest to do," is, in these men's judgments, to no purpose, and can give no security to the penitent; seeing it dependeth on an uncertain condition. He opposes "the absolute power of the keys," and adds; "To think that it lieth in the power of any priest truly to absolve a man from his sins, without implying the condition of 'his believing and repenting as he ought to do,' is both presumption and madness in the highest degree."

Usher especially controverts the idea, on which the above statements are grounded, of attrition being made contrition through grace given in confession. "Now that contrition is at all times required for obtaining remission of sins and justification, is a matter determined by the Fathers of Trent. But mark yet the mystery. They equivocate with us in the term contrition, and make a distinction thereof into perfect and im-

F 2

perfect. The former of these is contrition properly;
the latter they call attrition, which, howsoever in itself
it be not true contrition, yet when the priest, with his
power of forgiving sins, interposeth himself in the
business, they tell us that 'attrition, by virtue of the
keys, is made contrition,' that is to say, that a sorrow
arising from a servile fear of punishment, on such a
fruitless repentance as the reprobate may carry with
them into hell, by virtue of the priest's absolution, is
made so fruitful that it shall serve the turn for obtaining forgiveness of sins, as if it had been that godly
sorrow which worketh repentance to salvation not to be
repented of. By which spiritual cozenage many poor
souls are most miserably deluded, while they persuade
themselves that upon the receipt of the priest's acquit-
tance, upon this carnal sorrow of theirs, all scores are
cleared until that day; and then by beginning upon a
new reckoning, they sin and confess, confess and sin
afresh, and tread this round so long till they put off all
saving repentance, and so the blind following the blind,
both at last fall into the pit."[1]

It must be borne in mind, that the question here proposed is not whether these divines state fairly, without
prejudice or exaggeration, the particular points of Roman
doctrine which they controvert. They may, or not, err
in this respect without in the least affecting the conclusion to establish which their evidence is adduced. The
object of these quotations is simply to prove, that these
writers, and consequently the schools of English theology which they represent, in condemning certain de-

[1] Usher's Works. Oxford Edit., vol. iii. 91.

tails of the modern system of confession, do not thereby
condemn confession itself, and that their desire manifestly is to distinguish, and separate off, views of later
growth from the essential features of the original institution which they uphold.

It is moreover to be observed as a most remarkable and
pregnant circumstance, that the same difficulties and objections on the question of Confession have been felt both
within and without the Roman Obedience; for the points
of doctrine and practice controverted by our divines
coincide with those which, as already has been shown,
formed the subjects of attack from the earlier Reformers
before the Reformation. This agreement between our
own divines and the opponents of the schoolmen proves,
that our dissent from Rome is but a continuation of
the same protest which many of her children, and those
of great learning and ability, raised within her own
communion, until the Council of Trent silenced all
questionings. In both cases, before and after the Reformation, the resistance has been not to Confession
itself or any one of its original essential principles,
but to certain incidental, though in themselves and in
their effect upon confession most momentous, features,
which can be proved to have been developed in mediæval times, and to be at variance with primitive
belief.

Should it therefore ever in the tender mercies of
God come to pass, that the heart of Rome be turned
to her fathers, stirred to test her doctrines by their
teaching, seeking the reunion of Christendom by a return to the revelations once and for ever delivered to
the saints, the basis of agreement must be laid in the

principles to which many of her own leading theologians referred in the controversies which preceded the unhappy separation of so large a portion of the western world from her communion, and which are still our justification and support in the witness which, however painfully, we are constrained to bear in defence of the Apostolical traditions entrusted to us.

CHAPTER VI.

TO fix the conditions of Communion, was the question of greatest practical moment to be determined at the time of the Reformation in England. For upwards of 300 years, from 1215 to 1548, there was no approach to the Blessed Sacrament without habitual confession. This rule was repealed in England in the first year of Edward VI. But it was not intended that confessions should therefore cease. The contrary is clearly implied in the Royal Injunctions issued in the course of the same year. It is therein enjoined; "They (the clergy) shall in confessions every Lent examine every person that cometh to confession to them, whether they can recite the articles of their faith, the Pater Noster and the Ten Commandments in English; and hear them say the same particularly; wherein if they be not perfect, they shall declare them, that every Christian person ought to know the said things, before they should receive the Blessed Sacrament of the altar."[1] Confession therefore was intended to be continued as a general practice.

The first Prayer Book was published in the year following, and it contained an invitation to confession. No necessity existed for mentioning the subject of Con-

[1] Cardwell's Documentary Annals, "Injunctions by King Edward VI." Vol. i. p. 10.

fession in the new Eucharistic Office. The ancient Liturgy, from which it was taken, contained no allusion to it. If the Reformers had designed to set aside Confession, they could most readily have effected their object by passing it over in silence. There would have been no omission, where there was no precedent for its introduction. The express allusion to it in connexion with the Holy Communion can hardly be explained, except on the supposition of a desire to secure its continuance, though under an altered rule.

The passage relating to Confession stood thus in the first Prayer Book: " If there be any of you whose conscience is troubled and grieved in anything, lacking comfort or counsel, let him come to me or some other discreet[1] and learned priest, taught in the law of GOD, and confess and open his sin and grief secretly, that he may receive such ghostly counsel, advice, and comfort, that his conscience may be relieved, and that of us, (as of the ministers of GOD and of the Church,) he may re-

---

[1] I am indebted to Dr. Irons for the following remarks on the word " discreet :"—

" This is a term well known in the canon law. It does not mean any common virtue which a man may attribute to himself; but *definite* virtues ascertained by the Bishop or Ordinary. 'Discreet' canonically means, 'approved by the Bishop as discreet,' and 'learned,' approved by the Bishop as learned. They are technical terms. Thus a priest may be discreet for one thing, and not for another; discreet for hearing confessions, and not discreet for matrimonial causes. Facciolati, or any Lexicon of mediæval Latin, would explain, discretus, to mean 'separated specially' for a particular thing; and hence the virtue itself came to be called *discretion*, i.e., including all the fitness required for the particular work . . . Lyndwood says that Rural Deans may hear confessions in their own parishes (because they are parsons), but they may not hear them elsewhere, because they are not *discreet*, i.e., specially commissioned for such an exercise of their powers."

ceive comfort and absolution, to the satisfaction of his mind, and avoiding of all scruple and doubtfulness : requiring such as shall be satisfied with a general confession not to be offended with them that so use to their further satisfying the auricular and secret confession to the priest; nor those also which think needful or convenient, for the quietness of their own consciences, particularly to open their sins to the priest, to be offended with them that are satisfied with their humble confession to GOD, and the general confession to the Church ; but in all things to follow and keep the rule of charity, and every man to be satisfied with his own conscience, not judging other men's consciences ; whereas he has no warrant of GOD's word to the same."

Two important principles were here asserted. (1.) Confession was declared to be no longer obligatory on the consciences of all alike, but dependent on the special needs of individual souls. (2.) Permission was given to confess to any priest, not necessarily, as before, to the priest of the parish.[1]

Probably a third point at variance with mediæval

---

[1] The Roman rule binds every one to confess to his own parish Priest, and decrees that an absolution given by any other is void. The Council of Trent grounds this rule on the principle of Priests exercising a strictly judicial function. If they are judges armed with authority within a particular sphere, those who are within their cure are subject to them, and thus bound to their ministry. " Quoniam igitur natura et ratio judicii illud exposcit, ut sententia in subditos duntaxat feratur, persuasum semper in Ecclesia Dei fuit, et verissimum esse Synodus hæc confirmat, nullius momenti absolutionem eam esse debere, quam sacerdos in eum profert in quem ordinariam aut subdelegatam non habet jurisdictionem." That this is but a law of discipline, depending on Church rule, not a principle inherent in the institution, is clear from this, that in case of mortal sickness any Priest

practice was intended, viz., the restricting the objects of confession to absolution and spiritual counsel, no mention being made of satisfaction, or compensation for the temporal penalties of sin, which had formed so material a part of the mediæval idea of Penance.

The closing paragraph, most characteristic of the temper of the English Reformation in its earlier stage, before foreign divines entered in to disturb its native and legitimate tendencies, conveys a salutary warning to those who confess, not to disparage those who struggle on, as they suppose more healthfully, without it; and on the other hand to those who reject confession, not to regard those who use it, as on that account worse or weaker than themselves; but that each should esteem the other in the grace of charity, they who confess, confessing to the LORD, and giving GOD thanks, and they who confess not, confessing not to the LORD, and giving

is permitted to receive the confession and absolve, and even remit sentences of excommunication imposed by the Bishop. "Verumtamen piè admodum, ne hac ipsa occasione aliquis pereat, in eadem ecclesia Dei custoditum semper fuit, ut nulla sit reservatio in articulo mortis; atque idem omnes sacerdotes quoslibet pœnitentes a quibusvis peccatis et censuris absolvere possunt." Sess. xiv. cap. vii., de casuum reservatione.

It is clearly then a disciplinary law which the Church has power to regulate at discretion. Our rule, "let him come to me or some other," &c., is framed on the idea that confession is of so private and confidential a character, that it is fair and reasonable to allow to every one liberty as to the choice of the confessor. One can readily perceive a propriety in the different use of the Roman and English Communions, arising from their different principles. Confession in the one case being an absolute rule, it necessarily involved an obligation in every one towards his immediate spiritual superior; in our own case being discretionary, it would naturally on this principle admit a greater freedom. See Dr. Pusey's letter to Mr. Richards (pp. 19, 33), where the question is fully argued, and our rule elaborately defended.

GOD thanks.   How much contention would have been spared, if this paragraph had been suffered to remain ! How far gentler and more forbearing a spirit would have been infused into the discussions which of late years have been rife among us !

The entire passage underwent material alterations in the second Prayer Book of the same reign.   The object of the leading divines of our communion at the time, was to win over the foreign Protestants, and those who held with them in England, some, no doubt, from sympathy with their views, but others manifestly influenced by the charitable hope of preventing a wider separation, and possibly, by avoiding controverted expressions, smoothing the way for their adoption of higher Church views.   The wording of the passage, when altered, became in consequence less full and definite, though its original principles are still preserved.   That the change of language implied no change of doctrine, is asserted by the revisers themselves in a document of so public and grave a character as to preclude the idea of haste or exaggeration.   In the "act" authorizing the second Prayer Book, it is declared that "the alterations were adopted with no intention of condemning the doctrine of the former book;" that "it" (the former book) "contained nothing but what was agreeable to the word of GOD and the primitive Church;" and that "such doubts as had been raised in the use and exercise thereof, proceeded rather from the curiosity of the ministers and mistakers, than of any other worthy cause."[1]

[1] Stat. 5 & 6 Edw. VI. c. i.   Hardwick's Reformation, pp. 199, 220, quoted by Procter, Book of Common Prayer, p. 32.

From this declaration it follows that the first Prayer Book contains in full the true principles of the English Reformation, and consequently that we are justified in referring to it for the authoritative explanation of any doubtful passages occurring in the second Book. The passage of the Exhortation in question assumed in the second Book the following shape. The new or altered expressions which are of any importance, are italicized for the sake of easier reference.

" Because it is requisite that no man should come to the Holy Communion but with a full trust in GOD's mercy and with a quiet conscience, therefore if there be any of you which by the manner aforesaid, cannot quiet his own conscience, but requireth further comfort or counsel; then let him come to me or to some other discreet and learned minister of GOD's word, and *open his grief*, that he may receive such ghostly counsel, advice, and comfort, as his conscience may be relieved, and that *by the ministry of God's word* he may receive comfort and *the benefit of absolution*, to the quieting of his conscience, and the avoiding of all scruple and doubtfulness."

The main differences between the first and the second Book are, (1) " grief" instead of " sin and grief;" (2) "open" instead of " confess and open secretly;" (3) " by the ministry of GOD's holy word," instead of "of us (as of the ministers of GOD and of the Church) ;" (4) " benefit of absolution " instead of " absolution ;" (5) " auricular and secret confession" omitted, as well as (6) the closing paragraph, " requiring such as shall be satisfied," &c.

The solemn testimony of the revisers themselves,

already referred to, requires us to interpret the altered terms in the sense of the words for which they were substituted. But even without this authority determining their interpretation, there is no change or omission which could warrant the supposition of change of doctrine. Though "sin and grief" are fuller than "grief" alone, yet the grief intended is manifestly such as burdens the conscience, which can be nothing else than sin. "Grief" implies the effect of the sin on the soul, as well as the sin which causes it.[1] "Open" is a more concise expression than "confess and open," but it is the stronger term of the two, as involving an unreserved confession. To "cover a transgression," the direct contrary to "open," is the Scriptural phrase for withholding a confession. The omission of the terms, "secret," "auricular," is a loss of definiteness, but it has been shown in tracing the history of Confession, that in very early days it became a secret act, and the long established custom at the time when these words were used, would have conveyed to all who heard them the idea of privacy as necessarily involved in that of Confession, no confession but of a private character being then known.

[1] Grief from gravis (grave peccatum) corresponds with the "weighty matter" of the rubric in the "Visitation of the sick." See Mr. Newland's "Confession as it is in the Church of England." Mr. Newland argues from this expression that the confession intended, is limited to the special burden weighing on the conscience. It will hereafter be shown that neither is confession thus limited by the Church of England, nor indeed from its very nature can it be. The question is not entered into in the text, the only object here being to prove that the expressions used respectively in the first and second Prayer Book are identical in principle. "Sin and grief" in the first, and "grief" in the second book, are alike in the singular number, and if the former book did not intend to confine confession to any one special burden on the conscience, neither did the latter.

(4.) "Benefit of absolution," instead of "absolution" simply, is the adoption of an older phrase, and rather connects the language of the revised exhortation more closely than before with the traditionary expressions of the Church. The phrase occurs, e.g., in the canons of the Council of Narbonne, A.D. 1374, and again in those of the Council of Tarragona, A.D. 1329.[1] In the reign of Mary Bonner used the same phrase in one of his Visitation articles, inquiring "whether any person have refused to be confessed, and receive at the priest's hands the benefit of absolution, according to the laudable custom of this realm."[2]

(3.) The phrase, "by the ministry of God's word," needs a fuller consideration. It is indeed often quoted to prove, that absolution is here represented as merely an exposition or application to individuals of the promises of Holy Scripture. If this be indeed the true interpretation, the language of the Prayer Book no longer admits of argument, at least with any consistent results. For the term, absolution, has for ages obtained a definite dogmatic meaning in Christianity, as an ordinance, or act of ministry. It was so understood at the time when the second Prayer Book came into use. The Prayer Book itself always represents it as an exercise of authority confined to the Priesthood, and gives the form in which it is to be administered. The Homilies speak of it, as will afterwards be shown, as a Sacramental ordinance. In primitive times it was a clearly defined ministry, in constant use, and held to

---

[1] Quoted by Dr. Pusey in his Letter to Mr. Richards, "The Church of England leaves her children free."—Pp. 41, 42.

[2] Cardwell's Documentary Annals. Vol. i. p. 130.

be of the greatest moment; and the English Reformation proceeded on the assumption of moulding itself
according to ancient custom. If, therefore, by the insertion of the phrase in question, the Reformers meant
to introduce a new theory of their own, and while retaining the ancient term, affix to it a new meaning,
such a course was not merely in direct contradiction
to their avowed intentions, but would have introduced
hopeless confusion into theological language.

But there is no difficulty in explaining the expression
consistently with the declaration, already quoted, which
affirmed an identity of doctrine in the two Prayer Books.
The expression, no doubt, was adopted, because while
calculated to conciliate the foreign Reformers, it commended itself at the same time, as both scriptural and
patristic. It has been already shown, that in the foreign
reformed Confessions of Faith, special prominence was
given to the word of GOD in connexion with the ministry
of Absolution,—the Lutherans explaining the effects of
this ministry by the power of GOD's word in producing
faith, the Calvinists making it consist altogether in the
declaration of the promises of forgiveness revealed in the
Gospel.

But the expression is also truly consistent with a
sacramental view of the ministry, and is so used in
Scripture and by the Fathers. S. Paul, e.g., speaks
of CHRIST in holy Baptism "cleansing" the Church
" with the washing of water by the Word;"[1] S. Peter
again of our "being born again, not of corruptible
seed, but of incorruptible, by the Word of GOD."[2] In
both cases the grace of the sacrament is referred, not

[1] Ephes. v. 26.   [2] 1 S. Pet. i. 23.

to the act of the minister, but to the Word used in his ministry. In like manner, our LORD ascribes the last Judgment not to His own act, but to His Word: " the word that I have spoken, the same shall judge him in the last day."[1] S. Ambrose preserves this same language; " Sins are remitted through the Word of GOD, of which the Levite is the interpreter and a sort of executor. They are remitted also through the office of the Priest, and the sacred ministry."[2] Again S. Augustine, commenting on our LORD's saying, " Now are ye clean through the word which I have spoken unto you," adds, "Why saith He not, Ye are clean through the Baptism wherewith ye have been baptized? saving that in water also the word cleanseth. Take away the word, and what is water, but water? The word is added to the element, and it becomes a Sacrament, which itself also is a sort of visible word."[3]

Hooker evidently understood the phrase in our Office in this sense, regarding " the word" as a part or instrument of the ministerial act in conveying the grace of absolution, not as a substitute for it. "They " (i.e., they who seek relief of the Priest according to his invitation) " are to rest with mind encouraged and persuaded concerning the forgiveness of their sins, as out of CHRIST's own word and power by the ministry of the keys."[4]

The passage in the Exhortation, when thus under-

---

[1] S. John xii. 48.   [2] De Spir. Sanc. iii. 10.

[3] In Joh. Tract. 80, § 3. This and the preceding passage of S. Ambrose are quoted by Dr. Pusey in his second sermon, " Entire Absolution of the Penitent," note to p. 9.

[4] Eccl. Pol. l. vi. c. iv. 15, vol. iii. p. 61, Keble's edit.

stood, comprehensively expresses the several parts of the ministry,—1. the agent, a Priest, " let him come to me or some other ;"[1] 2. the instrument of His ministry, " God's holy Word ;" 3. the blessing bestowed, " counsel, comfort, and the benefit of Absolution ;" and 4. the results, " the quieting of his conscience and avoiding of all scruple and doubtfulness."

It is further urged, that the Absolution spoken of in the Exhortation is, not the private, but the public act of this ministry, as used in the daily Prayers and the Eucharistic Office. This opinion is grounded on the fact, that no form of private Absolution is appointed, except for the case of sickness ; and this fact is considered all the stronger, because in the Office for the Visitation of the Sick in the First Prayer Book there was a rubric directing, that the form there appointed should be used also " at other times," and this rubric disappears in the second Book. This studied omission of the rubric, it is urged, proves the Church's intention to discontinue the practice of private absolutions, except in sickness, more decisively than if the original order had never been given.

Against this argument the following reasons apply. (1) There is no question, but that private Absolution was intended in the passage in the Exhortation, as it stood in the first Prayer Book, and the framers of the second Book, as already shown, expressly disclaim any change of doctrine. But the doctrine of Absolution is

---

[1] The Priest alone can here be intended from the wording of the earlier part of the Exhortation : " *I* purpose, through GOD's assistance, to administer," &c. A Priest alone can read it, as a Priest alone can celebrate.

a main feature of Christianity, and the relative value of special and general absolutions is, as will hereafter be proved, a material part of the doctrine. (2) The clergy living at the time when the second Prayer Book was introduced, and therefore reading the Exhortation both in its original and altered forms, must have used the same words (for the words offering absolution were not changed) in two different senses, and yet no explanation was given to indicate such an important difference. Persons coming to them for confession on the terms of the first Prayer Book, knew that they might receive special private absolution. The very same invitation was given in the second Prayer Book; and is it conceivable that persons coming as before were intended to find the private ministry refused, and a different ministry employed? (3) The offer to come to God's minister to "open their grief," is addressed to Church goers, i.e., persons in the habit of receiving general absolutions, but yet unable by this means to obtain peace of conscience. They seek the private ministry, because the public service has failed to meet their need. To bid such persons go back, and rest satisfied in what they had already found to be inadequate, would be to acknowledge that the Church had no proper means to supply their special want. Yet the words of the invitation, when simply received,—"let him come to me or to some other . . . that he may receive the benefit of absolution,"—certainly would seem to hold out to such persons the promise of some further special form of the ministry of absolution, not before, or otherwise, within their reach. (4) The supposed change would be a departure from primitive practice, and the establishment of a new form of the ministry of reconciliation. For although, according to primitive rule, after a confession made in private the penitent might receive absolution in public, yet the absolution was always in such case given by individual application with imposition of hands. A special confession of sins when special absolution was sought, involved, according to all ancient practice, a personal and individual application of the power of the keys.

(5) The Church of Ireland is united with the Church of England, because of their common faith, and sameness of principle in their common reformation. They have the same Prayer Book and a common ritual.[1] Now among the Irish Canons drawn up by Bramhall, Usher being Primate, A.D. 1634, and re-enacted in 1701, when Marsh was Primate, there is one referring to the Exhortation in question, and enacted with the view of enforcing, and reducing to practice, the invitation to confession which it contains. This canon manifestly implies, that the special private ministry of absolution was intended. It is as follows: "Canon XIX. Warning to be given beforehand for the Communion. Whereas, every lay person is bound to receive the Holy Communion thrice every year, and many notwithstanding do not receive that Sacrament once a year: we do require every minister to give warning to his parishioners, publicly in the church at Morning Prayer, the Sunday before every time of his administering the Holy Sacrament, for the better preparation of themselves, which said warning we enjoin the said parishioners to accept and obey under the penalty and danger of the law.

[1] See Palmer's History of the Church, vol. i. sec. 550, 1.

And the minister of every parish, and in cathedral and collegiate churches some principal minister of the church, shall the afternoon before the administration give warning, by the tolling of the bell or otherwise, to the intent that if any have scruple of conscience, or desire *the special ministry of reconciliation,* he may afford it to those who need it. And to this end the people are often to be exhorted to enter into a special examination of the state of their own souls; and that finding themselves either extreme dull or much troubled in mind, they do resort unto GOD's ministers *to receive from them as well advice and counsel* for the quickening of their dead hearts, and the subduing of their corruptions whereunto they have been subject, *as the benefit of absolution likewise by the power of the keys which Christ has committed to the ministers for that purpose."*

The "special" ministry of reconciliation evidently denotes the personal or individual, as distinguished from the general, ministry, and the close connexion between "advice," &c., and "the benefit of absolution," marked by the particles, "as well," "as likewise," proves that the two are supposed to be given at the same time. It is moreover observable, that the expression, "ministry of GOD's Word," is not used in the canon, but "the power of the keys" is substituted for it, a term implying that the ministry intended is an exercise of the strictly priestly office.

It is anticipating the subject of the following chapter, to touch on the question of the rubric alluded to in the "Visitation of the Sick" of the first Prayer Book; but as the objection urged against the use of private absolution in preparation for Holy Communion, rests mainly on the removal of that rubric, it is impossible to settle the point now under consideration, without entering into the question.

The point to be determined is, with what view the rubric was omitted? If the purpose was to prevent special private absolution being given, as before, after confession, in preparation for Communion, thus modifying the meaning of one formulary of the Church by a sidelong move in the construction of another, it would be an instance of subtle policy of which there is no other instance in the Prayer Book. It is at once fairer to the character of our Reformers, and more natural, to look for the explanation of the change in the service itself, rather than in another disconnected part of the Prayer Book. Now it is observable, that at the very time when the rubric in question, following the absolution, was omitted, the rubric preceding the absolution was altered. The rubric preceding the absolution stood thus in the first Prayer Book : "After which confession the Priest shall absolve him after this form." In the second Prayer Book "after this form" was altered into "after this sort." The change was made in order to meet the objections raised against the compulsory use of this particular form of absolution. The indicative form was unpopular, because supposed to imply too great authority in the Priest. Our Reformers upheld the form itself as a true expression of the Church's doctrine, but at the same time they were not unwilling to meet the scruples of the objectors by allowing a liberty in its use, such as existed in primitive times.

Marshall gives several forms of special absolution[1] in-

---

[1] See Marshall's Penitential Discipline, Appendix, No. iv. to end.

differently used in the early Church, proving the discretionary power then exercised by the Priest. Following
this precedent our Reformers, while upholding the standard form, as most fully expressive of the authority and
virtue of the ministry, yet allowed the Priest to exercise
a similar discretion,—a principle acted on in the case of
the Exhortations in the same service, liberty being given
to substitute in the place of the form given any other
which the Priest may consider more appropriate to the
special case. On the same principle "this form" was
changed to "this sort." But when this change was
made, the rubric following the absolution could not
stand as before, for in such case this particular "form"
would have been enjoined, without power of choice, in
all other private absolutions, freedom to vary it being
given only in the case of sickness. By omitting the
suffixed rubric a similar discretion was given in both
cases. For the sick a form of absolution was provided,
the minister being free to choose another form of a like
"sort," if he prefer it. In the preparation for Communion the Priest is enjoined to give the "benefit of
absolution," but he is left free to select a form. It
is more consistent with the mind of our Reformation, to suppose such a liberty given in the choice of
a form, than that the mere absence of a form should
be construed into a repeal of an express order; for
absolution was ordered to be given, though no form was
prescribed. Nor can it be otherwise shown that the
Reformers adhered in this case to primitive Catholic
rule. For it would have been no greater deviation from
primitive usage, to deny special absolution in case of
sickness, than to deny it in preparation for Communion;

for the use of special absolution in sickness was but preparatory to the reception of the Blessed Sacrament.

To return to the Eucharistic Office. The passage under consideration remained unchanged for upwards of a century. It was under review in 1560, the first year of Elizabeth, when the Prayer Book underwent further revision; again in 1604, at the Hampton Court Conference, and lastly, in 1661, at the Savoy Conference. No change however was made in the passage under consideration till the last revision of all. The wording was then condensed, and more material alterations were made in the order of the sentences. The result will be best appreciated by quoting the paragraph, as it stood in the second Prayer Book, bracketing the words omitted in the last revision, and italicising those of which the position was changed. It will stand thus; "Let him come to me, or to some other discreet and learned minister of God's Word, and open his grief, that [he may receive such ghostly counsel, advice and comfort, as his conscience may be relieved, and that] by the ministry of God's holy Word, he may receive [comfort and] the benefit of absolution, *together with ghostly counsel and advice*, to the quieting of his conscience and avoiding of all scruple and doubtfulness." By this change, "ghostly comfort and advice," which had previously occupied the most prominent position, and thus was set forth as the primary object of confession, now sank into a subordinate place, and " the benefit of absolution," which had been last, became first. The term, " comfort," moreover was omitted, the result of which was still further to fix attention more pointedly on the absolution itself, as the ground of comfort, rather than on the comfort which was its result. The significance of these changes proves that the mere curtailing a lengthy sentence could not have been the object in view.

At the same time a material alteration was made in the directions for the use of the two Exhortations. In the first Prayer Book there had been but one Exhortation, and it was ordered to be read only in case "the people be negligent to come to the Communion." But in the second Book an additional Exhortation was inserted, and this contained no allusion whatever to confession or absolution. Moreover the new exhortation was placed first in order, with the following rubric prefixed. "Then shall follow this Exhortation at certain times, when the Curate shall see the people negligent to come to the Holy Communion." The original Exhortation was at the same time placed second, and a new rubric prefixed to it; "And some time shall be said this also, at the discretion of the Curate."

In consequence of this change the Exhortation inviting to confession, was read only as an occasional and discretionary substitute, the new form in constant and ordinary use containing no mention of it. If the parish Priest desired to discourage confession, the Exhortation recommending it might never be read at all.

But at the Savoy Conference the order of these two Exhortations was reversed, the one containing the invitation to confession being placed first, and a new rubric inserted, making its use compulsory, as the ordinary rule: "When the Minister giveth warning for the celebration of Holy Communion (which he shall

always do upon the Sunday or some holyday immediately preceding,) after the sermon or homily ended, he
shall read the Exhortation following." The other Exhortation took the second place, and was to be read only
"in case he (the Priest) shall see the people negligent to
come to the Holy Communion." Thus the invitation
to Confession ordinarily became obligatory, and was to
be read to the people in constant connection with the
notice to prepare themselves for Holy Communion.

The effect of these successive revisions has been
to reaffirm repeatedly the principle of Confession, the
invitation always being in the Office, whether, or not,
put forward prominently, while the last and final change
stamped it with even greater definiteness than before.
The invitation, when at first introduced, was, be it well
observed, an entirely voluntary insertion on the part of
the framers of the Office. Their successors not only
preserved it, but invested it with increased significance.
It now abides as an enduring testimony to a long established truth, confirmed by repeated acts of those
who had chief authority within the Church. "They
are," as it has been eloquently said, "living words;
they are an actual reality; they are renewed whenever they are pronounced; they speak whenever they
are read; they have spoken to thousands and tens of
thousands of broken, anxious, burdened hearts; they
are the voice of the Church of England, and of GOD
through her, speaking to people's consciences, and they
are heard and understood."[1]

---

[1] Dr. Pusey' Letter to Mr. Richards, page 121.

NOTE.

The successive changes in the concluding portion of the Exhortation will be more clearly seen when shown in parallel columns. The rubric, determining the use of the Exhortation, is given in italics.

First Prayer Book of Edward VI.	*Second Book of Edward VI.*	*The Revision of 1661.*
If upon the Sunday or holy day the people be negligent to come to the Communion, then shall the Priest earnestly exhort his parishioners to dispose themselves to the receiving of the Holy Communion more diligently, saying these or like words unto them :—	*And some time shall be said this also, at the discretion of the Curate :—*	*When the Minister giveth warning for the celebration of the Holy Communion (which he shall always do upon the Sunday or some holy day immediately preceding), after the sermon or homily ended, he shall read this Exhortation following :—*
. . . And if there be any of you whose conscience is troubled and grieved in anything, lacking comfort or counsel, let him come to me, or to some other discreet and learned priest, taught in the law of GOD, and confess and open his sin and grief secretly, that he may receive such ghostly counsel, advice, and comfort, that his conscience may be relieved, and that of	. . . And because it is requisite that no man should come to the Holy Communion but with a full trust in GOD's mercy, and with a quiet conscience ; therefore if there be any of you which by the means aforesaid cannot quiet his own conscience, but requireth further comfort or counsel; then let him come to me, or some other discreet and learned minister of GOD's word, and open his grief, that he may receive such ghostly counsel, advice, and comfort, as his conscience may be relieved, and that by the ministry of GOD's word, he may receive	. . . And because it is requisite, that no man should come to the Holy Communion, but with a full trust in GOD's mercy, and with a quiet conscience ; therefore if there be any of you, who by this means cannot quiet his own conscience herein, but requireth further comfort or counsel, let him come to me, or to some other discreet and learned Minister of GOD's word, and open his

us (as of the ministers of GOD and of the Church) he may receive comfort and absolution, to the satisfaction of his mind, and avoiding of all scruple and doubtfulness; requiring such as shall be satisfied with a general confession, not to be offended with them that do use to their further satisfying the auricular and secret confession to the priest; nor those also which think needful or convenient, for the quietness of their own consciences, particularly to open their sins to the priest, to be offended with them that are satisfied with their humble confession to GOD, and the general confession to the Church; but in all things to follow and keep the rule of charity; and every man to be satisfied with his own conscience, not judging other men's minds or consciences; whereas he hath no warrant of GOD's word to the same.

comfort, and the benefit of absolution, to the quieting of his conscience, and avoiding of all scruple and doubtfulness.

grief; that by the ministry of GOD's holy word he may receive the benefit of absolution, together with ghostly counsel and advice, to the quieting of his conscience, and avoiding of all scruple and doubtfulness.

CHAPTER VII.

OFFICE FOR THE VISITATION OF THE SICK.

THIS Office is taken, with some material alterations, from the original Latin form, which, as Mr. Palmer has proved, may in its substance "be traced to the primitive ages;"[1] and the resemblances as well as the differences in the two Offices are striking and instructive.

In the Latin Office the Priest was directed to examine the sick person, especially in reference to faith, charity, and restitution. After which he thus addressed him; "Dear brother, if thou desirest to attain to the vision of GOD, it is necessary above all things to be clean in heart, and pure in conscience, for CHRIST saith in the Gospel, 'Blessed are the pure in heart, for they shall see GOD.' That thou mayest attain to this purity and peace of conscience, confess all your sins."

In the English Office, as originally constructed in the first Prayer Book, the Priest was directed to institute the same inquiry as to faith, charity, restitution, &c. Then followed this rubric: "Here shall the sick person make a special confession, if he feel his conscience troubled with any weighty matter."

The Offices differed in two respects. The Latin re-

---

[1] Palmer's Orig. Liturg., vol. ii. chap. vii. p. 220.

presented Confession as absolutely necessary to purity of heart; the English required it only if the conscience were "troubled," &c.   Again, the Latin Office expressly required "all" (universa) sins to be confessed, leaving no discretion to the Priest or the penitent.   The English simply directed a "special confession" to be made. This change of terms was probably intended to counteract the prevailing idea, already noticed, of the necessity of "numbering," or exact enumeration, of sins, not so much for the purpose of unburdening the conscience, or exercising a deeper repentance, but in order to form the subject matter of satisfaction.   In 1661 this rubric was altered, and it then assumed its present shape. The variations are marked by italics.   "Here shall the person *be moved to* make a special confession *of his sins*, if he feel his conscience troubled with any weighty matter."

It is important to note that these alterations of 1661 brought back the rubric to a closer agreement with the old Latin form.   Instead of leaving Confession to the sick person's own discretion, as in the first reformed Office,.the Priest was directed, as before the Reformation, to take the initiative, and, if he thought the case required it, himself induce the sick person to confess. The original rubric merely gave an opportunity of Confession, if desired.   "Here shall the sick person," &c. The new rubric required the Priest to urge it.   "Here shall the sick person be moved," &c.

The rubric is still opposed to the Latin rule, in maintaining the principle of discretionary confession, with this additional variation—that in the Latin order the motives to be urged by the Priest are embodied in the directions given; in the English the Priest is left to choose his own grounds of persuasion. They agree however in this—that in both cases the Priest is equally ordered to exert his influence, and suggest reasons calculated to act on the sick man's conscience. The insertion with regard to the sick person, that he " be moved,'' &c., was apparently made in order to counteract the growing tendency to evade Confession, as well as to compel the Clergy to maintain the practice, as far as possible, and overcome any scruples they might feel in pressing it. Mr. Stretton observes, "This addition was made because in practice it was found that the clergy were slow and backward of themselves to perform a painful duty, nowhere by the letter of their vows enjoined upon them; since the priest perhaps in many cases might not deem it any part of his office by the terms of the rubric to exhort the sick man to confession, and to receive absolution."[1]

A similar return to the old Latin use appears in the insertion, "of his sins," after, " special Confession." The sick person was directed before the Reformation to " confess all his sins." The only difference, therefore, remaining after this insertion, was in the omission of the word, " all."

That this was not a mere incidental change without a special object, is evident from the cotemporaneous introduction of fresh matter of a corresponding kind in the earlier part of the rubric. The rubric originally commenced as follows: " Then shall the Minister examine whether he (the sick person) be in charity with all the world," &c. On the revision the following

[1] Stretton's Guide to the Infirm and Sick, p. 102.

words in italics were added, and it stood thus; "Then shall the Minister examine whether *he repent him truly of his sins,* and be in charity with all the world." This addition was doubtless intended to explain the mind of the Church on a practical question of considerable moment, which had. been left undetermined in consequence of the omissions made in the first reformed Office.   It was uncertain, according to the terms of the original rubric, whether, or no, the Priest receiving "a special confession," should confine himself to the one matter weighing on the sick man's conscience. The uncertainty was removed by the alteration of the rubric; for it then expressly extended the inquiry to the sick man's "sins," thus involving a review of his life as a whole.

This fuller explanation supplied an omission of great practical moment. Forgiveness is not of individual sins, separately viewed, but of the person who has sinned. It implies a state or condition of repentance, a capacity for the reception of grace. Any one unrepented sin is inconsistent with such a state, and is consequently a hindrance to the gift of GOD. Repentance is the condition in which sin, as sin, and so all sin alike, is hated and renounced by the renewed will. It is not applicable to one fact only in the soul's history. Unless it comprehends sin itself in all its developments, as existing in the person, so far as they can be ascertained, it is not rightly felt towards any one sin. Consequently Confession cannot be confined to any one matter, unless the Priest has otherwise reason to be convinced of the true penitence of the person confessing. It is not. indeed the fulness or exactness of detail on which the value of Confession depends. Nevertheless the Priest has to form a judgment whether the sense of sin be, humanly speaking, full and complete, or he cannot rightly absolve. He is not to run the risk of casting pearls before swine; he is not to hazard saying, " Peace, peace, where there is no peace." The Priest is therefore of necessity bound to test the general state of the person confessing, and not merely the one sin more especially burdening his soul, before he can exercise the ministry of reconciliation. He may see cause to dispense with the enumeration of other sins, or their details, to any extent, according to his discretion in any individual case; but the rule of a full confession, where confession is made at all, ordinarily applies. If the rule be relaxed, it is so only because the mind of the Priest is otherwise satisfied. He is responsible that he " lay hands suddenly on no man," lest himself become " partaker of other men's sins;" and Confession, or a readiness to confess, combined with such practical conditions as he may see fit to require, is to him the guarantee of the truth of the repentance, which the act of his ministry affirms.

The object of these changes therefore was twofold. They gave a fuller and more definite rule to the Priest. They also pressed the use of Confession with greater authority and distinctness, in counteraction of the neglect into which the ordinance had fallen in the interval between the Reformation and the Savoy Conference.

The English Office, moreover, corresponds with the Latin, with the exception of only a few significant modifications, in the order concerning Absolution. In the

Latin Office the direction is as follows: "Then let the priest absolve the sick person from all his sins, thus saying—Our LORD JESUS CHRIST of His great mercy absolve thee, and by the Authority of the Same our LORD JESUS CHRIST, and of the blessed Apostles, Peter and Paul, and by the authority committed to me, I absolve thee from all the sins which with a contrite heart and with thy mouth, thou hast confessed to me, and from all thy other sins which if thou hadst remembered, thou wouldest fully have confessed, and I restore thee to the Sacraments of the Church; in the Name of the FATHER, the SON, and the HOLY GHOST. Amen."

The English order, according to our first Prayer Book, was as follows : " *After which Confession, the Priest shall absolve him after this form. And the same form of Absolution shall be used in all private Confessions.*" In the second Prayer Book, as already stated, the expression, "*after this form,*" was changed into, " *after this sort,*" and the last clause of the rubric was erased.

The Absolution itself is expressed in the same terms in both the first and second Prayer Books, and is as follows :—" Our LORD JESUS CHRIST, Who hath left power to His Church to absolve all sinners which truly repent and believe in Him, of His great mercy forgive thee thine offences, and by His authority committed unto me, I absolve thee from all thy sins in the Name of the FATHER, and of the SON, and of the HOLY GHOST. Amen."

It is most remarkable that this, the indicative, form of Absolution was preserved equally in the second, as in the first, Prayer Book. That it should have survived the full pressure of foreign Protestantism during the latter days of Edward VI. is a most convincing proof, that the central principles of the Catholic doctrine of Confession were preserved intact by our Reformers, the dispute turning only on certain incidental features. The strongest possible argument, consistently with the acknowledged appeal to Antiquity, might have been urged for its rejection; for the indicative form only dates from the thirteenth century.[1] The earlier forms of absolution were universally, as they still are in the East, precatory or optative. As the English Reformation took its stand on the teaching and practice of the primitive Church, it would have been strictly in accordance with this principle, to have substituted one of the earlier precatory forms. The opponents of the indicative form, and they were then doubtless many, would have made an unanswerable appeal in favour of such a substitution. The unquestioned adoption by our Reformers of the indicative form can be accounted for only on the supposition that they regarded it, notwithstanding its comparatively modern use, as a true expression of the primitive faith.

The variations in the English order, though few, are significant. " By the authority of the Blessed Apostles, Peter and Paul," is replaced by, " Who hath left power to His Church ;" thus bringing out the idea of the Body of the Church, as the organ of the HOLY GHOST, instead of seeming to confine the transmission of His grace to

[1] Othobon, the Roman Legate, in A.D. 1268, first decreed in England; " Let all who hear Confessions expressly absolve their penitents by pronouncing the underwritten words,—' By the authority of which I am possessed, I absolve thee from thy sins.' " See a later chapter where the question is more fully considered.

individual Apostles. "All thy sins," is substituted for "all the sins which thou hast confessed to me, and from all thy other sins, which, if thou hadst remembered, thou wouldest fully have confessed;" thus apparently excluding the positive obligation of "numbering" sins. "All sinners who truly repent and believe in Him," is inserted instead of, "with contrite heart and with thy mouth;" the latter expression being removed, perhaps as seeming to imply that oral confession is itself an essential condition, and title to forgiveness. Lastly, "I restore thee to the Sacraments of the Church," is omitted, because properly applicable only where Church censures had been imposed.

The language and construction of this solemn form of Absolution is one striking instance, among many, of the force and completeness of expression, which marks our Prayer Book translations from the original Latin. Mr. Maskell pays an honourable tribute to its compilers in special reference to this Absolution. "The form," he says, "thus condensed and completed, is as perfect an expression of the truth of the ministry as can well be conceived, and is unequalled in the ritual of any portion of Christendom. There is the declaration of the power of Absolution, and of the qualifications necessary to the recipient; a short prayer that our LORD would forgive the penitent; an assertion by the minister that to him individually this power has been committed; the exercise of that power, closing with the awful Name of the Blessed and Undivided Trinity."[1]

It has been urged, and no ordinary authority pleaded

[1] Maskell on Absolution, p. 250.

in favour of the opinion, that this solemn form of Absolution relates, not to sins, but to Church censures.

The mere solemnity of the language would seem to
be irreconcilable with such an interpretation, but the
following reasons moreover combine to disprove it.

(1.) The corresponding terms in the Latin Office had
undoubtedly reference to sin; for ecclesiastical censures
were mentioned in a separate clause in the same form
of Absolution. "I restore thee to the Sacraments of
the Church," was subjoined to, "I absolve thee from
thy sins." If the Reformers had intended to limit the
Absolution to a release from Church censures, why
retain the latter, and omit the former, phrase? Or if
they thought to adopt the latter with an altered meaning, how could such an intention be understood, unless
it were explained? But no such explanation is given.

(2.) The whole context relates to sins. The Priest
is to inquire into the sick man's "sins." The sick man
is to be "moved" to confess "his sins." Can the term,
"sins," be used in one sense in the rubric, and in a
totally different sense in the Absolution? Throughout
the Office no mention occurs of Church censures. Nor
can Church censures be meant as the "weighty matter"
troubling the sick man's conscience, which occasions the
Confession.

(3.) The sins alluded to, as the special reason for
Confession, are from the very nature of the case, secret.
They are such as the Priest knows only through the
penitent's confession made at the time. But sins involving ecclesiastical censures must be notorious, such
as had either been previously confessed, or were so
public as not to need it.

(4.) It is no part of a Priest's office to release from Church censures. He needs for the purpose a special commission from his Bishop. But there is no indication of any commission being here supposed, and the Absolution is enjoined to be given, when desired, as an act of ordinary priestly authority.

(5.) In 1641, and again in 1661, when the Prayer Book was under review, the Nonconformists raised objections to this indicative form of Absolution, and desired that it might be made declaratory. Mr. Cooke, remarking on the circumstance, well observes; "How easy it would have been for the Bishops to have answered, that nothing but a release from Church censures was meant, if such had been considered to be the object of the Absolution." The very ground of the objection was the use of such a form in the forgiveness of sin—it being supposed, though erroneously, to imply some personal power in the Priest—and it is inconceivable that the difficulty should not have been removed by so ready an explanation, if such were the meaning of the terms. But the answer of the Bishops to the objectors, while supporting the use of the authorised form, clearly affirms the contrary. "The form of absolution," thus they replied, "is more agreeable to the Scriptures than that which they desire, it being said in S. John xx., 'Whose sins ye remit, they are remitted,' not, 'whose sins ye pronounce remitted;' and the condition needs not to be expressed, being always necessarily understood."[1] It is clear that both the objectors and the respondents alike felt the keenly questioned words to

[1] Cardwell's History of Conferences on the Book of Common Prayer. P. 361.

H

relate to the actual forgiveness of sin in the ordinary
acceptation of the terms. There could have been no
possible objection to the use of the indicative form in a
release from ecclesiastical censures.

(6.) The chief authority for the supposed interpretation is Wheatley, and he is the first Commentator on
the Prayer Book who takes this view. Such an interpretation is the more extraordinary in Wheatley, who
explains the Absolution at Matins and Evensong to be
" an actual conveyance of pardon at the very instant of
pronouncing it, to all that come within the terms proposed." Can we possibly admit the solemn act in the
Visitation of the Sick after special confession, to be
below that which is daily ministered in our Common
Prayer?

Bingham, whose knowledge of antiquity is unquestioned, and whose sympathies are well known to have
been in favour of the lower view of Absolution, entirely rejects this interpretation, when advanced by Fell. " Bishop
Fell indeed," thus Bingham writes, " has a more singular notion of the form ' absolvo te ;' he supposes that
in every crime there are two things to be considered,
viz., the offence against GOD, and the offence against
the Church; the former of which is forgiven by GOD
alone upon men's prayers and repentance, but the latter
by this authoritative form, 'I absolve thee.' But this,
though it may be true with respect to crimes which
fall under public discipline, cannot well be the meaning
of the form, as it is used in our Liturgy, in the Office
of the Visitation of the Sick. For in private sins there
is no offence given to the Church, and yet it is private
sins, confessed privately to a minister, for which that

rubric orders absolution to be given in this form, 'absolvo te.' "[1]

A further change in the same rubric, made at the revision of 1661, deserves notice. The parenthetical sentence requiring an expression of desire for Absolution on the part of the sick person ("if he humbly and heartily desire it,") was then for the first time inserted. Its object was evidently to prevent the risk of profanation in the case of so solemn an act, by guarding the Priest against the possibility of a mere perfunctory service, and by stimulating in the sick person the sense of his own concurrence in the act of absolution, as an indispensable qualification for its due reception.   Mr. Stretton thus explains the purpose of the order; " Lest the Priest should, through carelessness, haste, or from any other like unpardonable cause, pronounce absolution on one, who although he has confessed his sin, has yet given no sufficient proof of penitence, and lest the sick man be ignorant of the nature of the action, or rite performed over him, what the benefits thereof, and what are the recipient's qualifications for its efficacious use, it is ordered that absolution be not given unless ' he humbly and heartily desire it.' "[2]

The addition is one among many evidences, manifested throughout our Offices, of the care taken to make the ministry of reconciliation a living and intelligent service on the part both of the Priest and the penitent.

[1] Bingham's second letter on Absolution, ad finem.   Vol. viii. p. 414, 8vo. edit.

[2] Stretton, Visitatio Infirmorum.   Introduction.

There is a yet further correspondence to be noted between the Latin and English Offices. In both alike the Absolution is followed by the collect which had been in use for at least 1000 years before the Reformation throughout the Western Church, in reconciling dying penitents.[1] It was still retained after the introduction of the indicative form of Absolution, though necessarily taking a subordinate position. The following is an exact version of the original. The more important alterations only, made in our translation, are here given, in italics, and bracketed :—

"O most merciful GOD, Who, according to the multitude of Thy mercies, dost blot out the sins of those who are penitent, and extinguish by the grace of forgiveness the stains of past transgressions, look mercifully upon this Thy servant, who with a truly contrite heart desireth the remission of all his sins. Renew in him, most loving FATHER, whatever hath been decayed by the fraud of the devil, and restore [*preserve and continue*] this sick member to [*in*] the unity of the Church through the remission of his sins. Pity, O LORD, his groanings, his tears, his tribulation of heart, and forasmuch as he putteth his full trust in Thy mercy, admit him to the sacrament of reconciliation [*impute not unto him his former sins, but strengthen him with Thy Blessed Spirit, and when Thou art pleased to take him hence, take him unto Thy favour*], through JESUS CHRIST our LORD. *Amen.*"

It has been urged, that this collect is incompatible with the idea of forgiveness being conveyed through the preceding Absolution, because it is itself a prayer for

---

[1] It is found in the Sacramentary of Gelasius, A.D. 494. See Palmer's Orig. Lit. c. viii., vol. ii., p. 226.

forgiveness. This objection applies equally to the Latin, as to the English Office; for in both it stands in the same relative position. But there is no question, that in the Roman Church this collect has always been considered compatible with the fullest belief in the efficacy of the previous Absolution. Our Reformers were but perpetuating the pre-Reformation use in retaining it. But where is the necessity for supposing more inconsistency in the use of such a collect after absolution, than would be felt in the use of the LORD's Prayer, which contains a petition for forgiveness? A precisely parallel case occurs in the Office for Adult Baptism. In the collect immediately succeeding the act of Baptism, there follows the petition; "Give Thy HOLY SPIRIT to this person;" and yet the act itself of Baptism is before described as the "renewing of the HOLY GHOST." The explanation of such a petition following after Baptism, is founded on the momentous truth, that the gift of the HOLY GHOST is not an isolated or completed gift, but a continuous and progressive act of GOD. It is therefore a petition for perpetuating and perfecting a work already begun. In like manner this collect, following the act of Absolution, impresses the equally momentous truth, that the remission of sins, and repentance, which is its condition, are not completed, but progressive and advancing states; that all absolutions in this world must ever be in a measure imperfect, inasmuch as they are but anticipatory of, and dependent on, the final Absolution of the day of Judgment, given in a state which can never be altogether free from liability to err even in the very act of reception.

It is observable, however, that our Reformers felt the

inconsistency of the collect as it previously stood, and
the changes which they made are evidently grounded
on the idea of a previous conveyance of forgiveness.
For how, except under this idea, can we account for the
substitution of the terms, "*preserve and continue* this sick
member," instead of, "*restore ;*" and "*in,*" instead of
"*to,*" the unity of the Church, words manifestly implying the belief, that the penitent was already re-united by
a living grace to the Church, as the organ and Body of
CHRIST, and only needed the preservation and continuance of that vital bond; or, again, for the omission of
the closing petition, "admit him to the sacrament of
reconciliation," and the substitution in its stead, of
"*impute not unto him his former sins,*" (a deprecation
of merited punishment notwithstanding the forgiveness)
"*but strengthen him with Thy blessed Spirit ?*"   This
last alteration is most remarkable, and conclusive as to
the point at issue; for it implies a clear belief, that the
penitent had been already admitted to the " sacrament
of reconciliation," and that he only needed thenceforth
a deliverance from the temporal consequences of his sin,
and a continued increase of the grace of the HOLY
SPIRIT.

Mr. Stretton observes that this collect, " in the case
of special confession and formal absolution, completes
and confirms the absolution; in all other cases it sup-
plies and takes the place of this rite."[1]   Comber took a
similar view, and Bishop Mant by quoting him adds his
own authority to the explanation.   He remarks ; " That
this comfortable dispensing of remission," viz., the
" formal absolution" before given, " may not want its

[1] Visitatio Infirmorum.   Introduction, p. xcix.

due effect, we add a prayer after it, to beg of GOD to ratify His own act, and to declare that He hath done so by other testimonies of His favour, by renewing in the sick person the graces of faith, hope, devotion, and sincere obedience."[1]

The facts recorded in this and the preceding chapter sufficiently refute the supposition, that the mention of Confession in our Prayer Book was an accommodation to temporary circumstances, and intended to satisfy a lingering attachment to long established habits, while our Reformers really had the covert desire, that the practice should die out, as soon as the people were prepared for the more complete change, which, if practicable, they would at once have established. We find on the contrary that a full century after the Reformation, when its purpose was matured, after Puritanism had risen to its height of power, for a while even overwhelming the Church, and suppressing the Prayer Book ; when there could have been no popular pressure in favour of the recommendations to Confession—these various provisions and rules were, not only not withdrawn, but renewed with increasing definiteness, and brought into greater prominence than before. Nor is it to be forgotten ✓ that the very persons who superintended this final revision, had given the surest proof of their loyal attachment to the Church, by adhering to her in her lowest period of abasement, themselves proscribed, banished, or able only to use her offices in secret, and with every temporal inducement to abandon her either for one of the sects, or for the then more prosperous Church of Rome.

[1] Mant's Book of Common Prayer. Ad loc.

NOTE.

A comparative view of the rubrics and forms of Absolution referred to.

Latin Office.	1st and 2nd Book of Edward VI.	Revision of 1661.
Deinde dicet sacerdos : Carissime frater, si velis ad visionem Dei pervenire, oportet omnino quod sis mundus in mente et purus in conscientiâ ; ait enim Christus in Evangelio ; Beati mundi corde, quoniam ipsi Deum videbunt. Si ergo vis mundum cor et conscientiam sanam habere, peccata tua remisse confitere. *Deinde absolvat sacerdos infirmum ab omnibus peccatis suis hoc modo dicens :* Dominus noster Jesus Christus suâ magnâ piętate te absolvat ; et ego auctoritate ejusdem Dei Domini nostri Jesu Christi et beatorum Apostolorum Petri et Pauli, et auctoritate mihi tradita, absolvo te ab omnibus peccatis his de quibus corde contritus et ore mihi confessus es ; et ab omnibus aliis pec-	*Here shall the sick person make a special Confession, if he feel his conscience troubled with any weighty matter, after which confession the Priest shall absolve him after this form; and the same form of absolution shall be used in all private confessions.* / *absolve him after this sort.* / Our LORD JESUS CHRIST, Who hath left power to His Church to absolve all sinners which truly repent and believe in Him, of His great mercy forgive thee thine offences ; and by His authority committed to me, I absolve thee from all thy sins, in the Name of the FATHER, and of the SON, and of the HOLY GHOST. Amen.	*Then shall the minister examine whether he repent him truly of his sins, &c.* . . . . *Here shall the sick person be moved to make a special confession of his sins, if he feel his conscience troubled with any weighty matter. After which Confession, the Priest shall absolve him (if he humbly and heartily desire it) after this sort :* Our LORD JESUS CHRIST, Who hath left power to His Church, &c.

catis tuis de quibus si
tuæ occurrerent me-
moriæ libenter con-
fiteri velles; et Sa-
cramentis ecclesiæ te
restituo : In nomine
Patris, et Filii, et Spi-
ritus Sancti. Amen.

If it should appear to any that too much stress has been laid on minute changes in the Rubrics and Offices, or that too much has been claimed in support of High Church teaching from the history of these changes, let the thoughtful and pregnant words of Alexander Knox, in reference to a strictly kindred subject, be carefully weighed.

"The distress of the English Episcopal Church during the Usurpation had more than ever endeared her to her genuine children. A revision, therefore, of the Liturgy being called for, the revisers seized the opportunity, (contrary to what the public was reckoning upon) of introducing changes, not more puritanical, but more Catholic. They effected this, no doubt stealthily, and to appearance by the minutest alteration; but to compare the Communion Service as it now stands, especially its Rubrics, with the form in which we find it previously to that transaction, will be to discover that without any change of features that could cause alarm, a new spirit was then breathed into our Communion Service, principally by a few significant circumstances in the manner of conducting the business, which were fitted to impress the devout, though certain to be fully understood only by the initiated. Who can doubt of this transaction being, in all its bearings, providential? And yet it was clearly insufficient to produce any extended or striking effects. It has actually escaped general observation. Wheatly on the Liturgy notices the changes; but though himself a High Churchman, overlooks their import. What then can we suppose, but that these changes were meant by Providence to subserve ulterior movements, to lie dormant, as it were, until nearer the time of the end, when it might suit the order of Providence, that what was before deposited as seed should grow up into a rich and luxuriant harvest?"—Remains of Alexander Knox, vol. i. p. 59.

CHAPTER VIII.

ORDINATION SERVICE FOR PRIESTS.

THE Ministry of Confession presupposes a Divine commission. It is necessary, therefore, to consider the powers which, according to our Ordination Office, are committed to Priests.

The form in which the Commission in conveyed, is as follows :—

"Receive the HOLY GHOST for the office and work of a Priest in the Church of GOD, now committed to thee by the imposition of our hands. Whose sins thou dost forgive, they are forgiven, and whose sins thou dost retain, they are retained. And be thou a faithful dispenser of the word of GOD, and of His holy Sacraments; in the Name of the FATHER, and of the SON, and of the HOLY GHOST. Amen."

This form is divisible into two distinct parts; (1.) Our LORD's own words of ordination, unceasingly reiterated from age to age with ever fresh creative powers; "Receive ye the HOLY GHOST," &c.; and (2.) the voice of the Church describing the sphere of action within which this commission is to be exercised; "and be thou a faithful dispenser," &c.

These latter words are to be viewed in connexion with the third question previously put to the candidates for

the Priesthood "touching their duties;" "Will you
give your faithful diligence always so to minister the
doctrine and sacraments and the discipline of CHRIST,
as the LORD hath commanded, and as this Church and
realm hath received the same according to the commandments of GOD; so that you may teach the people
committed to your cure and charge with all diligence to
keep and observe the same?"

Three Priestly functions are thus clearly specified;
the ministry (1) of the Word of GOD, (2) of the Sacraments, and (3) of the Discipline of CHRIST.

The words of ordination; "Whose sins thou dost remit, they are remitted," &c. are, according to the
Church's uniform tradition, to be understood in two
senses, one comprehensive, embracing the whole sphere
of the ministry; the other, restrictive, as specially de-
noting those offices which were ordained for the remission of sins, as their characteristic object.

Dr. Pusey quotes S. Cyril, as an authority for both
interpretations of the words. Summing up S. Cyril's
teaching as to the first, or more general sense of the
words, he says; "S. Cyril unites the office of teaching
as one part of this gift of the HOLY GHOST, or rather
he contemplates that gift, as a whole, in its varied bearings. Authority, power to forgive sins, working of miracles, wisdom, and all the divers operations of the Spirit,
are thus included in this gift. Yet this does not of
course involve any confusion; S. Cyril passes from one
to the other."[1] Explaining the same words in their

[1] Dr. Pusey's Sermon on the "Entire Absolution of the Penitent,"
note 3, to p. 29. 1846.

restricted sense, S. Cyril says; "Guided by the Spirit
they remit or retain sins in two ways, as I suppose.
For either they call those to Baptism, who, for the seem-
liness of their life, and their approved faith, ought to
obtain it, or they hinder and exclude from the Divine
grace (i.e. Baptism) some who are not as yet worthy of
it. Or in another way they remit and retain sin, correcting the children of the Church when sinning, and
pardoning them when repenting, as Paul delivered the
fornicator at Corinth to Satan for the destruction of the
flesh, that the spirit might be saved, and again received
him."[1]

S. Ambrose also interprets the words in this more
restricted sense; "God is able, when He willeth, to forgive us sins, even those which we think cannot be forgiven. Seemeth it impossible that water should wash
away sin, or that sins should be forgiven through penitence? Christ granted this to His Apostles, which
from the Apostles was transmitted to the office of the
Priest; that therefore was rendered possible which
seemed impossible."[2] Again; "Why baptize ye, if sins
may not be remitted through man? For in Baptism is
the remission of all sins. Where is the difference,
whether through penitence, or through the laver, the
priests exert this power given to them? One is the
mystery in both. But thou sayest, that in the laver the
grace of the mysteries worketh. What in penitence?
worketh not the Name of God?"[3]

These eventful words gradually acquired a yet more

[1] S. Cyril in loc. quoted in the note to the same sermon, p. 32.
[2] S. Ambrose de Pœnit. ii. 2, quoted in the same sermon, p. 7.
[3] De Pœnit. 18, § 37, quoted in the same sermon, p. 7.

specific sense, which became more emphatic when the Novatian heresy arose; for the dispute between the orthodox Fathers and the Novatians turned on the question, whether these words of our LORD applied as fully to the ministry of Penance as to that of Baptism. And as the Novatians denied this interpretation, the orthodox Fathers were led to lay the greater stress on their application to Penance. Thus S. Chrysostom employs the words as if they were limited to the one grace of Absolution. " Through the Priests of GOD do we put on CHRIST; are buried with the SON of GOD, and become members of that Blessed Head; by them we are not only regenerated, but the sins after this they have power to *remit*."[1] Hooker also applies the words in this more restricted sense, when enumerating the priestly offices in his well known description; "What angel in heaven could have said to man as our LORD did to Peter, ' Feed My sheep. Preach, Baptize. Do this in remembrance of Me. Whose sins ye retain, they are retained; and their offences in heaven pardoned, whose faults you shall on earth forgive?' What think we? Are these terrestrial sounds, or else are they voices uttered out of the clouds above?"[2] During the middle ages both the maintainers and opponents of the new scholastic doctrines, while differing in matters of detail, agreed in deducing from these words the principles of sacramental Confession and Absolution. The Roman advocates, as we have seen, even grounded on them their belief of the necessity of Confession, and they are quoted in the canons of the Council of Trent, as the Scriptural proof of this necessity.[3]

[1] De Sacerdotio, iii. 6.   [2] Eccl. Pol. l. v. 77.
[3] " By Confession is understood the declaration which the penitent

I

The careful retention therefore of these words in the English Ordinal proves, that our Reformers had no desire to abandon the essential features of the ministry in question. To retain these words in their original position in the Ordinal, and at the same time hope to disconnect them from the ministry of forgiveness of sins, would have been vain. Nor was there any obligation, according to primitive Catholic use, to retain these words as the form of Ordination. They were not in the Ordinal in primitive times. They were introduced in comparatively recent days. For at least 1000 years the grace of Ordination was conveyed by the imposition of hands with prayer.[1] Our Reformers, therefore, grounding their judgment on primitive cus-

---

makes of his sins to a priest; the obligation of which evidently follows from the words of CHRIST, when, instituting the sacrament of penance, He breathed on His disciples and said, ʻReceive ye the HOLY GHOST; whose sins ye forgive,ʼ &c. For to what purpose was this given, if it imposed not on the sinner the obligation of making known his sins? Or how could that power be exercised, if no sins were communicated?" Conc. Trid. Sess. xiv., cap. v. De Pœnitentia.

[1] Palmer (Antiq. of the Engl. Rit. ch. xii. sec. vii.) says, on the authority of Martene, that these words have been used at least since the tenth century. Procter ("on the Book of Common Prayer,") supposes that they are not older in this use than the 12th century, and quotes Marshall, iii. p. 20, (note.) Palmer observes, that they are found in Western Pontificals written 600 years ago, which agrees with Procter's and Maskell's supposition. The older form of ordination was by the prayer still used in the Latin Office after the first imposition of hands: the second imposition of hands, as well as the words, "Receive ye the HOLY GHOST," &c. being a later addition. In the East the Greeks and Syrians still use only prayer for the gift of the HOLY GHOST, as originally in the West: the form of words differing; nor have they ever adopted into their ordinal the words, "Receive ye the HOLY GHOST," &c. See Courayer, cap. vi., The Form of Ordination, p. 96. Oxford edit.

toms, in contrast with those of later date, might, in perfect consistency with their position, have abandoned these words, and returned to the simple primitive use. It was a precisely similar case with the indicative form of Absolution in the Visitation of the Sick. Both forms were mediæval; both were identified with High Church views. The words of the form of Ordination were indeed our LORD's own words, and therefore could not themselves be set aside; but had they been altogether falsely applied, or abused, they might have been removed from the position in which, if retained, this false application or abuse would certainly be perpetuated. The only reasonable account of their retention is, that this special application was held by the Reformers to be substantially true. They therefore carefully retained them, only guarding them against certain modern interpretations and inferences which had become entangled with them, by protests and appeals to primitive testimony elsewhere sufficiently recorded.

Neither were these words retained without a full consciousness of the unsacramental theories, which at the time of the Reformation were associated with them. The advocates for change in our Ordinal at the present day are not more opposed to the sacramental view, than were the ultra-Protestants of the Reformation period. Zwingle, e.g., paraphrasing these words, said; "It is as though CHRIST said, 'To whomsoever ye preach the Gospel and they receive it, to them sins are remitted.' For in the last chapter of S. Mark He expresses this more clearly; 'Preach the Gospel to every creature,' 'he that believeth shall be saved,' i.e., whoso believeth the Gospel preached by you. The remitting sins then is ascribed to the Apostles, because they preach that through which sins are remitted; for they preach the Gospel as Christ Himself, or the grace of God through Christ, by which sin is remitted."[1] And Calvin to the same effect; "It is clear that in these places (S. Mark xvi.; S. John xx.) the power of the keys is simply the preaching of the Gospel."[2] Again Peter Martyr, whose influence with the English Bishops was one chief cause of the changes made in the First Prayer Book, says : "The key is twofold, the one of preaching the Word of God, the other of believing it when heard : one doth not open or remit sins without the other. That key is in truth nothing else than the Word of God, not given to Priests more than others, but to all Christians."[3]

In opposition to such doctrine the voice of the Church of England was heard at the very same time, speaking in the clearest and most express language, affirming the direct contrary to the teaching of these foreign reformers. The Homily for Whit-Sunday says; "Christ ordained the authority of the keys to excommunicate notorious sinners, and to absolve them which are truly penitent."[4] Cranmer's Catechism teaches the same truth more fully; "Now God doth not speak to us with a voice sounding out of heaven, but He hath given the keys of the kingdom of heaven, and the authority to forgive sin by the ministers of the Church. Wherefore let him that is a sinner go to one of them; let him acknow-

---

[1] In Hist. Dom. Res. Quoted by Dr. Pusey in note B. pp. 71, 2, at the end of his sermon, "Absolution of the Penitent."

[2] Instit. iv. 1—22, quoted by Dr. Pusey in the same note, p. 72.

[3] Serm. in S. John xx., quoted by Dr. Pusey, ibid. pp. 72, 73.

[4] Homily 2nd, for Whit-Sunday.

ledge and confess his sin, and pray him that according
to God's commandment, he will give him Absolution
and comfort him with the word of grace and forgiveness of his sins.   And when the minister doth so, then
I ought stedfastly to believe, that my sins are truly forgiven me in heaven, and such a faith is able to stand
strong in all skirmishes and assaults of our mortal
enemy, the devil; forasmuch as it is builded on a sure
rock, that is to say, the certain word and work of God.
For he that is absolved, knoweth for a surety that his
sins be forgiven him by the minister, and he knoweth
assuredly also that the minister hath authority from
God Himself to do so.   And, thirdly, he knoweth that
God hath made this promise to His ministers, and said
to them; ' To whom ye forgive sins on earth, to him
also they shall be forgiven in heaven.'   Wherefore despise not Absolution, for it is the commandment and
ordinance of God, and the HOLY SPIRIT of God is present and causeth these things to take effect in us and
to work our salvation.'"[1]

Cranmer published his Catechism in 1548.   In 1549
he with his colleagues prepared the Ordinal.   The one

---

[1] "On the power of the keys," Catech. Cranmer's works, vol. iv.
p. 283. Ed. Jenkyns.

Cranmer's vacillations of mind are often and justly urged against
arguments drawn from his expressions of opinion. A distinction, however, ought to be made between his private writings, and the public
documents which he was authorised to draw up. But further, Mr.
Cooke has shown that *on the point in question*, involving the doctrine of
the Priesthood, and the Ordinal, his finally settled views coincided with
those expressed in his Catechism. " In 1540, Cranmer had expressed
decidedly Erastian views, adding however, as if doubtful of their sound-
ness, 'This is mine opinion and sentence at this present, which nevertheless I do not temerariously define, but refer the judgment thereof

is therefore explanatory of the other.   In 1562 the
Homily for Whit-Sunday was published.   These documents therefore together form an authoritative catena
of doctrine, stretching throughout the crisis of the Reformation.   Jewel is often quoted as an authority in
favour of an opposite view, but even he, in one of his
strongest passages on preaching, which he describes as
an exercise of the " power of the keys," implies that
Absolution is also an exercise of the same ministry.
"The keys," Jewel says, " by which they (the Priests)
are able either to close or open the kingdom of heaven,
we, as Chrysostom, say that they are ' the knowledge
of the Scriptures ;' or as Tertullian, ' the interpretation
of the law ;' or as Eusebius, ' the word of GOD.'
Moreover that the disciples of CHRIST received this
power, not that they should hear the private confessions
of the people, or listen to their whisperings, as all
Priests now everywhere do, and do it so, as if in that
wholly and alone (in eo toto) *lay all the virtue and use of
the keys :* but that they should go, that they should

wholly to your Majesty.' Several of the divines who assisted Cranmer
in drawing up the Ordinal, expressed opinions in 1540, diametrically
opposed to the Archbishop. In 1543, a book was put forth by the
King and Convocation, called ' A Necessary Doctrine,' which defines
' order' to be ' the gift or grace of ministration in CHRIST'S Church,
given of GOD to Christian men by the consecration and imposition of
the Bishop's hands,' and declares the succession to be perpetual even
to the end of the world. In 1548 Cranmer himself put forth the Catechism in which Apostolic succession and the power of the keys are set
forth, and insisted on most strongly. ' It is plain,' Bishop Burnet remarks, ' that Cranmer had now quite laid aside those singular opinions
which he formerly held of the Ecclesiastical functions ; for now in a
work of his own, without the concurrence of any other, he fully sets
forth their divine Institution.' " Mr. Cooke's Power of the Priesthood,
p. 63.

teach, that they should publish the Gospel."[1]   Jewel's reference to the Fathers, S. Chrysostom, Tertullian, and Eusebius, shows that he intended his words to be understood in their sense, and his expressions prove that he was not denying a "real virtue and use of the keys" in Absolution, but only condemning so exclusive an application of the words to that one ministry as to result in a practical disparagement of the earnest and intelligent preaching of the Word of GOD in its power of co-operation towards the same end.

The ultra-Reformers sought to magnify preaching to the detriment of the inner ministry of confession.   The leading directors of the English Reformation rather aimed at restoring the balance between the two, seeking earnestly to develop an intelligent use of the Word of GOD, as the truest means of giving life to sacramental ordinances,—a characteristic feature of the mind of the Church of England, which Dr. Wordsworth thus expresses; " A right sentence is the only one which CHRIST has authorised, and the only one which He will ratify, by giving it validity spiritually and internally. 'Clavis potestatis nihil operatur sine clave sententiæ.' The key of knowledge and direction is necessary to give effect to that of power.   No one can be admitted through the door of pardon, who has not passed through that of penitence. CHRIST alone 'openeth and no man shutteth, and shutteth and no man openeth,' and He turns the key in the hand of His minister only when it is used aright."[2]

The several functions of the Priesthood, as a threefold power of ministry, set forth in the Ordinal, correspond with the description given in the Homilies of

---

[1] Jewel's Apology.   [2] Theophilus Anglicanus, xiv. " Absolution."

the "notes" of a true Church. "And it (the Church) hath always had three notes and marks whereby it is known; pure and sound doctrine, the Sacraments ministered according to Christ's holy institution, and the right use of Ecclesiastical discipline."[1]

We are here concerned only with the third or last "note" of the Church, to which, as we have seen, a special application of the words of ordination has always been made. "Discipline,"[2] which in the above passage of the Homily, as in the Ordinal, is indicated as the third function of the Priesthood, is expressed likewise in the "Injunctions" of Queen Elizabeth, drawn up by Parker and his fellow Bishops, under the corresponding term, "the authority of the keys." "The pure Word of God is preached, and the Sacraments are administered according to Christ's institution, and the authority of the keys is retained."[3] The threefold division is the same, though the language varies. The same expression is again used in "certain principal Articles of Religion appointed to be read by parsons, vicars, and curates, at their first possession taking," dated A.D. 1559. "I do acknowledge the Church to be the Spouse of Christ, wherein the Word of God is truly taught, the Sacraments orderly administered according to God's institution, and the authority of the keys duly used."[4]

---

[1] Homily for Whit-Sunday.

[2] The term "discipline" was thus used by the Fathers, as e.g., by S. Augustine; "Disciplinam qui abjicit, infelix est, qui negat, crudelis est." Serm. xiii. And again; "Ecclesiastica Disciplina medicinalis vindicta, terribilis lenitas, charitatis severitas." In Ps. lxiii., IV. 895, quoted by Wordsworth. Theoph. Anglic. ch. xiii., Power of the Keys.

[3] "The Interpretations and Further Considerations of Queen Elizabeth's Injunctions." Cardwell's Document. Annals. No. xliii.

[4] See Cardwell's Document. Annals. No. xlvi.

Ecclesiastical "discipline" has been explained by our Church, and the explanation is of great moment in our inquiry, to be not merely a means of correction for the sake of moral order or example, but a spiritual ministry affecting the soul's life before GOD. The Commination Service declares the object of "Penance" to be, "that their souls may be saved in the day of the LORD." In the form of excommunication drawn up under the supervision of Archbishop Tenison, and approved by Convocation, it is spoken of as " a certain anticipation of that which would be passed in heaven."[1]

It is further to be noted that the history of " discipline" in the Church of England closely resembles what occurred in the early Catholic Church. Public Penance was the mode of discipline first established, and earnestly sought to be maintained, by the Fathers both of the East and West. When it failed, they fell back on the private ministry as the only practicable, but still, as they judged, the sufficient, means of exercising the power of the keys. The rulers of the Church of England from the Reformation down to the times of Bishop Wilson,—who as Dr. Wordsworth says; " Of all witnesses which have raised up their voices in our Church, in support of discipline, not only in his writings, but in his practice also, presents the fullest and most valuable testimony,"[2]—used their utmost efforts to restore what the Fathers had so earnestly desired, though in vain, to uphold. The

[1] Quoted by the Bishop of S. Andrew's, Dr. C. Wordsworth, in an Appendix to his Sermon, "Evangelical Repentance," No. 36. The Appendix is specially valuable for its full details on the subject of Church discipline.

[2] Ibid. p. 97.

Church of England, like the Church of old, failing to accomplish this object has in like manner fallen back on the private ministry of Confession, as the only resource for carrying into effect this necessary function of its ministerial powers.

It can hardly fail to be a matter for serious reflection to those who cannot recognize in private Confession a legitimate ministry of the power of the keys, that according to their views, during the present abeyance of public Penance, the Church of England has entirely forfeited what she yet asserts to be a "note" of the true Church. The only escape from this conclusion is, to suppose that the desire for the restoration of public Penance as a thing "much to be wished," once in the year expressed in our public penitential service, when years as they pass by give no improving prospect of such restoration, is a sufficient guarantee for the virtual possession of this essential ministry. They on the contrary, and they alone, who hold, that every one within the Church of England seeking it, may now, as of old, find the full benefit of forgiveness of post-baptismal sins personally applied to their great comfort through special private Confession and Absolution,—testify by such belief, that the Church is still true in her claim to be in possession of a Priesthood fully empowered, and with sufficient means at command, to minister this vital sacramental grace.

CHAPTER IX.

THE Twenty-fifth Article is often quoted as irreconcileable with sacramental or sacerdotal views of Confession. The words referred to are as follows:

" There are two sacraments ordained of CHRIST our LORD in the Gospel, that is to say, Baptism and the Supper of the LORD. Those five commonly called sacraments, that is to say, Confirmation, Penance, Orders, Matrimony, Extreme Unction, are not to be counted for sacraments of the Gospel, being such as have grown partly of the corrupt following of the Apostles, partly are states of life allowed in the Scriptures; but yet have not like nature of sacraments as Baptism and the LORD's Supper; for that they have not any visible sign or ceremony ordained of GOD."

The language of this Article is obscure; but, while denying Penance to be a sacrament equal to Baptism, or the LORD's Supper, it does not follow that it therefore represents it as devoid of sacramental virtue. If this were so, the statement would be inconsistent with the Thirty-third Article, which affirms that an excommunicate person is " to be reconciled by penance ;" and also with the judgment of Parker, from whose hands the Articles took their last shape, who in his Visitation

Articles of 1567 reckons as one among "unwholesome, erroneous, and seditious doctrines," the position, "that mortal or voluntary sins, committed after baptism, be not remissible by penance."[1] For the virtue implied in the gift of remission or reconciliation is a spiritual grace, and therefore the form or means of imparting it must be sacramental. It is no sufficient answer to say that public Penance is meant in these places. The Article makes no distinction. Moreover, public Penance had practically ceased for many centuries before the Reformation, and the term would certainly be understood of the practice then in ordinary use. Moreover, where such a distinction was intended by the Church, it was carefully specified, as in the Commination Service, which speaks of " public and open" Penance, as distinct from the private ministry. Nor again can it be meant that Penance, in its essential features of Confession and Absolution, arose " from a corrupt following of the Apostles;" for we have seen that it is traceable to the purest Christian antiquity, and to the Holy Scriptures, as an unquestioned Ordinance of the Gospel. It follows then that not Penance, whether public or private, simply considered, but some incidental doctrines, which had become intimately associated with the term, and formed part of the practical system then prevailing, are repudiated in the Article.

Moreover, the language of the Article is carefully guarded. It affirms "that there are two sacraments," but explains the principle of this limitation by adding,—and so distinguishing those specially intended from all others, —"*ordained of Christ our Lord in the Gospel*," as in the

---

[1] Cardwell's Documentary Annals, xlvi.

Catechism again similarly'it is stated, that there are two only *"as generally,"* i.e., universally or in all cases, *"necessary to salvation,"* the very distinction, attributed to the two, implying the existence of other sacramental ordinances, not equally necessary. Moreover, the Article says of " the five," not that they are not sacraments, but only not " sacraments of the Gospel," a technical expression of which more will be said hereafter.

The sacramental theory on which the Article is based, is more largely drawn out in one of the Homilies, and the passage, in which the explanation is given, may fairly be regarded as illustrative of the Article, because the Second Book of Homilies, in which it occurs, was published the same year in which the Articles underwent their final revision.

" As for the number of them, (the sacraments,) if they be considered according to the exact signification of a sacrament, namely, for visible signs, expressly commanded in the New Testament, whereunto is annexed the promise of free forgiveness of our sins, and of our holiness and joining in CHRIST, there be but two, namely, Baptism and the Supper of the LORD. For although Absolution hath the promise of forgiveness of sins, yet by the express word of the New Testament, it hath not this promise annexed and tied to the visible sign, which is the imposition of hands. For this visible sign (I mean laying on of hands) is not expressly commanded in the New Testament to be used in Absolution, as the visible signs in Baptism and the LORD's Supper are; and therefore Absolution is no such sacrament as Baptism and the Communion are, and though the Ordering of Ministers hath this visible sign and promise, yet it lacks the promise of remission of sins, as all other sacraments, besides the two above named do. Therefore neither it, nor any other sacrament else, be such sacraments, as Baptism and the Communion are. But in a general acceptation, the name of a sacrament may be attributed to anything whereby a holy thing is signified. In which understanding of the word, the ancient writers have given this name, not only to the other five, commonly of late years taken and used for supplying the number of the seven sacraments, but also to diverse and sundry other ceremonies, as to oil, washing of feet, and such like; not meaning thereby to repute them as sacraments in the same signification that the two forenamed sacraments are. And therefore S. Augustine, weighing the true signification and exact meaning of the word, writing to Januarius, and also in the third book of the Christian Doctrine, affirmeth, that the sacraments of Christians, as they are most excellent in signification, so they are most few in number; and in both places maketh mention expressly of two, the sacrament of Baptism and the Supper of the LORD. And although there are retained by order of the Church of England, besides these two, certain other rites and ceremonies about the institution of ministers in the Church, Matrimony, Confirmation of children, by examining them of their knowledge in the Articles of the faith, and joining thereto the prayers of the Church for them, and likewise for the Visitation of the Sick, yet no man ought to take these for sacraments in such signification and meaning as the sacraments of Baptism and the LORD's Supper are; but either for godly states of life necessary in CHRIST's Church and therefore worthy to be set forth by public action and solemnity by the ministry of the Church, or else judged to be such ordinances as may make for the instruction, comfort, and edification of CHRIST's Church."[1]

The same careful language is employed here, as in the Article. The " other rites and ceremonies," which " no man ought to take for sacraments," are only excluded from being so called "*in such signification and meaning as* the sacraments of Baptism and the LORD's Supper are." Again, "*the number of them*" is limited to the two, only *if* they be considered according to *the exact signification* of a sacrament. This "exact signification" is determined by a careful definition of the term, which includes not only "a visible sign expressly ordained by our LORD," but also, as the inward grace, "forgiveness of sin, sanctification," and also "union with CHRIST." It is only when measured by this standard that Baptism and the LORD's Supper alone are considered to be sacraments. They alone correspond with the exact significa-tion of the term, when understood in its technical sense determined by the definition, and therefore they have their peculiar pre-eminence. But the Homily, while confining the term, sacrament, in its fullest, strictest sense, to these two, and allowing that it has been em-ployed more widely to express anything " whereby a holy thing may be signified," recognises at the same time an intermediate class of sacraments, or sacramental ordi-nances, of which Absolution and Orders are mentioned as instances. These are indeed classed in the Homily under the common description, " rites and ceremonies," from a jealousy of applying the term, sacrament, to any

[1] Homily of Common Prayer and Sacraments.

ordinance falling short of its "exact signification;" but the graces, specifically assigned to them, necessarily involve a sacramental virtue. "Absolution" is affirmed to "have the promise of forgiveness of sins," and "Orders" to convey the grace of the Priesthood. These are therefore sacraments of the intermediate, or secondary, class.

One sentence only appears to be inconsistent with this explanation. After the statement, that "Absolution hath the promise of forgiveness of sins," it follows within a few lines; "all other sacraments, besides the two above named (Baptism and the LORD's Supper), lack the promise of forgiveness of sins," words which, literally taken, deny to Absolution this specific grace, and thus expressly contradict the previous statement. Mr. Cooke notices the inconsistency and suggests an explanation. He supposes the Homilist to be speaking of ordinances which possess visible signs expressly instituted by GOD to accompany and seal the promised grace, of which he instances Orders, the "laying on of hands" being its "visible sign" according to divine appointment; and then to state that there is "no promise of forgiveness of sin annexed or tied to this visible sign, i.e. in Orders; nor have any other sacraments, except Baptism and the LORD's Supper, the promise of remission of sins tied to any outward sign." "This," he adds, "undoubtedly must be the meaning of the passage. We cannot suppose the writer of the Homily to be so strangely inconsistent, as to assert within the short space of fifteen lines, that Absolution *has*, and *has not*, the promise of forgiveness of sins. Such a flagrant self-contradiction would make the passage, if not the whole

Homily, utterly worthless, and far from 'wholesome doctrine.' Therefore if we wish to uphold the authority of the Homily, the sentence,—' it lacks the promise of remission of sins, as all other sacraments besides the two above named do,'—must be interpreted as meaning, that 'the promise (i.e. in the case of Absolution) is not tied to an outward sign,' i.e. not by divine authority."[1]

Mr. Cooke has not noticed the omission of Absolution from the list of secondary ordinances, given at the close of the passage, which may also seem to some to present a similar difficulty. But there can be no doubt, that this ordinance is intended to be included under the expression, "the Visitation of the Sick," of which it practically forms the cardinal point, and in regard to which alone that Office becomes, strictly speaking, sacramental. Supposing Absolution to be intended by this expression, it is classed in this passage under the same general head with "Orders" and "Confirmation," and is therefore considered of similar importance and virtue.

Moreover, the reference to S. Augustine, which the passage of the Homily contains, proves, that the above statements are intended to be in harmony with his, and therefore with Catholic, teaching. To rest on such testimony for the pre-eminent distinctiveness of Baptism and the LORD's Supper, implies that the same authority is to determine the comparative value of the other means of grace. And it is clear that S. Augustine taught the sacramental virtue of Absolution.[2]

[1] Power of the Priesthood in Absolution. P. 76.
[2] "In Confession, the accusation of oneself is the praising of GOD. Some one says, In what doth the Church benefit, if already he who con-

K 2

The Homily could not therefore deny it, without denying the authority, on which the main substance of its doctrinal statement is based.

It appears then that, according to the judgment of the Homily, Absolution is not to be counted a sacrament in the "exact signification" of the term, because (1) its visible sign, ordinarily used in the primitive Church, is not ordained in Holy Scripture; (2) it conveys not the whole, but only a certain measure, of the graces of the New Covenant, being inferior in this respect to Baptism and the Holy Eucharist. But inasmuch as Absolution is represented as having the promise of accompanying grace, i.e., "forgiveness of sins," the Homily implies, that it possesses a sacramental virtue, and is thus to be distinguished from those "rites and ceremonies," which are merely symbols of invisible things, not channels of grace.

The Church of England therefore recognises three classes, or grades, of holy ordinances; (1) the complete sacraments, conveying CHRIST Himself, and in Him all grace, through signs of His own institution—Baptism and the Eucharist alone constituting this first class;

fesses comes forth resuscitated by the voice of the LORD? In what doth the Church benefit, to which it is said, 'What things ye shall loose on earth, shall be loosed in heaven?'" (Serm. viii. on S. Matt. Vol. x., p. 19.) Again. "Let no one flatter himself, and say, I confess in private to GOD, and GOD that knows my heart, will pardon me, though I never confess at all to the Priest. Hath GOD in vain said, 'Whose sins ye remit, they are remitted?' Hath GOD in vain given the Priest the power of the Keys? Shall we by our neglect go about to make void the promise of CHRIST?" (Serm. viii. 392, 23.) Quoted by Sparrow in his Cambridge Sermon on "Confession of sins and power of Absolution."

(2) sacramental rites, conveying certain special kinds of grace—Absolution, Orders, and Confirmation, falling under this head; (3) rites and ceremonies, or simple symbolic forms of spiritual things, which the Church of her own will uses as instructive and edifying, though not endued with any spiritual gifts. The term, "sacraments of the Gospel," is employed as a dogmatic phrase, specially appropriated to the first class, because they alone contain and convey the full graces promised in the Gospel, and therefore satisfy the complete definition.

The whole question thus depends on the meaning attached to the term, sacrament. The history of the term marks successive variations of doctrinal definition. The Fathers applied the term indiscriminately to all visible signs of spiritual things. There was no need of distinction, where there was no controversy; no risk of confusion, where the living faith of the people preserved the substantial ideas of each separate ordinance. The schoolmen of the middle ages devised the theory of the seven sacraments, and excluded from their list all other visible signs, classing the seven alone under the one common term. This theory arose from the reverence attached to the number seven. Seven petitions compose the LORD's Prayer. The seventh day is the holy day of the week. Seven is the sacred number connected with the work of creation. Seven graces are identified with the Gift of the HOLY GHOST. The Spirit Himself is symbolised by the "seven lamps burning before the Throne." Seven was therefore selected as the number by which to classify the spiritual and corporal works of mercy, and the deadly sins. The same rule was applied to the sacraments.

But in the lapse of time evil arose from this classification of the sacraments, just as evil has arisen from
the like classification of the deadly sins, it being open
to the supposition that others were not deadly,[1] because
not included in the list. What were thus classed as
alike distinct from all other ordinances, came to be regarded as co-equal one with another. The greater were
confounded with the less. The pre-eminent dignity of
Baptism and the Eucharist was by the comparison obscured to the popular mind. The two only absolutely
necessary means of perfect union with CHRIST were thus
disparaged. In particular, Penance having become, by
the changed law of the Church, as necessary for all
persons as Baptism and the Eucharist,—it popularly
assumed a place of equal authority. When the full
scholastic doctrine of Penance, with its elaborate details
stretching into all spheres of life, and determining even
the judgments of the world to come,—was developed, it
gradually acquired enlarged proportions, filling up almost
the entire view of religion in its practical bearing on
the people. Our Reformers sought to restore the true
balance between the several ordinances, and the statements we have been considering are the fruit of this
endeavour. But to apprehend these gradations of the
Divine mysteries, requires an enlightened and well-dis-
ciplined mind. And it is because of the comparative
rarity of such an endowment, that evil has arisen from
this latter and more exact attempt to classify the sacraments, as before evil arose in an opposite direction from

---

[1] It is scarcely to be doubted, that the sin of lying has suffered in
estimation, because not classed among the deadly sins, though unquestionably so condemned in Scripture. (Rev. xxi. 9.)

the scholastic mode of statement. The human mind, ever impatient of distinctions, passes rapidly into extremes. And, just as the scholastic view, seeming to equalise the ordinances of grace, operated practically to depress the two greater sacraments, by elevating unduly those of inferior virtue, so the dogmatic exposition of our Reformers, separating off the two greater sacraments, according to their peculiar prerogatives, as alone properly claiming the name of sacraments, has seemed to reduce the lesser sacramental ordinances to the level of mere rites and ceremonies.

But the English Reformers selected the true basis for constructing a dogmatic statement of the means of grace, although it cannot be enforced with the certainty attaching to the Articles of the Creed. Where there are no conciliar decisions of Œcumenical authority to which to appeal, as is the case with regard to the sacraments,—because in earlier days they were too well known to need any formal definition, and, being uncontroverted, required no guarding,—the only recourse is to holy Scripture, the general teaching of the Fathers, and the practice of the earliest antiquity. But doctrinal statements founded on such a basis, cannot possess the weight which attaches only to articles of faith expressly defined, and sealed, by the authority of the undivided Church. For this reason, among those who, agreeing in the use of the same ordinances, and thus practically and essentially one, are yet divided as to their dogmatic definition, the greatest mutual forbearance ought to be cherished, and the utmost latitude of kindly consideration allowed.[1] Differences of view in such a case can

[1] The memorable words in which Mr. Keble, at the close of his trea-

hardly but exist. The mere varieties of education, of spiritual life and intelligence, would alone suffice to account for great divergence.

Nevertheless, for all of us who rest in simplicity on the judgments of their own Communion, which, subject to the authority of the undivided Church, is the teacher vouchsafed to us of GOD, sufficient guidance is given as to the specific virtues of these several sacramental ordinances. We are taught in our dogmatic records how to distinguish one ordinance from another, and to fix the relative value of each, with sufficient precision for all practical purposes. The two pre-eminent sacraments are shown, while containing all grace, to have nevertheless each its distinctive gift; and the lesser sacramental ordinances are also distinguished as to their own special virtues. Thus Baptism is described to be

---

tise on "Eucharistical Adoration," has recorded his opinion for our encouragement in the midst of our sad divisions on the question of sacraments, bear materially on the subject matter of the text. "Whether it be that the sacramental system does not require to be doctrinally known in order that its benefits may be received, any more than a person need be able to analyze what he eats and drinks, before he can have it for 'food and gladness,' or for other causes unknown to us, it pleased Providence that the Church should enter on its era of sad divisions, without any œcumenical decision primarily and directly pronounced on the subject. And therefore that portion of CHRIST's truth has not come down to us in distinct dogmatical assertions guarded by anathemas, as the statements concerning the Trinity and the Incarnation have; and it is consequently a more adventurous thing and more largely partaking of the boldness of private judgment, to denounce any person as a heretic in respect of the former class of errors. It is not so plainly our duty to withdraw from his communion, as it would be if he had been distinctly excommunicated by the Church. Materially he may be in heresy, but formally he is not yet so,—a distinction acknowledged by all theologians." P. 169.

the means of "remission of sins by spiritual regeneration."[1] The Holy Eucharist, viewed in the same distinctiveness, is "the strengthening and refreshing of
the soul by the Body and Blood of CHRIST, Which are
verily and indeed taken and received by the faithful."[2]
Thus again, Confirmation is "the increase of the HOLY
SPIRIT."[3] Orders is the communication of " the HOLY
GHOST for the Office and work of a Deacon, or a Priest,
in the Church of GOD."[4] Matrimony is consecrated to
an "excellent mystery, signifying unto us the mystical
union which is betwixt CHRIST and His Church."[5] And
so, lastly, "Absolution *hath*," i.e., not merely declares
or assures, but also *is* the means of conveying, "the
promise of forgiveness of sins."[6]

[1] Baptismal Service.
[2] Catechism.
[3] Office of Confirmation. Form of Blessing in the imposition of
hands.
[4] Ordination Services.
[5] Office for Holy Matrimony.
[6] Homily of Common Prayer and Sacraments.

CHAPTER X

ONE passage in the " Second part of the Sermon on Repentance," often quoted as expressing the mind of the Church of England in contradiction of the views here expressed, needs in consequence of the importance attached to it, to be here brought under review. In order to enter into its true meaning, the whole context must be considered. The passage runs as follows :

" And where they (the Roman teachers) do allege this saying of our SAVIOUR JESUS CHRIST unto the leper, to prove Auricular Confession to stand on GOD's Word, 'Go thy way, and show thyself unto the Priest,' do they not see that the leper was cleansed from his leprosy, before he was by CHRIST sent unto the Priest for to show himself unto him? By the same reason we must be cleansed from our spiritual leprosy, I mean our sins must be forgiven us, before that we come to confession. What need we then to tell forth our sins into the ear of the Priest, sith that they may be already taken away? Therefore holy Ambrose, in his second sermon upon the 119th Psalm, doth say full well, *Go show thyself unto the Priest*. Who is the true Priest, but He which is the Priest for ever after the order of Melchizedeck? Whereby this holy Father doth understand that both the priesthood and the law being changed, we ought to acknowledge none other Priest for deliverance from our sins, but our SAVIOUR JESUS CHRIST, Who being our Sovereign Bishop, doth with the Sacrifice of His Body and Blood offered once for ever upon the altar of the Cross, most effectually cleanse the spiritual leprosy, and wash away the sins of all those that with true confession of the same do flee unto Him. It is most evident and plain, that this auricular confession hath not the warrant of GOD's Word, else it had not been lawful for Nectarius, Bishop of Constantinople, upon a just occasion to have put it down. For when anything ordained by GOD, is by the lewdness of men abused, the abuse ought to be taken away, and the thing itself suffered to remain. . . . Moreover these are S. Augustine's words : 'What have I to do with men, that they should hear my confession as though they were able to heal my diseases? a curious sort of man to know another man's life, and slothful to correct and amend his own. Why do they seek to hear of me what I am, which will not hear of thee what they are? And how can they tell, when they hear by me of myself, whether I tell the truth or not, since no mortal man knoweth what is in man, but the spirit of man which is in him?' Augustine would not have written thus, if auricular confession had been used in his time. Being therefore not led with the conscience thereof, let us with fear and trembling, and with a true contrite heart, use that kind of confession which GOD doth command in His Word, and then doubtless, as He is faithful and righteous, He will forgive us our sins, and make us clean from all wickedness. I do not say but that, if any do find themselves troubled in conscience, they may repair to their learned curate or pastor, or to some other godly learned man,[1] and show the trouble and doubt of their conscience to them, that they may receive at their hand the comfortable salve of God's Word; but it is against the true Christian liberty, that any man should be bound to the numbering of his sins, as it hath been used heretofore in the time of blindness and ignorance."

It was remarked in reference to the passage quoted from the Homilies in the last chapter, that its statements are based on Patristic authority. The same is the case here. It is to S. Ambrose, S. Augustine, and Nectarius, that the Homilist appeals in proof of his doc-

---

[1] This expression is sometimes urged as a proof, that our Church, like the Swiss communities, recognises Confession to a layman equally as to a priest. There is nothing in any of our Offices to bear out such a conclusion. The expression, " godly learned man," clearly means a clergyman, and corresponds with "some other discreet and learned minister of God's Word," in the Exhortation before Communion. In both cases the expressions follow in precisely the same relation to the mention of the Parish Priest. " Let him come to me or to some other discreet and learned," &c., corresponds with the injunction of the Homily, "they may repair to their learned curate or pastor, or to some other godly learned man." The expression was commonly used at the time. Thus William Turner, Dean of Wells, a reformer, writes: "If any doubt arise in your conscience, whom ought we rather to go to, to ask counsel, than the *head man* of our souls?" The same writer in another place says: "Let the Bishops appoint *learned men* to hear confessions, and not blockheads, and then the people shall come to the priests by heaps and swarms." "The old and new learning." Tracts of Anglican Fathers. Vol. ii. p. 196.

Chillingworth uses the same term in a like connection: "Come not to him (the spiritual physician) only with such a mind as you would go to a *learned man* experienced in the Scriptures, or one that can speak comfortable quieting words to you, but as to one that hath authority delegated to him from God Himself, to absolve and acquit you of your sins." Serm. vii.

trine. The whole statement therefore is at least intended to be in harmony with Catholic teaching.

Moreover, the drift of the argument evidently culminates in the closing sentence, " it is against the true Christian liberty, that any man should be *bound* to the numbering of his sins." That this is the point which the writer seeks to disprove, is evident from the stress laid on the case of Nectarius. Nectarius was Bishop of Constantinople, A.D. 237, and during his Episcopate serious scandal was caused by a case of grievous sin which had been confessed to the Penitentiary, who imposed on the penitent public Penance. This led to the exposure, and eventually the deprivation, of a deacon, causing, as it was thought, great injury to the Church, by the dishonour cast on one of the clergy. The Nestorians were ready to make the most of any exposure of evil within the Church. Nectarius, alarmed, and anxious to prevent the recurrence of such cases in future, abolished the office of Penitentiary in Constantinople, and his example was followed throughout the East. The effect of this measure, as Marshall explains it, was, that " the confession of *secret* sins, which gave no scandal, was left thenceforward to the discretion and conscience of those who had committed them." He adds: " They (the people) were still, I presume, at liberty to use the advice of a ghostly counsellor, if they found themselves in want of it, only there was thenceforward no peculiar officer, whose distinct business it should be to receive such applications, which brings the case pretty nearly to that of our own establishment in the particular now before us."[1]

[1] Marshall's Penitential Discipline, pp. 43, 44. Marshall quotes Socrates the historian, expressing his apprehension of the hurtful effects

The case is perfectly conclusive on the point for which the Homilist adduces it, viz., against a rigid law of compulsory Confession as of divine right, which the Church had no discretionary power to modify. But at the same time the very circumstance of discontinuing the special office, establishes the fact of the existence of private Confession in the early Church. The original public system had been already superseded by the appointment of a Priest specially commissioned to receive private confessions, in order to judge whether the public Penance should be undergone. The change was in suppressing this special authorised receiver of private confessions. It proves the Church's power of modifying its rule regarding Confession, but it equally proves the original use and prevalence of the system.

Again, the emphatic sentences,—"*this* auricular confession hath not the warrant of GOD's word;" "the numbering of sins, *as it hath been used heretofore in the times of blindness and ignorance,*"—manifestly imply that, not private Confession simply considered, but a particular

---

likely to follow the suppression of the Penitentiary; "When Eudæmon (who had advised the suppression) told me what I have laid before my reader, I presently replied to him, 'Whether your advice will be of use, or detrimental to the Church, GOD only knows.' But now I see plainly that it hath given a handle, and an occasion, for discontinuing that wholesome practice of reprehending one another's sins, and for neglecting that Apostolical precept which directs us 'to have no fellowship with the unfruitful works of darkness, but rather reprove them.' " Hooker (Eccl. Pol. l. vi. c. iv. 12,) describes the matter, as though private confession was cut off by abolishing the Penitentiaries, but his words may be intended only to imply the discontinuance of private confession to a Priest specially authorised, and not such as might be made to the ordinary Parish Priest. Certainly the rule of private confession has continued in the East since the days of Nectarius, equally as in the West. Under either supposition the argument in the text applies.

system of it, was before the writer's mind ; for the "times of blindness and ignorance" cannot mean the primitive ages, and it is the sanction then given to the principle of Confession with which we are concerned. The expressions show, that the Homilist is speaking of the system of his day, and of the generations immediately preceding. The complex code of rules, often doing violence to the conscience ; the enforced spiritual influence bound, by the law of the Lateran Council, without the possibility of escape, about the closest relations of domestic and political life ; the dispensations and indulgences extending into the unseen world ; the possible interference with the soul's inner yearnings for unfettered communion with GOD,—this later system claiming, as it did, a divine authority, and not anything that we now see, or are likely to see, or which could possibly arise under a discretionary law of Confession, however widely extended, was the idea which the Homilist sought to dislodge from the popular belief.

This conclusion is yet further proved by the fact, that the writer is speaking of what was "not used in S. Augustine's time," which, as already sufficiently proved, could not be said generally of Confession, whether public or private, for both ministries were recommended by the Saint ; though true of the particular system in use immediately before the Reformation.

Again, the quotation from S. Ambrose intended to disprove the priestly claim to remit sin, on the ground that it is a disparagement of our LORD's Priesthood, can only be directed against some supposed idea of an absolute power in the Priest. It has no application against the doctrine of a Priesthood which professes

only to be the organ and instrument of our LORD's
Priesthood, nor against absolution, as an act of ministry
dependent on the free grace of GOD.   Where the two are
viewed as co-operating together, and the one claims only
to be subordinate to the other, there is no room for contrast.   S. Ambrose is as strong in asserting the efficacy of
the commissioned Priest's derived ministry in remitting
sins, as he is in denying to him any absolute power.   He
says, in a passage already quoted; "To the remission
of sins *men supply their ministry*, yet do not exercise the
right of any power; for they do not forgive sins in their
own, but in the Name of the FATHER, and the SON, and
the HOLY GHOST.   They pray; GOD giveth: *the execution is through man*, the richness of the gift is from the
power on high."[1]

The retort with which the Homilist rebuts the use of
such a text as our LORD's command to the leper, "Go,
and show thyself to the Priest," to prove a divine obligation to confess to a Priest, as the only means of obtaining forgiveness, showing how the incident really tells
the other way, inasmuch as the leper was cleansed before he reached the Priest—is indeed a just repudiation
of attempts to strain holy Scripture without reference
to its context, in order to support a foregone conclusion.
But it is perfectly consistent with, or rather it positively
affirms, the belief—already claimed as that of the primitive Church, and therefore our own,—that sin may
be forgiven by GOD alone, on true contrition, while yet
the Priest's absolution is to be sought in order to assure
and attest the gift.   It is only inconsistent with the
idea of forgiveness being solely and indissolubly annexed to the priestly ministry.

[1] S. Ambrose de Spir. Sanc. iii. 18, § 137.

NOTE.

An important passage in Becon's "Potation for Lent" proves what has been shown in the two preceding chapters, that even the Ultra-Reformers of the English Reformation did not seek to remove Confession, but only certain incidental features of the system then in force, nor even stumbled at the term, auricular. Becon's opinions may be judged by the fact that he explained "the use of the keys" to "consist in preaching," and our LORD's words, "Whatsoever ye shall loose upon earth, shall be loosed in heaven," to mean, "He hath committed to them the office of preaching the Gospel." (Works of Becon. Catechism, pp. 556, 566.) His views on the value of Confession are therefore the more remarkable.

Philemon. Why auricular confession should be condemned and exiled from the bounds of Christianity, I see no cause; but that it should be approved, retained, maintained, and used, I find causes many, yea, and these right urgent and necessary.

"*Christopher.* Much absurdity and wickedness hath both been conspired, learned, practised, and done in this auricular confession, as historians make mention, neither want we experience of this thing.

"*Phil.* I cannot deny these things to be true. There is nothing so good and of so great excellency, but it may be abused. The abuse thereof is to be taken away, and not the thing itself. That confession hath been greatly abused, it cannot be denied, as many other things in the Church have been also; yet ought it not therefore to be rejected and cast away, but rather restored to the old purity, and the use for the which it was first instituted. And so shall it not only not hurt, but also profit very highly, and bring much utility and profit to the Christian congregation . . . . . But I pray you, mark what I shall now say unto you concerning this auricular confession. That auricular confession is a thing of much weight, and grave importance, it appeareth well, inasmuch as it bringeth to men divers ample commodities and large profits.

"*Theophilus.* I pray you what are those?

"*Phil.* First, it engraffeth in us a certain humility, submission, and lowliness of mind, and depresseth all arrogancy and pride, while we humbly are contented to confess to our ghostly father such offences as wherewith we have offended GOD. Secondly; it incuteth and beateth into our hearts a shamefacedness, whereby we are so ashamed of our faults heretofore committed, that we utterly abhor them, and are wholly

inflamed with the love of virtue. Thirdly; it bringeth us to the knowledge of ourselves, while we hear those things of the Priest, that are necessary to be known of every Christian man. Fourthly: in confession
we do not only learn to know how heinous and detestable a thing sin is
before GOD, but also means and ways to eschew it. How many, think
you, are there which, if this auricular confession were taken away,
would not care how they lived, neither would they regard any part of
CHRIST'S doctrine, but live like brute beasts, without any fear of GOD
at all, or study of innocency, wallowing and tumbling themselves daily
in sin, not once having a respect unto the correction of their old and
wicked manners? Fifthly; if we be in doubt of anything, in confession we may learn the assurance and certainty of it. Sixthly; in confession, the ignorant is brought unto knowledge, the blind into sight,
the desperate into salvation, the presumptuous unto humility, the troubled unto quietness, the sorrowful unto joy, the sick unto health, the
dead to life. What need I make many words? Confession bringeth
high tranquillity to the troubled conscience of a Christian man, while
the most comfortable words of Absolution are rehearsed unto him by
the Priest." (Parker Society Edit., p. 100.)

Mr. Benjamin Shaw, in a pamphlet published in 1858, (Rivington,)
quotes an extract from Bullinger's letter to Bishop Horn in 1565,
in proof that auricular confession ceased to be used in England at the
commencement of the Reformation. The extract quoted says; "Not
only will all ecclesiastical order be disturbed, and the number of most
abused ceremonies be increased, but even images (which we know are
defended by the Lutherans) will be restored; the artolatry in the
LORD'S Supper will be re-introduced, private absolution, and after this
auricular confession will creep in by degrees; and an infinite number
of other evils will arise," &c. (Zurich Letters. Parker Society, p. 342.)
Mr. Shaw adds, "There seems no reason to doubt, that this is unex-
ceptional historical evidence of the state of things at the time; it was
apprehended by this writer that private absolution and auricular confession might creep in. It follows that in the actual state of affairs
they could not have been generally in use." Yet Becon, whose words
involve so different a view of the state of things, was Cranmer's chaplain. It should be noted that Bullinger writes not from England,
but from Zurich; that he was a Zuinglian minister, and that it does
not appear he ever was in England, and so extreme was the party with
which he sympathised, that he, like Calvin, "objected to the surplice,

to private baptism, churching of women, the ring in marriage," and other " hurtful and offensive ceremonies," as Calvin afterwards called them. (See Cardwell's Preface to the Two Liturgies of King Edward VI. compared p. xxxiii., in note.) Bullinger therefore must have received his information from some extreme party correspondents in England, who represented the progress of opinions among themselves as a type of the state of the Church. At this very time " private absolution" was ordered in the Prayer Book to be given whenever desired; and yet Bullinger speaks of it as an abuse which, he feared, might creep in again.

L 3

CHAPTER XI.

THE COMPARISON OF OFFICES.

EVIDENCE of an important kind intimately bearing on the question before us, is to be derived from the contrast between our own Offices, and others drawn up either about the same time, or subsequently. Such evidence is of the greatest weight in the case of formularies directly derived from our own. Doctrinal variations can then be accounted for only by difference of belief, or from the influence of causes less favourable for the assertion of truth. As from the retention of primitive Catholic usages in our own Prayer Book we argue the unbroken transmission of primitive doctrine, so from the absence of such usages in other cases we argue its loss or rejection.

One instance from the Offices of foreign Reformed Communities will sufficiently illustrate the marked distinction between our own, and their, views of the ministerial Commission.

The Middleburgh Booke of Common Prayer was drawn up in 1586, for the use of certain foreign Protestant Communities, and was for some time largely used in England. The Ordination Service of this " Booke" has the following order; " He, (the Pastor elect) is to be ordained by the laying on of the hands of the eldership of that congregation, and the ministers appointed for that purpose, whereof one is to pronounce these words : " According to this lawful calling, agreeable to the word of God, stand thou charged with the pastoral charge of this people, over which the HOLY GHOST hath made thee overseer, to govern this flock of God, which He hath purchased with His blood." The Commission contains no gift of the HOLY GHOST; no claim to the ministry of remission of sins. The only special charge given is the exercise of spiritual government.

John Knox's book, which was adopted by the Scotch Kirk, closely corresponds with that of Middleburgh, and is equally devoid of any allusion to those mysterious powers which the Catholic Church has ever associated with holy Orders. In this book the Commission is thus given; " Prayer ended, the rest of the ministers, if any be elders of that Church present, in sign of their consent, shall take the elected by the hand. The chief minister shall give the benediction as followeth; 'GOD the FATHER of our LORD JESUS CHRIST, Who hath commanded His Gospel to be preached to the comfort of His elect, and hath called thee to the office of a watchman over His people, multiplie His graces with thee, illuminate thee with His Holy Spirit, comfort and strengthen thee in all virtue, governe and guide thy ministry to the praise of His holy name, to the propagation of CHRIST's kingdom, to the comfort of His Church, and finally to the plaine discharge and assurance of thy own conscience, in the Name of the LORD JESUS, to Whom,' " &c.[1] Preaching is the promi-

---

[1] Edit. Edinburgh, 1611. 8vo. cum privilegio. Both this and the preceding extract are quoted from Mr. Maskell's " Doctrine of Absolution." Pp. 208, 209.

nent idea embodied in this Commission, accompanied only with a general pastoral charge.

It has been observed, as " a significant thing," that in the requisitions which were more than once presented to Convocation during Queen Mary's reign, to restore doctrine and discipline as they had been before King Edward's time, Confession was scarcely alluded to, as though there was no ground for desiring change in this respect in the Church of England's rule, even in the estimation of Roman Catholics. The observation is the more instructive, as coming from one who, shortly after his book was written, left us to join the Church of Rome. "The only notice," Mr. Maskell says, " that I remember, is to the effect that Confession be again made, as it had been, obligatory. Much less is there complaint made, that people had been of late years taught, that the blessings and grace of (special?) sacerdotal absolution were to be obtained after the public repetition of general confessions. The order to confess once a year was again insisted on, and this was all."[1]

In the reign of William III., an influential body of the clergy, backed by the King, attempted an alteration of the Prayer Book, with the view of producing "a good agreement between the Church of England, and the Protestant Dissenters." It was the first attempt at a comprehension; the first fruits of the compromise sought to be established between religious parties after the Revolution. A Commission was issued to ten Bishops and twenty divines, " to prepare such alterations of the Liturgy and Canons, &c. . . . . . as might most conduce

[1] Maskell's "Doctrine of Absolution," pp. 130, 131.

. . . . to the reconciling as much as possible all differences." The Commissioners had before them all the
objections and demands which had at various times
been offered by opponents of the Prayer Book. Among
the concessions contemplated was the omission of the
mention of private absolution in the Exhortation of the
Eucharistic Office. It was proposed that the passage
should stand as follows; "let him come to me, or to
some other minister of GOD's Word, and open his grief,
that he may receive such spiritual advice and comfort,
as may tend to the quieting of his conscience, and his
better preparation for the Holy Communion." "The
benefit of Absolution," which in our Prayer Book is
the first object mentioned, is wholly omitted. In the
"Visitation of the Sick," the term, Confession, as well
as the direction to "move" the sick person to it, were
to be omitted, and instead a series of questions to be introduced, of which the last was; "Is your conscience
troubled with any weighty matter, in which you desire
my advice and assistance?" "Advice and assistance"
take the place of remission of sins. After these questions was to follow the prayer—"O most merciful GOD,"
&c., and then the indicative form of Absolution, but
with this alteration, that instead of, "I absolve thee,"
should be read, "upon thy true faith and repentance I
pronounce thee absolved."[1]

The manifest object of these proposals was to remove
points of doctrine or practice unpalatable to nonconformists. No amount of pastoral intercourse, no strictness of outward discipline, would have offended them.
The stumbling-block was sacramental Confession with
its accompanying promise of remission of sins; and it

[1] Procter on the Book of Common Prayer, pp. 144, 152—156.

is therefore clear that in the judgment both of Churchmen and Dissenters of that day, the words proposed to
be omitted or changed, and which still stand in their
place, involved its use.

About the same time the Nonjurors separated from
the Church. Some of the chief, such as Hickes and
Collier, adopted the first Prayer Book of Edward, but
the greater number continued to use our present Book
with such changes as they deemed necessary to adapt it
to their views. They introduced prayers for the dead,
the invocation of the HOLY GHOST, the prayer of Oblation in the Communion Office, chrism at Confirmation, and the use of oil in the Visitation of the Sick.
But they made no change whatever in the parts relating
to Confession and Absolution. There can be no question as to the views of the Nonjurors on these points.
The fact can be explained only on the idea, that they
regarded the Church of England's existing rule as an
adequate expression of the Catholic doctrine.[1]

The same conclusion follows from the history of the
Scotch Prayer Book. Changes were made under Laud's
direction in the Communion Office, such as the introduction of the invocation of the HOLY GHOST, with the
view of restoring certain Catholic usages, which had
been abandoned in the 2nd Prayer Book. But no change,
no addition, was made in reference to Confession or Absolution; and this, we may presume, because in his judgment none was needed.

All these facts tell in one and the same direction;
and they mark a uniform interpretation put upon our
rule both by friends and opponents for upwards of 200
years immediately subsequent to the Reformation.

[1] See Procter on the Book of Common Prayer.

The comparison with the American Prayer Book, brings down the chain of evidence to the close of the last century. The preface to this book indeed states, that in the following Offices "the doctrines of the Church of England are preserved entire." But the changes which were made are considered to be a subject of great regret by the many faithful Churchmen in the United States; and Mr. Procter, an unexceptionable witness on such a point, has not scrupled to characterise them as being, "some meant to conciliate the new Government, some perhaps admissible as improvements, but others decidedly objectionable and suspicious."[1] At first both the Athanasian and Nicene Creeds were omitted. The article, "He descended into hell," was erased from the Apostles' Creed. Only on the strong representations of the English Bishops, who refused on any other condition to consecrate Bishops for the United States, were they re-inserted. But even then the Creed of S. Athanasius, as also the sign of the Cross in Baptism, were left discretionary, to be used or not as the minister pleased. The modifications made in the practice of Confession and Absolution still remain unaltered, and they are as follows. The rubric before the general Absolution in the Daily Service, "The absolution or remission of sins to be pronounced by the Priest standing," &c. is changed into "A declaration concerning the forgiveness of sins to be said," &c. In the Ordinal, "Receive ye the HOLY GHOST; whose sins ye remit," &c., is allowed to be omitted, and the Bishop, if he choose, may say instead, "Take thou authority to execute the office of a Priest in the Church of GOD, now committed to thee," &c. In the Exhortation before

---

[1] See Procter on the Book of Common Prayer, p. 163.

Holy Communion, those who cannot quiet their own consciences are invited to come to the minister of GOD, " to receive such godly counsel and advice as may tend," &c. " The benefit of absolution" is omitted. In the Visitation of the Sick, the Rubric directing the minister to " move" the sick person to Confession, and also the indicative form of Absolution, are expunged, and nothing substituted in their place.[1]

The different modes of expression which have been noticed in these many forms of service, as either suggested, or actually adopted, are unquestionably indications of a distinct line or school of thought; and, when contrasted with the expressions of our own Offices, they together mark the working out of two principles which, from the time of the Reformation, have striven for the mastery in the West,—one, preserving the priestly office entire, with its Apostolic exercise of the power of the keys; the other, a re-action, as extreme, from the extreme Roman view of Penance, limiting pastoral intercourse to mere confidential conversation on the side of the penitent, counsel and exhortation on that of the Priest. A constant effort has been made to introduce into our Offices this latter mode of dealing with penitents, as the sufficient and more desirable exercise of the priestly office. The Church has uniformly and

---

[1] See Procter on the Book of Common Prayer. It should be observed, as some, and no inconsiderable, compensation for such serious losses as those mentioned in the text, that happily, through the influence of Bishop Seabury, the prayers of invocation and oblation omitted in the Communion Office of our own Prayer Book, were re-inserted in the American Office, as previously they had been introduced in the Scotch Office.

steadily resisted it. We may thankfully rejoice in the unvarying success attending such resistance; but at the same time, while our principles have been upheld true and clear, we have to acknowledge with painful regret, that the pressure which failed to alter the language of the Church, has yet succeeded in associating it in the minds of our people with a novel and uncatholic interpretation. The desired result has, to a large extent, been effected, though not in the way intended. The language of antiquity is faithfully preserved, while a dissenting interpretation has been forced upon it. But a change of language would have been far more disastrous; for many have received the Church's teaching in the Church's sense, and the time may come—is it not even now hastening?—when the rightful interpretation shall be justified of all her children. The pressure for change was successfully resisted so long as the Prayer Book was under revision. And still for those who have ears to hear, and hearts to understand, these records of a true Catholic penitential system are preserved among the many treasures of the marvellous Book, around which the strife for Catholic principles has been waged in England for upwards of 300 years, and yet ceases not,—links preserving us in connexion with the Saints of generations long at rest, and with CHRIST, and with His members also on earth in other lands, for visible communion with whom, alas! we must needs still wait, watching the movements of His Providence, Whose intercession in the heavens ceases not, that " all may be one," even as Himself and His FATHER " are One."

CHAPTER XII.

IT is often said that the mind and temper of the
Church of England are better criterions of her
teaching, than can be obtained by theological arguments,
or the wording of formularies. But what is meant by
the "mind" of the Church? What era in her history
is to be chosen, as its standard or type? Is the reign
of the Stewarts, or of the Georges, the truest represen-
tative? If the former be taken, which of the contend-
ing parties are to be considered the exponents of English orthodoxy, the Bishops who presided at the Savoy
Conference, or the Puritan clergy, who protested against
their decisions? If the rule which our Church has followed, in ascertaining the mind of the Catholic Church,
viz., the teaching of the earliest centuries of her history,
be applied to herself, the generations immediately succeeding the Reformation will supply the expression of
her mind; and since the Episcopate is the divinely
ordained guardian of doctrine, and the Bishops of those
times were mainly concerned in constructing our formularies, then their acts and judgments may be taken,
as the truest exponents of the actual teaching of our
Church during the supposed normal period, or at least
the fairest and most practicable approximation to it.

It has already been shown, in tracing the history of those passages in our Offices which relate to Confession from the year 1545 to 1660, that the changes made subsequently to the issue of the second Prayer Book, uniformly tended to give increased prominence and encouragement to the practice. Such changes were calculated, more than any other acts to fix the teaching of the Church; for her Service-books are the most authoritative and expressive elements of her actual life. But these provisions were not merely recorded on paper. They were brought to bear on the practice of the Priesthood and the habits of the people, by the injunctions of the Bishops at their Visitations. The "Articles of inquiry" issued on such occasions are not to be regarded as mere expositions of the Bishop's private opinion. Their historical value consists in this, that where they are in force, they illustrate the recognised law and custom of the Church.

Reference has been already made to the Visitation Articles of Archbishop Parker, but they need to be here dwelt on more fully. Parker held the primacy of England during the first sixteen years of Elizabeth, and was the chief authority in deciding questions of doctrine during that eventful period. During his primacy, in the year 1567, he instituted a formal inquiry throughout his Province as to the reception and progress of the reformed doctrines. He prefaced his injunctions to his Suffragans by saying, " you shall inquire of the doctrine and judgment of all and singular heads and members of your Church, whether any of them do either privilie or openlie preach or teach any unwholesome, erroneous, or seditious doctrine, ... or in any other point do persuade or move any not to conform themselves to the order of religion reformed, restored, and received by public authority in the Church of England." Among the chief subjects of inquiry he specifies, as examples of heterodoxy, "that every Article in our Crede, commonly received and used in the Church, is not to be received of necessity, or that mortal voluntary sins be not remissible by Penance;"[1] thus classing the rejection of the power of the keys in the remission of post-baptismal sin, in closest proximity with the denial of the authority of the Apostles' Creed.

There are extant Visitation Articles, among others, of Overall, Bishop of Norwich, 1619; Andrewes, Bishop of Winchester, 1625; Cosin, as Archdeacon of York, 1627; the Bishop of Peterborough, 1636; the Diocese of Norwich, 1636; Montague, Bishop of Ely, 1686.[2] In all these alike there are inquiries of the following kind: "Whether doth your minister before the several times of the administration of the LORD's Supper, admonish and exhort his parishioners, if they have their consciences troubled and disquieted, to resort unto him, or some other learned minister, and open his griefe, that he may receive such ghostly counsel and comfort as his conscience may be relieved, and by the minister he may receive the benefit of absolution, to the quiet of his conscience, and avoiding of scruple. And if any man confesse his secret and hidden sinnes, be he sicke or whole, to the minister, for the unburthening of his con-

---

[1] Cardwell's Documentary Annals. No. lxviii.

[2] Quoted in Dr. Pusey's Sermon, notes; Letter to Mr. Richards, p. 117; Mr. Cooke's Power of the Priesthood, pp. 108, 109; and in Mr. Maskell's Doctrine of Absolution, p. 136.

science, and receiving such spiritual consolation, doth
or hath the said minister at any time revealed and
made known to any person whomsoever, any crime or
offence so committed to his trust, contrary to the 113th
canon." " Doth the minister visit the sick ? Doth
he upon their confession, repentance and faith, (being
thereunto desired,) absolve them ?"
    Provincial canons are still more important. They
are the acts of the Church in Synod. For this reason
the 113th canon of 1603 is of material weight in our
argument.   It relates to presentments for ecclesiastical
censure, and states as a ground of exemption the laws
against breaking the seal of confession. " Provided
always that if any man confess his secret and hidden
sins to the minister, for the unburdening his conscience,
and to receive spiritual consolation and ease of mind
from him, we do not in any way bind the said minister
by this our constitution, but do straitly charge and
admonish him, that he do not at any time reveal and
make known to any person whatsoever, any crime
or offence so committed to his trust or secresy (except
they be such crimes as by the laws of this realm his
own life may be called into question for concealing the
same) under pain of irregularity."[1]
    Canons are not enacted except in reference to prac-
tices in ordinary use. They are not framed to meet
isolated cases. Confession must not merely have been

[1] " *Pain of irregularity*, as the canonists tell us, not only doth deprive
a man of all his spiritual promotions for the present time, but makes
him utterly incapable of any for the time to come ; and therefore it is
the greatest penalty except degradation from the Priesthood, which
possibly a clergyman can be subject to."—Dr. Peter Heylin on the
Creed, p. 480.

publicly recognised, but sufficiently frequent to affect the clergy in general, if such a provision were felt to be necessary. Still more important is the resolution passed in the Convocation of 1640, and recorded by Heylin, though the acts of that Convocation were not confirmed by Royal authority, and so are not formally constituted canons. But they equally show the mind of the Convocation of that day. " It was made," Heylin says, " one of the inquiries in the Book of Articles, established in the Convocation of the year 1640, for a perpetual rule and standard in all Episcopal and Archidiaconal Visitations, and proposed to the Churchwardens; viz. Have you ever heard that your said priest or minister hath revealed and made known at any time to any person whatever any crime or offence committed to his trust and secresy, either in extremity of sickness, or in any other case whatsoever, (except they be such crimes as by the laws of the land, &c.) ? declare the name of the offender, when, and by whom you heard the same." Such a resolution passed, and intended to be a perpetual rule for Episcopal Visitations throughout England, sufficiently proves both the extent of the practice of Confession at the time, and the supposition of its continuing to be an abiding part of the pastoral care.

A document of considerable interest enables us to carry down the evidence derived from the acts of the Episcopate, to the reign of William III. In the year 1696, two persons of note, Sir John Friend, and Sir William Parkins, were under the sentence of death for conspiracy against the life of the king. Before their execution certain priests gave them absolution, although they had made no special confession. A declaration was immediately issued censuring this proceeding in the following terms :

" For those clergymen that took upon them to absolve these criminals at the place of execution, by laying, all three together, their hands upon their heads, and publicly pronouncing a form of absolution; as their manner of doing this was extremely insolent and without precedent either in our Church, or any way that we know of, so the thing itself was altogether irregular.

" The rubric in our Office of the Visitation of the Sick, from whence they took the words then used, and upon which if upon anything in our Liturgy, they must ground this their proceeding, gave them no authority, nor no pretence for the absolving these persons ; nay, as they managed the affair, they acted in this absolution far otherwise than is there directed.

" That rubric is concerning sick persons, and it is required, first, that the ' sick person shall be moved to make a special confession of his sins, if he feel his conscience troubled with any weighty matter, and then after such confession, the priest shall absolve him, if he humbly and heartily desire it.' But here they absolved, and that publicly, persons condemned by law for execrable crimes, without so much as once moving them to make a special confession of their sins, at least of those sins for which they were condemned. And on the other side here were persons absolved, that did not humbly desire absolution, as feeling any such weighty matter to trouble their conscience. If these ministers knew not the state of these men's souls, before they gave them absolution, as it is manifest two of them did not—how could they without manifest transgression of the Church's order, as well as the profane abuse of the power CHRIST has left with His ministers, absolve them from their sins ?

" If they were acquainted with these men's sentiments declared in their papers, then they must look upon them either as hardened impenitents, or martyrs.

" We are so charitable to believe that they would not absolve them under the former notion, for that had been in effect, sealing them to damnation.

" April 10th, 1696."[1]

This declaration is signed by Tenison, Archbishop of Canterbury ; Sharpe, Archbishop of York ; Compton, Bishop of London ; and eleven other Bishops ; thus constituting it a formal act of a majority of the Bishops of England, headed by their two Primates.

The Declaration is aimed specially against absolving without previous confession. But it bears, moreover, on several questions which have been under our consideration, illustrating the Church's belief at the time on the following points.

It proves the belief (1) that absolution is a real ministry of grace committed by CHRIST to His Ministers; (2) that the effect of absolution is a release, not from Church censures, but from sins ; (3) that the consequence of an unworthy reception of absolution—they term it, " a sealing to damnation,"—is what could be attributed only to the profane reception of a sacramental ordinance ; (4) that these results are applicable to individual per-

[1] Wilkins' Concilia, vol. iv. p. 629.

sonal absolution, given, not in the congregation, but as a private act; (5) that the rule specially laid down by the Church for the sick, is as truly applicable to the whole, the offence being not that they applied the rules of the Office to persons not contemplated by it, but that they misapplied the rule by not requiring previously either confession of sins, or an expression of desire for forgiveness.

We are thus brought to the very opening of the 18th century with the clearest consensus of authority for the use of Confession, as a living part of English Church life; and this continued downward in an uninterrupted line from the Reformation.

CHAPTER XIII.

D EVOTIONAL books are an additional means of ascertaining the "mind" of the Church. They do not help us to measure the extent of a religious practice, but they mark the recognised constituent elements of a religious life, and the habits of the more devout. It is therefore of great moment to note, that the manuals of devotion, which have survived the 17th century, and were therefore, as we may presume, the most popular in their day, uniformly recommend Confession, and speak of it as in ordinary use.

Thus Bishop Andrewes, in his private thanksgivings, offers praise to GOD Who " hast given me good hope for the remission of my sins, by repentance, by the works of repentance, and by the power of the holy keys."[1] George Herbert says of his " Priest to the Temple ;" " In his visiting the sick, or otherwise, he followeth the Church's counsel, namely, in persuading them to particular confession, labouring to make them understand the great good use of this ancient and pious ordinance, and how

---

[1] Bishop Andrewes's Devotions. And so again in his daily thanksgiving, 2nd part : " Thou hast opened to me the gate of hope, when I confessed, and besought Thee by the gift of inspiration and of the keys."

necessary it is in some cases."[1]   Andrewes died in 1626, and Herbert in 1632.

Again, Bishop Taylor in his " Holy Living" says ; " Because we may very much be helped, if we take in the assistance of a spiritual guide, therefore the Church of GOD in all ages hath commended, and in most ages enjoined, that we confess our sins, and discover the state and condition of our souls to such a person whom we or our superiors judge fit to help us in our need."[2] Connect with this the advice given in the " Holy Dying :" " Whether they be many or few that are sent to the sick person, let the curate of the parish, or his own confessor, be amongst them . . . . he that is the ordinary judge cannot safely be passed by in his extra-ordinary necessity, which in so great portion depends upon his whole life past."[3] Corresponding directions are given in the " Guide to the Penitent," which is usually bound up with the " Golden Grove," though whether the work of Jeremy Taylor, or of Bishop Duppa, is uncertain : " You are advised by the Church, under whose discipline you live, that before you are to receive the Holy Sacrament, or when you are visited with any dangerous sickness, if you find any one particular sin or more, that lies heavy upon you, to disburden your-self of it into the bosom of your confessor, who not only stands between GOD and you, to pray for you, but hath the power of the keys committed to him, upon your true repentance, to absolve you in CHRIST'S Name from those sins which you have confessed unto him." Bishop Cosin in his " Devotions" states

---

[1] The Country Pastor, c. xv.   [2] On Repentance, ix. 5.
[3] C. 352, 4.

it even as one of the "precepts of the Church," "to receive the Blessed Sacrament of the Body and Blood of CHRIST with frequent devotion, and three times a year at least, of which Easter shall be always one, and for the better preparation thereto, as occasion is, to disburden and quiet our consciences of those sins that may grieve us, or scruples that may trouble us, to a learned and discreet priest, and from him to receive advice and the benefit of absolution." Jeremy Taylor died in 1667, and Cosin in 1678.

Again, Bishop Patrick, in his book for beginners, advises; "If he still find he is not safe, he must after all advise with some discreet minister of GOD's Word, as with a spiritual physician; desiring to know what course to take, that he may get the mastery of those unruly lusts which are too hard for him. And when he comes for this ghostly counsel and advice, let him not be ashamed plainly to confess his sins, and to open the whole state of his soul before him whom he consults; relating how and by what means he comes to be thus entangled in the snare of the devil, that he cannot get out of it. Be sure you conquer the loathness you will find in yourself to make this discovery, for fear it disgrace you in his opinion, and convince yourself that you ought the rather to confess your sins ingenuously, that you may take shame to yourself, and lay yourself low in the presence of GOD and His minister." Patrick died in 1707.

Still more remarkable are Chillingworth's (the author of the "Religion of Protestants") strong expressions, if we consider his free handling of Church doctrines: "In obedience to His gracious will, and as I am warranted, and even enjoined by my holy mother the Church of England, and expressly in the Book of Common Prayer, in the rubric of Visiting the Sick, I beseech you that by your practice and use, you will not suffer that Commission which CHRIST hath given to His ministers, to be a vain form of words, without any sense under them, not to be an antiquated expired commission, of no use nor validity in these days, but whensoever you find yourselves charged and oppressed with such crimes as they call, *peccata vastantia conscientiam*, such as do lay waste and depopulate the conscience, that you would have recourse to your spiritual physician, and freely disclose the nature and malignity of your disease, that he may be able, as the cause shall require, to proportion a remedy; either to search it with corrosives, or comfort and temper it with oil."[1] Chillingworth died in 1644.

The close of the 17th century preserved the same traditionary teaching.   John Isham, whose " Daily Office for the Sick" was published in 1694, and republished in 1696, and again in 1702, repeats the strongest passages of Bishop Taylor.   " Though our Church presseth particular confession to the priest only when the conscience is disquieted with sins of deeper malignity, yet it doth not discountenance the more frequent use of it, and this, too, in so comprehensive a case as to take in great numbers that neglect it; and it is the declared judgment of the learned and pious Bishop Taylor, that confession being useful in all cases, and necessary in some; and encouraged by Evangelical promises, by Scripture precedent, by the example of

[1] Serm. vii. 83.

both Testaments, and prescribed by Apostolical injunctions, and the canons of all Churches and the example
of all ages; and taught us by the analogy to the
ministerial power, and the very necessities of every man;
he that for stubbornness, or any other criminal weakness, shall decline it in the days of his danger, is near
death, but very far off from the kingdom of heaven."

The " Whole Duty of Man," which was first published before the close of the 17th century, contains
the same counsels.   Referring to the Exhortation in the
Communion Office, it is observed : " This is surely such
advice as should not be neglected, neither at the time
of coming to the Sacrament, nor any other when we
are under fear or reason of doubt concerning the state
of our souls.   And for want of this many have run into
very great mischief, having let the doubt fester so long,
that it hath either plunged them into deep distress of
conscience, or, which is worse, they have, to still that
disquiet within them, betaken themselves to all sinful
pleasures, and so quite cast off all care of their souls."
(Of the LORD's Supper, p. 22.)

It is interesting to note, in connection with these extracts from the devotional manuals of the 17th century,
the records which have been preserved of the practice
of churchmen during the same period.

It is recorded e.g. of Dr. Reynolds, A.D. 1607, who
had appeared in behalf of the Dissenters at the Hampton Court Conference, that he " being absolved before
his death, and not being able to speak, kissed the hand
wherewith he was absolved;" of Mrs. D. Holmes, in a
funeral sermon by Bishop Cosin in 1623, that her

" preparation to her end was by humble contrition and
hearty confession of her sins, which when she had done,
she received the benefit of absolution, according to
GOD's ordinance, and the religious institutions of our
Church ;"[1] of Lord Derby, when going into battle with
the rebels in 1651, that he desired " Mr. Greenhaugh to
read the Decalogue, and at the end of all the commandments made his confession, and received absolution ;"
of Lady Capel, A.D. 1660, that being absolved " she
showed a heavenly comfort and peace after it ;" of
Lady Anderson, A.D. 1661, being absolved on her death-
bed, " to her no little comfort ;" of Lord Digby, " desiring of all things in his last extremities to receive the
Holy Sacrament, and priestly absolution, according to
its (the Church of England's) order and appointment ;"
of Hooker and Dr. Saravia being " supposed to be confessors to each other," and that at Hooker's deathbed,
" after a conference of the benefit, the necessity and
safety of the Church's absolution, it was resolved the
Doctor should give him both that and the Sacrament
the day following ;" of Bishop Sanderson, A.D. 1663,
" receiving absolution of his chaplain ;" of Kettlewell,
" requesting and receiving absolution at the hands of
Bishop Lloyd in the form contained in the Office for
the Visitation of the Sick ;" of Evelyn, in his Diary,
March 16, 1685, recording how he had found, among
the papers of his deceased daughter, " one to a divine
to whom she writes that he would be her ghostly father,
and would not despise her for her many errors and the
many imperfections of her youth, but beg of GOD to
give her courage to acquaint him with all her faults,

[1] Cosin, Vol. i. p. 28.

imploring his assistance and spiritual directions," to which he adds, "I well remember she had often desired me to recommend her to such a person, but I did not think fit to do it as yet, seeing her apt to be scrupulous, and knowing the great innocency and integrity of her life;" and lastly, of Bishop Wilson, referring to the death of his wife, in 1705, and thanking GOD for " His mercies to her in the time of sickness, the opportunities of receiving the Blessed Sacrament, the prayers of the faithful, the ministry of absolution, &c."[1]

Among those whose advice or example has been here adduced, will be recognised some whose names have become as household words amongst us; whom an hereditary reverence has honoured as types of the truest English theology, and of that calm, chastened piety, which our Church specially has loved to cherish. Their testimony in favour of Confession is not limited to the probable extent it may have actually attained in their own day, as if that was the measure which they desired. Although the instances given prove an extent of use such as we have now no experience of, men of highest note were at the same period complaining of the neglect into which Confession had even then fallen. Bishop Cosin in the sermon before referred to, speaks of Confession as " a thing that the world looks not after now, as if confession and absolution were some strange superstitious things among us, which yet the Church has taken such care to preserve, and especially to be preparatives to death." Again, Dr. Sparrow in his Sermon

[1] These anecdotes are collected together by Mr. Stretton in his Preface to the " Visitatio Infirmorum" and the " Guide to the Infirm."

preached at Cambridge before the University, on Confession of Sins, and Power of Absolution, 1637, says :
" Confess as the Church directs us. Confess to God ;
confess also to the priest, if not in private, in the ear,
since that is out of use, (*male aboletur*, saith a devout
Bishop, 'tis almost quite lost, the more the pity,) &c."

The importance of these two last extracts can hardly
be over estimated, if it be remembered that both
Cosin and Sparrow were Commissioners at the Savoy
Conference, when the Prayer Book underwent its last
revision. Their regrets at the prevailing neglect of
Confession are clear indications of the object of the
changes then made in our Offices, which have been
already dwelt upon in detail. They were intended, as
such expressions of the mind of their compilers show,
beside their own internal evidence, to give greater
definiteness to our Church's teaching, and strengthen
the provisions previously made for the encouragement
of Confession, which increasing negligence was rapidly
causing to become obsolete.

The neglect of this ordinance, which the divines of the
seventeenth century deplored, increased yet further with
the decay of spiritual life which marked the succeeding
century, till at length Confession not only fell into
almost universal disuse, but came to be regarded as a
practice detrimental to vital religion, and altogether
alien to the system of the Church of England.

We have entered into this tradition, and to many it
seems to be our normal state. Yet it cannot be deemed
any disparagement to a religious ordinance, if in seeking
precedents for its use, we have to pass over the eighteenth
century, and recur to days when George Herbert gave

M 3

the tone to the pastoral ministry, when Taylor shed over
the rules of holy living and holy dying the graces of his
own beautiful and fervent piety, and Hooker, Sanderson
and Bull lent the weight of their profound learning to
sustain the cause of the English Reformation.   Nor is
it in favour of those who now oppose the revived desire
for Confession, that the only century since our LORD's
death, which in its prevailing practice at all justifies their
conclusion, is the one out of the cold torpor of which
we are slowly struggling, when the Non-jurors had been
lost to the Church, when Convocation was silenced by
the State because of the dissensions between the two
Houses, when Wesley could find no place among us,
and the largest secessions ever known in England occurred, when the Church cared so little for the growing
multitudes still left to her, that the unprecedented passion for Church building of the last thirty years, has
failed to recover the lost ground; when with but rare
exceptions the dank and disfigured churches were closed
from Sunday to Sunday, and the state of our fonts and
altars bore unmistakeable and most melancholy testimony to the dishonour fallen even on the two most
indispensable sacraments, the pre-eminent mysteries
which communicate the full life of the Incarnation.

Yet even in that dreary period there were not wanting
witnesses of mark, who still sustained and transmitted
to us the more genuine teaching of the English Reformation. Archbishop Wake, who died in 1737, in his exposition of the doctrine of the Church of England, says;
" The Church of England refuses no sort of confession
either public or private, which may be any way necessary
to the quieting of men's consciences, or to exercising of

that power of binding and loosing which our SAVIOUR CHRIST has left to His Church. We have our penitential canons for public offences; we exhort men, if they have any the least doubt or scruple, nay, sometimes though they have none, but especially before they receive the Holy Sacrament, to confess their sins. We propose to them the benefit not only of ghostly advice how to manage their repentance, but the great comfort of absolution too as soon as they shall have completed it. When we visit our sick we never fail to exhort them to make a special confession of their sins to him that ministers to them, and when they have done it, the absolution is so full that the Church of Rome itself could not desire to add anything to it."[1] Bishop Wilson, who died in 1755, in his sermon on the great blessing of a standing ministry, says; "Absolution benefiteth by virtue of the power which JESUS CHRIST has given to His ministers. In short, our LORD having purchased the forgiveness of sins for all mankind, He hath committed the ministry of reconciliation to us, that having brought men to repentance we may in CHRIST's Name, and in the Person of CHRIST, pronounce their pardon. And this will be the true way to magnify the power of the keys, which is so little understood, and so much despised, namely, to bring as many as we possibly can to repentance, that we may have more frequent occasions of sealing a penitent's pardon by our ministry. And now, if the sick person has been so dealt with, as to be truly sensible of his condition, he could then be instructed in the nature and benefit of confession (at least of such sins as do trouble his con-

[1] Gibson's Preservative from Popery, vol. iii. p. 31.

science) and of absolution." Later still, Bishop Horne,
who died in 1792, says, "a soul when sick or wounded
by sin must be recovered and restored by godly counsel
and wholesome discipline, by penance and absolution,
by the medicine of the word and sacraments, as duly
and properly administered in the Church by the lawfully
and regularly appointed delegates and representatives
of the Physician of souls."[1]   And in our own day
Bishop Short, thus completing the catena, has expressed
his sense of the changed state of feeling which now
claims so untruly to be the genuine teaching of the
English Reformation.   "In the Church of England the
confession of particular sins is recommended in the
Exhortation to the Sacrament, and the Visitation of
the Sick; but so little are we accustomed to this most
Scriptural duty, that their recommendations are frequently unknown and generally neglected."[2]

[1] Discourse xviii. on Ephes. iv. 7.
[2] Hist. of the Church of England, p. 171, 5th ed.

CHAPTER XIV.

THE LIMITS OF CONFESSION.

IT is often urged that admitting the rules, and the encouragement for Confession in sickness and in preparation for Communion, to be as has been here stated, its use nevertheless is intended to be limited to these occasions. According to this view, the cases mentioned are regarded as special exceptions for definite purposes, and, by the fact of Confession being appointed for these cases, it is understood to be excluded in all others.

The following reasons are urged in support of an opposite view :—1. Mr. Palmer has observed that the passage in the Exhortation before Holy Communion "relates not so much to the practice of Confession in general, as to the particular custom of confessing before receiving the Eucharist,"[1] i.e., that it leaves the question of its general application untouched. The circumstances under which the Exhortation is enjoined seem to prove the truth of his remarks. The Exhortation is addressed to communicants. It contemplates only those who are intending to receive, and explains the manner of their preparation. It had a special pur-

[1] Mr. Palmer's Book of the Church, vol. i. p. 518 ; or part ii. chap. vii.

pose in reference to the law, then cancelled, of the necessity of Confession before Communion, and was in
truth a public announcement of the fact, that although
the access to the Blessed Sacrament was now free to all
who were not excommunicated, yet that Confession
was still under certain circumstances recommended to
communicants.   The Exhortation had no direct reference to non-communicants, or to those who had not at
the time the intention of communicating.

2. The Church has another and a special provision
for those who are not in living communion with her,
who in fact, or by express judgment, are excommunicated.   Public Penance, which our Church has so earnestly sought to restore for the sake of the unfaithful
members of her body implied, as we have seen, private
confession as a test of its need, or in preparation for its
due performance.   To desire to estàblish the one therefore was by implication to encourage the other, and
consequently this case was not excluded by the terms
of the Exhortation ; and, if this was not excluded, other
cases similarly may be left untouched by it.   It was
intended to meet a particular case, but decides nothing
as to cases not alluded to.

3. It has been shown that the directions relating to
Confession in the Visitation of the Sick were directly
copied with certain modifications from the ancient Latin
Office.   The Latin form was in use when Confession
was compulsory for all persons throughout life.   It was
not therefore at that time considered to be exclusive,
and if before the Reformation it was consistent with
a system of private confession in cases of health, it
could not necessarily militate against such a practice

after the Reformation. Moreover, a rule for sickness cannot from the nature of the case be limited to sickness. Such a rule is given as a preparation for death. But if for death preceded by sickness, why not also in readiness for sudden death? Why not even in preparation for sickness, lest the soul be then incapacitated for the effort by pain or mental exhaustion. We are taught to live as those who are prepared to die. The Church's directions for the sick are not less applicable to the whole, if the spiritual danger be the same. A guilty death is not more terrible than a guilty life, except that the one leaves space for repentance, and how to provide for a true repentance is the question at issue.

Commentators on our Office for the Visitation of the Sick have taken this enlarged view of our Church's meaning. Wheatley on the Visitation of the Sick says; "We may still, I presume, wish very consistently with the determination of our Church, that our people would apply themselves oftener than they do to their spiritual physician, even in the time of their health, since it is much to be feared, they are wounded oftener than they complain, and yet through aversion to disclosing their sin suffer it to gangrene for want of their help who should work their cure. But present cure is not the only benefit the penitent may expect from his confessor's aid; he will be better assisted in the regulation of his life, and when his last conflict shall make its approach the holy man, being no stranger to the state of his soul, will be better prepared to guide and conduct it through all difficulties that may oppose."[1] Thus also Comber; "We wish that the people even in time of

[1] Wheatley on the Book of Common Prayer.

health (when their conscience is troubled with some great sin, and their souls are assaulted with a violent temptation) would come and make their case known to their spiritual physician, to whom the Fathers elegantly compare the Priest in this case. . . . . But if we have omitted this before, we have more need to send speedily for God's ministers in our sickness."

Devotional manuals, and Visitation articles, previously quoted, take the same view of the case. Thus, e.g., George Herbert's recommendation of Confession was "in visiting the sick or otherwise." Jeremy Taylor's rule was, that "what is necessary to be done in one case, and convenient in all cases, is fit to be done by all persons." Chillingworth's advice is, "Whensoever you find yourself charged and oppressed."[1] The "Whole Duty of Man" enjoined the not neglecting it, "neither at the time of the Sacrament, nor any other when we are under any fear or reason of doubt concerning the state of the soul." Again, the Visitation Articles speak of Confession made "in any case whatsoever," "being sick or whole" "at any time."

It is sometimes assumed, that even allowing Confession to be thus freely open without any limit but what the need of souls and the directions of pastors determine, yet that the habitual and periodical practice of it is condemned at least by implication in the spirit of the Church of England's teaching. The question, be it observed, is not the expedience of such a use of confession, but its lawfulness, whether or no it be consistent with entire loyalty.

The arguments employed to disprove any limitation

[1] Chillingworth's Sermons, vii. 83.

as to special occasions, seem equally applicable to the question of frequency. Habitual and periodical Confession had been the custom previous to the time of the Reformation. The idea was implanted in the mind of the people; unless expressly prohibited, it would naturally have seemed still open to those who desired to continue their former habit. The compulsory rule was expressly repealed; nothing, however, was ruled with the view of limiting the frequency, or defining the period. It is indeed scarcely conceivable that at such a crisis, in the violent collisions of first principles involved in the Reformation, the Church could have undertaken to consider so delicate and abstruse a question; nor could the Church at any time enter upon such a question without a degree of interference with individual life that would universally be esteemed vexatious and intolerable. It would be felt, that if Confession were made a discretionary rule, its application and extent must also be left to discretion. True freedom on such a point must act both ways, equally in behalf both of those who reject, and those who desire it.

Our devotional writers, who have been quoted, evidently thus viewed this question. The " Golden Grove" gives as a rule, " that for the frequency of doing this you are to consult with your own necessities." Cosin, as to the time of so doing adds, " as occasion is." Patrick, in advising recourse to a " spiritual physician" says; " To him it will be necessary to repair on all occasions, that he may instruct and teach you in that whereof you are ignorant, or awaken you when you are sleepy, or refresh and cheer you when you are wrong, or cure you when you are sick or ill at ease, or resolve you in your doubts, or quicken your dulness, or bridle your fervour."[1]

Moreover, the term, "Confessor," commonly used by Jer. Taylor, "his own Confessor," beside "the Curate of the Parish," and by Isaac Walton, in reference to Hooker and Saravia, and even by Wheatley in a formal commentary of the last century;[2] the kindred terms, "ordinary judge," "spiritual guide," "physician," "private guide and judge," "ghostly father," (as by Evelyn's daughter), used indifferently in passages previously quoted, and Wheatley's reason just given for Confession, "in health, because the holy man being no stranger to the state of the soul, will be better able to guide and conduct it through all difficulties,"—all tend to the same conclusion.

The same reasoning applies to the question, whether habitual direction is sanctioned by our Church. Direction, if viewed simply in its first principles, is implied in "ghostly counsel and advice." The extent or duration of such counsel and advice is of necessity dependent on the circumstances of each individual case; and direction rightly understood, is but ghostly counsel and advice become habitual. The evils popularly associated with the idea of direction, and ordinarily intended to be condemned under the term, viz., the substitution of the priest's judgment for the true acting of the conscience of the person under his influence, and the con-

[1] Advice to a Friend, sect. 13, "When we are much indisposed to advise with our spiritual physician."

[2] The passages where these expressions appear are quoted in the last chapter. See Jer. Taylor's Holy Dying, chap. v. §§. 2, 4.

sequent loss of all sense or obligation of personal responsibility,—are but the abuse of a most sacred trust.
The true object of direction is not to preserve a hold on
the mind of the penitent, or habituate it to lean on
authority overruling its own powers of action by minute details of rule; but rather to develope true principles, and awaken dormant energies within the soul, so
as to enable it to judge and act more healthfully for
itself. The term, "director," is recognised by our
devotional writers, and is used indifferently with the
term, "guide." The former term may appear to imply a disregard of the free action of the conscience not
intended in the latter, but the difference arises only from
incidental abuses not necessarily identified with it.
Direction in its true and original sense means such
help as may strengthen and assist the soul in the
use of its renewed powers, not destroy them; quicken
its sense of responsibility, not paralyze it. It is impossible, of course, for the Church to direct her priests
in the fulfilment of such a charge, any more than she
can secure her preachers from indiscretion. Quis cus-
todiet ipsos custodes? The possible abuses in the one
trust are not greater, or more hurtful, than those incident to the other. It has seemed to our Church most
consistent with its own principles, and least open to
evil, to entrust to her children, in cases where the
parish Priest is either hindered by circumstances, or un-
equal to the charge, the responsibility of choosing their
own spiritual advisers, rather than commission certain
Priests of her own choosing, and binding all to have
recourse to them alone. "Let him come to me, or
some other," &c. Her system is to leave much to

individual discretion, and, as in the case of confession, so also in that of spiritual "counsel and advice," to allow the choice of the person consulted, and the frequency of the act, to be determined freely according to the circumstances of each individual case.

The trite saying, commonly urged as if settling the question of frequency, or of the use of confession at all, that it is the exception, not the rule; the remedy of disease, not the food of life,—only illustrates the nature of the ordinance, and defines nothing. Confession is essentially the exceptional and remedial element of Christianity. The Holy Eucharist, prayer and self-discipline, teaching and divine illuminations, are the proper rule, and ought to be the sufficient food of the life of the Baptized. Their intended effect is to refresh and strengthen, increase and perfect, by a progressive advance, the regenerate nature in its eventful course, till it attain its consummation of bliss in conscious union with GOD in CHRIST. More ought not to be needed. But because such grace is often hindered, or may decay, or even be lost, the remedial ordinances are given to renew the faded, or debilitated, or departed life. If the analogy of medicine were consistently carried out in respect to Confession, it would lead us far beyond what they who commonly urge it can intend. To the greater number medicine is a periodical necessity; to many an unceasing stay; few, if any, but must at some period of life have recourse to it. Nor again is it true to say, that Confession is to be identified with weakness, or an inferior standard of spiritual attainment. In a leading article of the *Guardian,* which appeared in the course of the late discussions on the subject of Confession, the writer, while strongly criticising the abuse to which he supposes Confession to be liable, vindicates it from this popular reproach; " We cannot," he says, "shut our eyes to the silly exigeant egotism, the unmanly shrinking from responsibility, the negligence of ordinary ties, which causes, as it is caused by, the resort to a confessor. But looking to the iron characters which abound in the Roman Church, it is childish to suppose a constant connexion between weakness and the confessional; or to doubt that the unceasing self-examination which that institution involves, its periodical self-abasement, and the ever present certainty that weak or sinful indulgence must soon be followed by that abasement,—must have made many a weak man strong, and have had a great share in forming that almost unparalleled mixture of determination with obedience, of pliancy with strength, which shines in the great characters of the Roman Communion."[1]

As experience shows that spiritual strength may be the fruit of Confession, so there is nothing to prove that the desire for its use necessarily presupposes spiritual inferiority. Neither sin nor weakness in themselves lead to a desire for relief, but a sensitiveness to the one or the other. And as sensitiveness to sin may be the result and mark of a growing sanctity, so consciousness of weakness may arise from deeper effort after greater holiness.

A more real scruple as to the modern use of Confession is derived from the ancient rule of Penance, which yet, as we have seen, is claimed as its prototype and

[1] This passage was copied at the time of its publication, but the date of the number was omitted to be taken down.

authority.   The ancient Penance was ordinarily allowed
but once in a lifetime, and this only for very grievous
sins.   How then can this custom be pleaded as the
warrant for a system which allows constant recurrence
at discretion to the same ministry, by the same persons,
and after even comparatively the lightest forms of
sin?   To this it may be answered, that the ancient
rule implied only, that Penance could not be twice
allowed, not that Confession might not be repeated.
Public Penance might extend over several years, and
repeated private confessions might be made during its
course.   Or private Confession might be made, and no
public Penance be enjoined.   It might be made in the
case of sins, to which the Penance was inapplicable.
There was no restrictive rule as to the use of Confession,
as there was to that of Penance.   The most rigid adherence therefore to ancient precedent would only limit
the use of Absolution in the case of the more grievous
sins.

Moreover, there appears to have been in the earliest
ages an amount of personal guidance and direct teaching, of which there is no parallel in the present day;
and the assistance thus of old given, is now sought
through Confession.   An active public discipline was
then exercising a constant influence on the inner life,
which the Church in the present day can supply only
through her private ministerings. The difference of circumstance between our own and the earlier ages is
therefore too great to admit of a conclusive argument
being drawn from such a comparison.

Moreover, it is clear from the many statements in
our formularies already considered, that our Church at

the Reformation accepted the modern usage of Confession, excepting only the particular points in its use which it especially excluded. It might have restricted its penitential system to the ancient laws of public Penance; but manifestly it did not do so. It rejected the idea of compulsion, and certain other details of the pre-Reformation system, but otherwise it sanctioned the later use. Experience had justified the new principle, as suitable under the existing circumstances of society and the Church. The loving readiness to apply at need in any case her healing ministry, seemed in her judgment the truest and most practical means, especially during the abeyance of the ancient discipline, "to comfort and help the weak-hearted, and raise up them that fall." And all acknowledge that the Church has power from GOD thus to adapt her ministry of reconciliation to the changing circumstances of the times. "The Church," says Hooker, "is not denied to have the authority of abridging or enlarging the use and exercise of that power."[1]

Notwithstanding however this free scope for Confession allowed in the English Church to those who desire it, there is a principle, lying deep in her system, which more or less modifies and restricts its use among us, and which is therefore always carefully to be considered in connection with the foregoing arguments. One object sought in the reconstruction of our Offices was to develope and cherish the soul's unfettered communion with GOD. Compulsory confession, and the prevail-

---

[1] Eccl. Pol. l. vi. iv. 15. The passage quoted with its context in the following chapter.

ing idea that remission of sin could not be had without it, must have tended to introduce confused views as to the relative importance of confession to GOD and to the Priest. The former would often be sunk in the latter. The subjective life of repentance might suffer from the force of the objective system, which constrained it. That there was ground at the time for special care in this matter can hardly be disputed, if it be considered how passages of Scripture relating to repentance were then interpreted to mean Penance, and allusions to confession necessarily to mean confession to a Priest.[1] This conviction actuated our Reformers in many of the changes which they introduced into our Offices. They sought to bring into increased prominence the idea of confession to GOD alone, not in order

---

[1] The following instances may be taken as examples. Thus μετανοεῖτε, which we rightly translate, "repent," is in the Vulgate, pœnitentiam agite; in the Douay version, "do penance." It is most remarkable that the following texts are assigned in the Canon of the Council of Trent, in proof of the Divine necessity of Penance. "Unde Propheta ait, Convertimini, et agite pœnitentiam ab omnibus iniquitatibus vestris; et non erit vobis in ruinam iniquitas. (Ezech. xviii. 30.) Dominus etiam dicit, Nisi pœnitentiam egeritis, omnes similiter peribitis. (S. Luc. xiii. 3.) Et princeps Apostolorum Petrus peccatoribus Baptismo initiandis pœnitentiam commendans, dicebat, Pœnitentiam agite et baptizetur unusquisque vestrum. (Act. ii. 38.)" Sess. xiv. c. 1, de pœnitentia.

Mr. Maskell adduces a remarkable instance of this mode of interpretation from Wilkins' Concilia, Tom. i. p. 579. "The Council of Durham, in 1223, thus interpreted the text, 'Let a man examine himself, and so let him eat,' &c., as enforcing Confession. 'Qui manducaverit carnem Domini et biberit sanguinem ejus indignè, reus erit corporis et sanguinis Domini: tenere nos potest terribilis hæc sententia. Propter hoc audite, filii carissimi, consilium Apostoli, quod tale est; probet autem semetipsum homo unusquisque per confessionem mundans et sanctificans, et sic de pane edat et de calice bibat.' "

to do away with sacramental confession, but to restore the balance which they thought had been disturbed. With this view the general confessions were enlarged, deepened in tone, and made congregational instead of being said, as before, by the Priest and assistants only.[1] The daily Exhortation teaching, that, "although we ought at all times humbly to acknowledge our sins before GOD, yet ought we most chiefly so to do, when we assemble and meet together;" the Exhortation in the Communion Office directing the people " wherein (they) shall perceive themselves to have offended, either by will, word, or deed, there to bewail (their) own sinfulness, and confess (themselves) to Almighty GOD;" and generally the use of the mother tongue in all our services, and the associating the people with the Priest in the acts of his ministry,—all tended to encourage and develop the idea of the soul's secret and independent communion with GOD. It is impossible to calculate how much of the spiritual life of England has been quickened and sustained by the constant use of such exhortations and such prayers, accompanied.with all the magic power of a native language ; nor how many thousands and tens of thousands, who would never have confessed to. a Priest, and perhaps only been driven further from GOD by the attempt to constrain them to it by force, have been thereby led to humble confession before their " FATHER which seeth in secret."

[1] In the " Ordinary of the Mass," the Priest alone says the confession : " Confiteor Deo omnipotenti, Beatæ Mariæ semper Virgini, beato Michaeli Archangelo, beato Johanni Baptistæ, sanctis Apostolis Petro et Paulo, omnibus Sanctis, et vobis, fratres : quia peccavi nimis cogitatione, verbo et opere, mea culpa, mea culpa, mea maxima culpa. Ideo precor," &c. The assistants then repeat the same confession for themselves.

N

This principle of secret confession is indeed so strongly implanted in us, that to many, and those often most truly devout, it appears irreconcilable with confession to a Priest. They have tasted the blessedness of communion with GOD in loneliness; they have felt the mysterious stay of a spirit casting the burden of its life on the Invisible, "where none was nigh, save GOD and one good angel;" and they are jealous of this secret joy. They fear lest through any created intervention, even one ordained of GOD Himself, their clear apprehension of His personal sympathy and support should be disturbed, or their own motives become less pure and simple. One cannot too highly esteem such scruples. Nor could there be any stronger proof that Confession was acting unhealthfully, and was unsuitable under the circumstances, if it were found to interfere with, nay, if it did not rather foster and deepen, this free and childlike intercourse of the Divinely-quickened spirit with its GOD. Experience unquestionably proves that various minds, and the same minds under various circumstances, take very different views as to the use of Confession. Our Reformers allowed for this variety. They willed that none should be forced to it, nor one judge another, as ·though one could necessarily be a rule to another, in such a matter. But on the other hand our Reformers seem never to have contemplated any incompatibility between this secret confession to GOD, and confession to a Priest. Otherwise they could not have encouraged confession to a Priest, except in the most urgent cases. They could not have advised its use in cases of mere " scruple and doubtfulness." Modern teachers would rather have been disposed to advise, that such lesser trials should be overcome by the soul's own effort; and such may often be sound advice in cases of the kind. But our Church suggests the use of Confession, not merely if the conscience be "troubled with any weighty matter," but also in these lesser spiritual difficulties. So far therefore from contemplating any incompatibility between the two, our Reformers must have considered that even in these latter cases confession to a Priest may, if rightly guided, rather tend to remove hindrances, and so prepare the way for more peaceful communion with God.

The true limitation therefore to the use of Confession in the Church of England is to be found, not in any restrictive rule, still less in any jealous disparagement, or distrust of a Divine ordinance, but in moral considerations, in the balance of the two forces, which her Offices seek to develop in harmonious co-operation, the one or the other acting with the greater power according to the special distinctive needs of individual souls.

CHAPTER XV.

IT has been already shown, that Holy Scripture gives no definite indication of the special sins, which need to be reconciled by the individual application of the power of the keys. The ministry was ordained indefinitely for the remission of sins, without distinguishing the cases to which respectively the general, or the individual, ministry of reconciliation applies. It was left to the guidance of the Spirit within the Church to determine its application. We have seen, however, that the same law which regulates the use of the individual ministry, determines at the same time the use of Confession, because the individual ministry of reconciliation involves Confession; and an uniform rule has guided the practice of the Church from the beginning on this momentous question.

It has been sufficiently shown that, where no deadly sin burdens the conscience, the individual ministry of reconciliation, and so Confession, is left as a question of discretion and spiritual experience. The Church of Rome has never regarded Confession in such cases as necessary, except as a rule of discipline, arising out of the canonical law which obliges every one to confess once at least in every year. The Council of Trent decreed, that "venial sins, i.e., such as do not exclude from the grace of GOD, and into which all fall more or less frequently, may remain unconfessed without fault, and be expiated by many other remedies, although to confess them is right and profitable."[1] Confession in such cases may be the means of advancing spiritual life, of increasing humility and contrition of heart, of greater knowledge of sin and of faults besetting the character, of more earnest carefulness and self-control, of deepened peace and more restful communion with GOD. But, on the other hand, it may also be the occasion of scrupulosity, of self-consciousness, or perplexity, and so become a hindrance to grace; it may be used merely for temporary relief without any purpose, or endeavour after a higher life, and so become even an encouragement to sin, or at least an alleviation of the sense of fear and self-reproach attending it, and thus a means of self-deception. Whether therefore Confession be beneficial or not, to one living in a state of grace, although with more or less of imperfection, and if so, at what periods of life, or with what frequency, it should be used,—are questions that need, and ought, to be determined by a wise and discriminating judgment, no constraint or definite rule being imposed by the Church.

But a clear and wide distinction has always been preserved between those lesser sins, which only hinder the

---

[1] "Venialia, quibus a gratiâ Dei non excludimur, et in quæ frequentius labimur, quanquam rectè et utiliter, citraque omnem præsumptionem, in confessione dicantur, quod piorum hominum usus demonstrat, taceri tamen citra culpam, multisque aliis remediis expiari possunt," &c. Sess. xiv. cap. v. de Confessione.

perfectness of a true and on the whole consistent course, and sins burdening the conscience as of a deadly character.[1] The strong, urgent appeals of the primitive Fathers for submission to Penance, as a necessary means of obtaining the remission of more grievous sins, although the original rule limited such necessity to only a few of the more extreme cases of this class, have already been noticed. The same distinction has been shown to prevail uniformly in all ages. This tradition has been preserved among us. Our best devotional writers and guides of souls have recognized this distinction, though without specifying nominatim the sins for which such remedy is necessary. They are of one mind in affirming, that for such sins as peril the grace of Baptism, and hinder communion with God, the individual ministry of the power of the keys, and therefore Confession, is the ordinary means of reconciliation, while for other cases it is only to be recommended as more or less expedient.

Bishop Cosin, commenting on the Office for the Visitation of the Sick, says : " The Church of England, howsoever it holdeth not confession and absolution sacramental, that is, made unto and received from a Priest, to be absolutely necessary, as that without there

---

[1] Jeremy Taylor thus expresses his mind as to our Church's view of this distinction : "Although we do, with all the ancient doctors, admit of the distinction of sins mortal and venial, yet we also teach that in their own nature and in the rigour of the Divine Justice, every sin is damnable and deserves God's anger : yet by the Divine mercy and compassion, the smaller sins which come by surprise, or by invincible ignorance, or inadvertency, or unavoidable infirmity, shall not be imputed to those who love God, and delight not in the smallest sin, but use caution and prayers, watchfulness and remedies against them." Dissuasive from Popery. Heber's Ed. vol. x. p. 209.

can be no remission of sins, yet by this place it is manifest, what she teacheth concerning the virtue and
force of this sacred action. The confession is commanded to be special, &c. . . . . Venial sins that
separate not from the grace of GOD, need not so much
to trouble a man's conscience. If he have committed
any mortal sin, then we *require* confession of it to a
Priest."[1] Bishop Montague, more fully to the same
effect says; "We refuse it to none, if men require it,
if need be to have it; we urge and persuade it in extremes; we *require* it in case of perplexity, for the
quieting of men disturbed in their consciences."[2] In
passages already quoted, Bishop Taylor uses the term
"necessary," urging among his reasons for confession;
"That it is by all churches esteemed a duty necessary
to be done in case of a troubled conscience;" and again
George Herbert's Country Parson, in dealing with his
parishioners, follows "the Church's counsel in persuading them to particular confession, labouring to
make them understand how necessary it is in some
cases."[3] Comber uses similar language: "Although
the sins be so secret, or the discipline so remiss, that no
public sentence passes on the offender, yet *every grievous
sinner* hath deserved to be censured, and is condemned
by his own conscience, and under the displeasure of
Almighty GOD, and therefore shall stand in need also
of absolution."[4]

---

[1] Commentary on the Offices of Common Prayer. First Series, vol.
v. p. 163. Library of Anglo-Catholic Theology.

[2] A Gag to a New Gospel, p. 82, quoted by Mr. Cooke, in his appendix to his pamphlet on the Power of Church Absolution.

[3] See ch. xii.

[4] On the Offices.

Our recognised rule, then, following the uniform tradition of the Church, affirms the individual ministry of reconciliation to be the proper and ordinary means of remission of grievous and deadly sins, and therefore morally obligatory in such cases, yet without denying the possibility of forgiveness without it. On this ground the Priest is ordered to " move" the sick person to confession, should his case be of this nature. It is lest he should lose the means specially ordained as a remedy for his great need. The same reason accounts for the Church bidding all persons to express the desire for the restoration of Penance every year at the beginning of Lent, that every one at that season, which earliest tradition has set apart for the renewal and perfecting of repentance, should have recalled to him his own possible need of such a remedy, and the belief of its saving efficacy.

While however this rule has been thus fixed, determining the cases in which Confession is to be regarded as obligatory, we must bear in mind how difficult it often is to draw any clear and certain line between classes or degrees of sin; how abstruse the distinctions between venial and mortal sins; how great the tendency of venial to lead to mortal; the possibility of the mere accumulation of venial sins constituting a state equivalent to mortal sin, and the manifold dangers of self-deception, in such a momentous case. A conscientious mind, earnestly stirred by the sense of sin, will continually doubt as to its character and extent. Doubtless with this conviction it was that Hooker spoke so strongly of the inducements operating on the soul to seek this means of reconciliation with GOD, even when

not conscious of any positively deadly sin. "Because
the knowledge how to handle our own sores is no vulgar
and common art, but we either carry towards ourselves
for the most part an over soft and gentle hand, fearful of
touching too near the quick; or else endeavouring not
to be partial, we fall into timorous scrupulosities, and
sometimes into those extreme discomforts of mind from
which we hardly do ever lift our heads again; men
thought it the safest way to disclose their secret faults,
and to crave imposition of penance, from them to whom
our LORD JESUS CHRIST hath left in His Church to be
spiritual and ghostly physicians, the guides and pastors
of redeemed souls, whose office doth not only consist
in general persuasions unto amendment of life, but also
in the private particular care of diseased minds."[1]

It may be questioned, whether the Roman rule of
compulsory confession, though unsupported by the
teaching or use of the early Church, as already sufficiently proved, nevertheless may not be practically the
more effectual exercise of the power of the keys, and
preferable to the free and discretionary system adopted
in the Church of England, even though our rule be
allowed to be more truly in accordance with ancient
precedent. Under our system undoubtedly many that
have been guilty of deadly sins, may yet approach the
Blessed Sacrament, or may die, without having been
reconciled to GOD through the appointed and ordinary
means, a case which, when the Roman rule can be fully
applied, would be impossible. To this it may be replied, that the compulsory rule to a great extent coun-

[1] Eccl. Pol. lib. vi. ch. iv. 3.

N 3

teracts itself, and becomes inoperative, by alienating multitudes from the Church's ministry, and even from the holy Eucharist; for to withdraw from Confession under the Roman system, is ipso facto to be excommunicated. The case therefore is by no means so clear as at first sight it may seem to be. It involves an alternative of difficulty. If, on the one hand, the absence of compulsion leads to the neglect of Confession in cases where according to the clearest Catholic tradition it ought to be made, on the other hand compulsion provokes resistance, and raises up a barrier hindering the approach to higher graces, where yet the soul may have been truly accepted of God. The risk lies between the consequences of an undue force laid upon the conscience, and the turning of liberty into licence. Either way evil may arise. The Church of England has chosen to run any hazard rather than attempt to bind what God has not bound, refusing to enforce by her own authority, as of divine right, a rule for which there appears to be no clear scriptural or primitive evidence. Moreover, the free action of the soul is of the very essence of contrition. An absolute rule, not necessarily indeed, yet practically may tend to produce a formal and forced use of what specially requires the full surrender of the renewed will, in order to be a living and acceptable service.

At the time of the Reformation the compulsory system of Confession had been fairly tested by a long experience. It is but fair to attribute considerable weight to the practical judgment of those who had witnessed its operation, and decided against it apparently with general consent. Our later experience of its working in foreign Churches, even with all the disadvantages of our present lax discipline, hardly presents so favourable a view, as to lead any thoughtful mind, however anxious for the freest use of confession, to the conclusion that it would be well to return to the compulsory law binding every one alike.

It may however be questioned, whether a modified rule compelling confession in the case of deadly sin alone, might not have been adopted. The reply is not difficult. (1.) Although the distinctive characteristics of deadly sin are clear in the Eye of GOD, yet no human judgment can avail to discern them with accuracy, and therefore cannot lay down any rule grounded on this distinction with any fairness. (2.) Even if the subject-matter of sin could be defined, it would be impracticable to apply any rule touching all cases equitably, without a free consent on the part of the sinner. For while there are deadly sins, open and notorious, " going before to judgment," which the Church may readily mark and censure, there are also whole classes of sins, equally deadly, which are perfectly secret, and can become known only by the free acknowledgment of the transgressor. To deal fairly in the two cases by an absolute rule would be impracticable, and without equity no discipline could be maintained. Not only then is the subject-matter on which the Church has to act, such as precludes the possibility of any general rules, but there are also no means of determining the persons whom she ought to coerce. In a choice manifestly beset with difficulties the Church of England has preferred the risk of a relaxed rule, content to apply her ministry to such as are themselves willing, rather than drive the heart into resistance, by the attempted assertion of an authority which can only be supported by questionable warrants, and which cannot in all cases at least be effectually enforced at all.

It may be doubted, whether the doctrine here advanced, as that of the Church of England, viz., of special Confession and Absolution, though not enjoined of necessity, yet being the ordinary means of remission of deadly sin after baptism, be in accordance with the language of the Exhortation, so often referred to, in giving notice of Holy Communion. We are there taught the ways and means of becoming a worthy communicant, which are "first to examine your lives and conversations by the rule of GOD's commandments, and whereinsoever ye perceive yourselves to have offended, either by will, word, or deed, there to bewail your own sinfulness, and to confess yourselves to Almighty GOD, with full purpose of amendment of life." After this, apparently as a secondary means, it is added; "if there be any of you who by this means cannot quiet his own conscience herein, but requireth further comfort and counsel," then "let him come to me or to some other &c., and open his grief, &c." The form of expression implies, so it is urged, that confession to GOD alone is the better way of obtaining pardon and peace; confession to a Priest the less desirable course, to be followed only if the former fails. The case is said to be all the stronger, because deadly sin is evidently referred to; for the cases specified are, "if any be a blasphemer of GOD, an hinderer or slanderer of His Word, an adulterer, or be in malice, or envy, or in any grievous crime,"—thus including sins which, according to the ancient rule, would certainly have needed to be "reconciled by penance."

In answer to this view of the passage, it is to be observed, that if the Exhortation were intended to discourage the use of special sacramental confession, in such grievous cases, advising it only as an aftercourse, and one less desirable, this would be irreconcileable with our Reformers' avowed purpose of a faithful adherence to primitive rule, as well as to positive affirmations in other parts of our formularies, already quoted, as to the virtue and moral obligation in the supposed cases, of the individual ministry of reconciliation. It can hardly be supposed that the Church should assert this ministry to be Divinely ordained for the remission of deadly sin, and yet actually discourage its use, or speak of it as a subordinate, or even a less desirable, course, in the very cases in which an unquestionable Catholic tradition determines its great benefit. If Discipline should ever be enforced in our Communion, it would without doubt include such cases. But the Exhortation, according to the supposed interpretation, would interfere with such restoration of Discipline, which yet the Church leads us year by year to plead before GOD, as a thing "much to be wished." Such Discipline, if restored, grounded as it must needs be on the ancient rule, would require confession to a Priest, as part of the "penance," to be followed by absolution, with the special promise, according to the teaching of the Homily, of "the forgiveness of sin." This position would altogether clash with the terms of the Exhortation, if, as supposed, it affirms the confession of sin before GOD alone to be the preferable course.

The solution of the apparent inconsistency is to be sought in the mixed character of the subject. It has been shown how in the early Church, there were concurrently held two principles in regard to the remission of sins, the covenanted promises attached to the sacramental ministry of Penance, and the inherent acceptableness of true contrition with confession to God only. According to the view of the Fathers the latter principle was not supposed to interfere with the laws of canonical discipline, or the special benefits derived through the power of the keys. So likewise in our own case, the virtue of sacramental confession and absolution are affirmed, while at the same time there is the assertion of the freedom of the soul's own secret communion with God alone. In our case, as in that of the Church of old, these two principles may be held together in harmony. There are special reasons why the latter principle, the acceptableness of contrition and confession to God alone, should, in this particular instance under our view, have been put forward. The Exhortation is addressed to persons who from the circumstances of the case are not excommunicate, nor at the time apparently disposed to place themselves under the private directions of the Priest, but purposing, it may be, to come to Communion on the following Sunday or Holy Day. The Exhortation is evidently directed against a low standard of preparation for Holy Communion. Its object is to quicken and stir up a more earnest sense and care. It seeks by solemn warning to guard those who are not in the habit of Confession against the risk of coming with grievous sins upon their souls. The sins specified, though of a deadly character,

are such as may be unknown to the Priest, and with
which therefore he could not deal by private remon-
strance. He is therefore bid to urge on such persons
the necessity of repentance before GOD, as the absolutely essential preliminary to an approach to the
Blessed Sacrament, and this accompanied with an
intimation of the "benefit of absolution," if the conscience should be stirred by the appeal. The solemn
warning is as "a bound set around the Mount," to
guard the sacredness of the Sanctuary against those
who from any cause may be careless, or, though needing
it, unwilling to avail themselves of the ordinary means
of reconciliation. It is a case in which such words as
those of S. Chrysostom apply. Speaking of the approach to the LORD's Table, and applying S. Paul's
words, he says, " Let each prove himself, and then let him
come, and he (S. Paul) biddeth us not prove ourselves,
the one to the other, but each himself, making the Judgment-seat private, the proof unwitnessed." (Hom. 28,
on 1 Cor. § 1.) And again; " But thou art ashamed
and blushest to utter thy sins; nay, but even were it
necessary to utter these things before men, and display
them, not even then shouldest thou be ashamed, (for
sin, not to confess sin, is shame), but now it is not even
necessary to confess before witnesses. Be the examination of transgressions in the thoughts of conscience.
Be the Judgment-seat unwitnessed. Let GOD alone see
thee confessing; GOD Who upbraideth not sins, but
remitteth sin on confession. But thou hesitatest even
thus and drawest back?" (Hom. non esse ad gratiam
concionand. § 3, t. 2, p. 663.)[1] And yet at the time

---

[1] Quoted by Dr. Pusey in note M, Tertull., vol. i. pp. 399, 400. 1842.

these words were uttered, the belief of the Church unquestionably was clear and strong as to the sacramental virtue of the ministry of Penance. The exhortation therefore to confession to God alone could not have been held to be inconsistent with that ministry. The circumstances of the time, the unwillingness of the people to come forward, as in earlier days of greater fervour, to undergo the humiliation of the public penance, rendered it expedient in the judgment of S. Chrysostom to urge the people to secret acts of penitence before God, as the most probable alternative. The prevailing belief of the efficacy of contrition without Penance, where the mind was indisposed to yield itself to such a course, would warrant the hope held out to any act of repentance, were it but sincere. And if this mode of dealing were approved in those earlier days, when Discipline still retained much of its primitive force and reverence, a similar course could not be deemed unwarrantable in our own case with far less means of carrying out the severer rule. The unwillingness in the case of the Church of the East, in S. Chrysostom's time, to enforce the Church's law of Penance, is a sufficient justification of our Reformers, at the far more difficult crisis which they had to meet, for a like accommodation to the circumstances of their time.

Hooker, alluding to this passage of the Exhortation, implies, that there was no intention of denying the profitableness of Confession, but only its supposed necessity, or its enforcement against strong prevailing prejudices. "Neither," he says, "any such opinion had of the thing itself (viz. special confession), as though it were either unlawful or unprofitable, saving only for those inconveniences which the world hath by experience observed in it heretofore, and in regard thereof, the Church of England hath thought it the safer way to refer man's hidden crimes unto God, and themselves only; *howbeit not without special caution* for the admonition of such as come to the holy Sacrament, and for the comfort of such as are ready to depart the world."[1]

Moreover, in allowing this freedom as to Confession, care was taken that no one should ever approach the Blessed Sacrament without receiving priestly Absolution, though not of an individual, yet a very solemn form of a public kind. The general confession and absolution of the Communion Office were framed for the express purpose of insuring some measure at least of the grace of this ministry to all who frequent the services of the Church, thus meeting, so far as is possible, the needs of those who, from whatever cause, make use of the liberty to confess themselves to God alone.

The old Latin forms of confession occurring in the daily Offices, and in the Mass, when translated and embodied in our own formularies, were enlarged and deepened in tone; and the absolutions previously said kneeling as in prayer, were ordered to be said standing, as in the exercise of special priestly authority. The change made in the absolution of the Mass is peculiarly significant. According to the Latin use the absolution is said twice, once by the assistant minister on behalf of the priest; and the second time by the priest on behalf of the assistant minister, and people, as though it were but a mutual expression of desire for each other's for-

[1] Eccl. Pol. lib. vi. 4, 15.

giveness.[1] In our Communion Office, on the contrary, it is said once only, and then by the Priest on behalf of the people; and our enlarged form expresses the special promise given to the Church's ministry in the exercise of its absolving power, thus marking it as an official act: "Almighty GOD, Who of His great mercy hath promised forgiveness of sins to all them that truly repent and turn unto Him," &c. The claim of the power of reconciliation, as being at the time exercised, is more definitely expressed in the absolution of our daily offices, which speaks of "the power and commandment given by Almighty GOD to His ministers, to declare and pronounce to all them that are penitent the absolution and remission of their sins."

Of the virtue of the public, in comparison with the private, absolution more will be said in the following chapter. But as to the efficacy of these public acts of the priesthood in supplying the lack of the individual ministry in the case of those who have been guilty of deadly sins, I would avail myself of the remarks of the learned and devout writer of an article which lately ap-

---

[1] The Latin forms at Mass—the same are used likewise at Prime and Compline—are as follows:

After the Priest's Confiteor then,

"Ministri R̂. Misereatur tui omnipotens Deus; et dimissis peccatis tuis, perducat te ad vitam æternam.

"Sacerdos dicit Amen, et erigit se. Deinde ministri repetunt Confessionem, &c.

"Postea Sacerdos junctis manibus facit absolutionem dicens:

"Misereatur vestri omnipotens Deus; et dimissis peccatis vestris, perducat vos ad vitam æternam. Amen.

"Signat se signo crucis, dicens; Indulgentiam, absolutionem, et remissionem peccatorum nostrorum, tribuat nobis omnipotens et misericors Deus. Amen."

peared in the "Ecclesiastic."[1] After strongly expressing his belief that "private absolution is the proper
exercise of the sacerdotal commission, and the one
proper mode of conveying the benefit of it," and that
the "blessings obtained by personal confession and
individual absolution are so distinct and great, that no
elevation of the general forms can bring them into
competition with them,"—he suggests that "the absolution of the general services, if they be received in
contrition, with faith and hope," may be the means of
conveying "renewed cleansing, releasing from the bonds
of sin, and relief from its effects;" and that repeated
confessions and absolutions "may tend even to the
putting away of deadly as well as venial sin." "The
subject," he proceeds to say, "is indeed a deep and
difficult one, both as regards the miserable effects of
sin, and the means for the removal of them. Far
should we be from underrating the great and supremely
high effects of proper absolution on confession. This
stands out in marked contrast to any other appointed
means when received, as is of course implied, in the
sincerity of penitence and faith. The benefit thus conveyed is definite, known and secured: for this is a
pledge, as well as a means, of forgiveness, not to mention the comfort and assurance given to the penitent
by the judgment of another rather than his own. With-

---

[1] No. XXXIX., March, 1849. The Doctrine of Absolution, pp. 169,
170. The article is known to have been written by one whom Oxford
counts among the noblest of her sons, illustrious in the defence of the
faith, and the promotion of true piety among her students, but now,
alas! lost to her, and to the Church on earth, though not yet taken
to his rest.

out this we must believe, that remission and release is gradual, and the assurance of it less certain and less definite, however hopeful and comforting." " But," he adds, " shall we fathom and limit either the manifold effects of sin, or the manifold means by which these effects may be removed? The Church prays for the remission of sins after absolution has been pronounced; she so prayed of old, she so prays in other branches of the Church besides our own. Surely there is some meaning in this. There is some meaning in the continual repetition of a prayer for forgiveness, in the words our LORD has taught us, in our daily service; still more in the recurring devotions of Lent, and in the Penitential Psalms. These prayers are not to be limited to sins of daily incursion, they run back over our whole lives, entreating for the forgiveness of the most deadly, even more than of venial sins, and they have their efficacy. Why then should not the absolutions, which are said to us in general, have some corresponding efficacy? The previous confession and prayer for pardon, the very acts of faith and contrition involved therein, have, as is admitted, an efficacy that way. Why should not the priest's absolution have the like effect? If it be said, it is a general absolution said for all alike, so, we may reply, is his benediction. Yet this has its effect, as we conceive the absolution has, when it comes upon a soul, duly prepared for the reception of it. If it be said, that the form is only a general declaration of GOD's forgiving the penitent, let it be remembered that the declaration is prefaced by an announcement of the sacerdotal commission: and then let the principle to which we have referred of the Church's intention, be

taken into account.   That the intention of the absolution in the daily service was to cleanse the worshippers,
we think, cannot reasonably be questioned.   That the
intention of the form before the Communion was so,
likewise appears clear.   Let us look then to the intent,
not to the mere words, and then we see a provision not
only for a cleansing from venial, but for some renewed
cleansing, or some assisting influence towards the entire
removal of the effects of the gravest sins to the truly
penitent."   The writer closes his observations with a
quotation from " the Catholic-minded Sherlock, the
teacher of Bishop Wilson," confirmatory of his opinion :
" After the confession (in the daily service) when the
minister comes to the words of absolution, bow down
your head, and say softly, in your heart, ' LORD, let this
pardon pronounced by Thy minister, fall upon my soul,
and seal thereunto the forgiveness of all my sins.' "

It is important to add to the foregoing remarks, what
Morinus notes as to the exceptional use of general absolutions in the remission even of deadly sins without
any special confession.   He states that " formerly in
many churches, chiefly Metropolitan and Cathedral
churches, it was customary every year at the holy Eucharist to offer, in the name of the whole congregation,
a general confession embracing all kinds of sins, after
which a general absolution, equally embracing all sins,
was solemnly given."   He adds, " that in many churches
this custom still prevailed in his time, as e.g., in the
Metropolitan church, and certain parishes of the diocese of Paris.   The form in which the absolution was
given, is grounded on the commission of our LORD;
' Whosesoever sins ye remit,' &c., thus implying the

full exercise of the priestly ministry, and it also com-
prehended all sins, whether in thought, word, or deed,
by omission or negligence."[1] Morinus remarks that
this absolution was evidently, not a release from excommunication, nor connected in any way with Indulgences, but a real remission of sins (vera realisque
remissio peccatorum). He supposes the intention of
this act of reconciliation originally to have been the
supplying any defect in previous absolutions given after
special confession, in consequence of questions arising
from the reservation of cases, on the part of the Pope
towards the people generally, or of an abbot towards

[1] This office is called in France "l'Absoute." The mode of administration is thus described by Morinus : "After a confession embracing
sins of every kind offered by the Priest in the name of the people,
he then bids each person present to make his own Confiteor, or, if he
does not know the words, then to say a 'Pater-noster' and an 'Ave
Maria,' after which the Priest thus proceeds :

" 'Through the merits of the Passion and Resurrection of JESUS
CHRIST our LORD, through the intercession of Blessed Mary ever
Virgin, and of All Saints, the Almighty GOD have mercy on you, and
forgive you all your sins, and bring you to everlasting life. Amen.
Pardon and absolution of all your sins, a contrite and truly penitent
heart, the grace and consolation of the HOLY SPIRIT, the Almighty
GOD grant to you. Amen.'

"Then stretching out his right hand towards the people, he says :
'Let us pray. Our LORD JESUS CHRIST, Who said to His disciples,
'Whosoever sins ye remit,' &c., in the number of whom He hath
willed me unworthy sinner to be a minister, through the intercession
of, &c.: may He absolve you through my ministry of all your sins,
whatever in thought, word, or deed, by negligence or omission, you
have done, and may He bring you released from all their bonds to His
heavenly kingdom, Who with the FATHER, &c. Amen. The blessing
of our LORD JESUS CHRIST descend upon you, and abide with you for
ever, in the Name of, &c. Amen.' "

This form is quoted from a manual published in Paris, A.D. 1615.

the members of his community; that therefore this general absolution is not to be viewed separately in itself, but as operative in connection with the special absolutions previously received.   At the same time he implies, that it is a relic of a former state of things, when absolution was given with less of limitation than the later use of the Middle Ages would warrant.   He closes his remarks by saying, " The ancients do not seem to have restricted absolution of sins within such narrow bounds as the scholastic doctors afterwards did."[1]

If notwithstanding the explanations here given, it should still appear to be a hurtful laxity to admit to the Blessed Sacrament without the security of special confession, from the great risk of the approach of unworthy communicants, and that the freedom allowed amongst us in doubtful cases has no parallel in the better ages of the Church's history, the following words of S. Augustine should be carefully weighed.   They imply that in his day it was thought better to run such a risk, casting the responsibility of the decision on the individual conscience, rather than assert in all cases a precarious power which might possibly diminish the sense of responsibility, and without any certain safeguard against self-deception, or evasion.   " Let no one suppose that he ought therefore to despise the counsel of this salutary

---

[1] Lib. viii. c. xxvi. xiii.   He adds the singular, but very significant and pregnant remark: " Nondum edocti erant (antiqui) artem illam de singulis rebus theologicis præcisè, definitè et quasi punctim, et circum-currente lineâ, disserendi.   Liberius vagatur corum sermo, attamen ἡ γλῶσσ' ἁμαρτάνουσα τ' ἀληθῆ λέγει."

Penance, because perchance he notices and knows, that many approach to the Sacrament of the Altar, whose such and such crimes he is not ignorant of. For many are corrected, as Peter; many are tolerated, as Judas; many are not known, until the LORD come, Who will illuminate the hidden things of darkness, and will make manifest the thoughts of the heart. For most persons are on that account unwilling to accuse others, while they wish by their means to excuse themselves. But most good Christians are for this reason silent, and suffer the sins of others which they know, because they often lack evidence, and are unable to prove to ecclesiastical judges, that which they themselves know. For although some things be true, yet they are not to be easily disclosed to the judge, unless they be shown by certain proofs. But we cannot hinder any one from communion (although this prohibition be not yet mortal, but medicinal,) unless either one that hath of his own accord confessed, or that has been named and convicted in some either secular or ecclesiastical judgment."[1]

It is important to remark, that our rubrical directions to the Priest for dealing with his people go, in strictness of rule, beyond what is implied in this last sentence of S. Augustine, and would, if faithfully carried out, raise our discipline above what seems to have been practicable in his day.[2]

---

[1] De Pœnitentia, sec. 10, quoted by Mr. Owen in his " Introduction to the Study of Dogmatic Theology," p. 433.

[2] See rubrics prefacing our Office for Holy Communion.

CHAPTER XVI.

ABSOLUTION.

THE doctrine of Absolution is so intimately connected with that of Confession, and so essentially complementary to its use, that although incidentally touched upon in the foregoing argument, the subject needs a separate and fuller consideration.

The Catholic Church has never defined Absolution, nor the distinctive efficacy of its several modes of administration. No controversy having arisen on these questions while the Church was yet one and undivided, there was no occasion for, and therefore no exercise of, an œcumenical judgment, such as sealed the articles of faith concerning the Nature of GOD, or the Person of our LORD. As Baptism and the Holy Eucharist were left undefined, so likewise and for the same reasons was Absolution. In this, equally as in those greater parallel cases, the Church's doctrine is to be gathered from her traditionary usages, and the writings of the Fathers.

That the power of Absolution was uniformly believed to be vested in the Priesthood, has been already sufficiently proved. Its connection with Baptism and the Eucharist has been also implied. Of the baptismal ministry it is, as it were, but an extension. Remis-

o

sion of sins is one part of the baptismal grace, and
therefore the absolving power necessarily enters into
its administration.   Absolution, as a subsequent and
distinct act, is the restoration of this baptismal grace,
when lost, or its renewal, when decayed.   It is essentially involved in Baptism, and its repetition is rendered
necessary by the universal liability to sin still besetting
the regenerate.   It is in like manner connected with the
holy Eucharist.   For the Body and Blood of our LORD
can be rightly received only by the pure of heart—" holy
things for the holy."   The incursions of evil, therefore,
such as unfit the soul for the mysterious reception of
its heavenly Sustenance, needing to be done away, and
special grace for this end to be sealed and ensured,—
a sacramental preparation suitable for the great sacramental gift,—it follows that an antecedent ministry is
required, at once to guard the approach, and to remove
the barrier, that so the penitent may without fear or
scruple, and with assurance of acceptance, partake of
the Divine Mystery.   If Absolution may be viewed on
the one side as the extension of Baptism, it may be
also regarded on the other as the anticipation of the
holy Eucharist.   The ordinance looks both ways, sin
necessitating it in both cases; in the one to restore
grace given, in the other to ensure yet greater grace to
come.

A theory at variance with this view has found acceptance with some divines, which supposes that the remission of sins is bestowed sacramentally only through
Baptism and the holy Eucharist.   That these pre-
eminent Sacraments involve this gift as containing all
the promises and graces of the covenant, is unquestion-

able; but it is equally certain, that the Church has ever held the special ministry of remission of sins, as a sacramental ordinance separate and distinct from them.

Mr. Freeman has carefully and clearly expressed this distinction, and the Church's uniform witness to its Divine appointment: "It is often objected, explicitly or otherwise, to the Church's doctrine concerning the remission of sins through CHRIST, that it is involved in some inconsistency; in that it ascribes that effect, on the one hand, to the due reception of the Sacraments" (the two only generally necessary to salvation are here evidently meant); "while yet on the other it recognises a personal commission, vested in a body of duly ordained men, to convey by word of mouth the same blessed reality. If the Sacraments contain in themselves full power for the remission of sins, by application of the Blood of CHRIST, to what purpose, it is not unnaturally asked, is 'power and commandment' given to CHRIST's ministers to 'declare and pronounce to the penitent,' and thereby actually to convey, the 'absolution and remission of their sins?' Or again, if this latter be effectual, what place remains for the operation of the Sacraments in the matter? Why do we, after such absolution, still seek in the holy Communion 'remission of our sins' among the 'other benefits of the Passion?'

"Now it is undeniable that our LORD did give, over and above the commission to administer the two Sacraments, a separate one, 'to remit and retain sins' by the power of the HOLY GHOST. And though it might be alleged that this was only to be exercised through

o 2

the administration of the Sacraments, it is certain that the Church has never understood it so. She has always had verbal absolutions, and never more solemn ones than in the prospect of celebration of Divine service, or in the course of it; and specially at the celebration of the Eucharist."[1]

Mr. Freeman also refers to the provisions of the Levitical law,—the typical pattern of the Gospel dispensation,—in further proof of this intermediate ministry in the remission of sins: "The means by which the individual, or the congregation, obtained access, of old, to the peculiar Presence have been already dwelt upon. The Altar, it is manifest, was the way to the Presence. But which was the way to the Altar? By what rules was that way fenced about, and to whom was the guardianship of it committed? The answer is, that the 'way' was through 'the door' of the Tabernacle court, and that it was freely open to every Israelite not disqualified by breach of covenant laws; but that in case of such disqualification, of which the conscience of the worshipper was the judge in the first instance, the Priest was constituted, in a very marked manner, the dispenser of absolution from it. The offender, on becoming aware, through self-examination or the warning of others,[2] of his fault, was to bring a stated offering; and the Priest, by the prescribed methods of offering and eating, procured, and probably announced, his forgiveness. As to what constituted disqualification, there were certain plain rules laid down, while in cases of

---

[1] Principles of Divine Service. Vol. ii.: Theory of Eucharistic Worship, ch. i. sec. 18.

[2] Lev. iv. 27, 28; v. 4; x. 11; Mal. ii. 6, 7.

doubt or difficulty, recourse was to be had to the Priest for counsel, as well as for remission."[1]

For reasons already given we may expect to find variations of opinion, and consequently of expression, in explaining the rationale of this ordinance. It necessarily presents itself in varying aspects to different minds, viewing it under different circumstances, one writer dwelling rather on one, another on another phase of the complex whole, while nevertheless, as differently coloured rays melt into one common light, their several views and statements may coalesce and harmonize in one truth. The Fathers were wont to represent Absolution under the instances which holy Scripture records of GOD's merciful dealing with uncleanness in the prefigurative appointments of the Levitical ritual, or of our LORD's miracles of healing. Thus, e.g., they likened

---

[1] Principles of Divine Service. Vol. ii.: Theory of Eucharistic Worship, ch. i. sec. 18.

I am indebted to a friend, whose name would carry with it deserved weight, for the following remarks. Referring to the spiritual results of the holy Eucharist, he observes; "Hooker indeed says; 'the effect thereof in us is a real transmutation of our souls and bodies from sin to righteousness.' (Vol. ii. p. 355.) But I have supposed that this statement is to be explained by the doctrine of S. Thomas, who distinctly teaches that, as deadly sin constitutes an 'impedimentum' to the vivifying and spiritual reception of the Sacrament, it cannot be considered to be remitted therein, unless in the case of a person who is guilty of sin in fact without knowing it. He holds, on the other hand, that the Eucharist does do away with venial sin; as S. Ambrose seems to teach, 'iste panis quotidianus sumitur in remedium quotidianæ infirmitatis,' in De Sacramentis. Sin must be forgiven before the Eucharistic Reception (whether with, or without private absolution). The Eucharist seals the forgiveness. It makes clean the body, and washes the soul from the lesser stains which do not suspend life," &c.

Absolution to the Priest's judgment of the leper, and to the Apostles' loosing the bands which bound Lazarus, when our LORD raised him from the dead. The one case represents Absolution as merely a declaration of what had been done, the other as an instrumental act in the chain of causes co-operating towards the fulfilment of the end.

Jeremy Taylor gives instances of this diversity of view from the writings of S. Jerome and S. Ambrose. The former commenting on S. Matt. xvi. 19, says: " In Leviticus the lepers were commanded to show themselves to the Priests, who neither make them leprous nor clean, but they discern who are clean and who are unclean. As therefore then the Priest makes the leprous clean or unclean, so here does the Bishop or the Priest bind or loose, i.e., according to their office; when he hears the variety of sins, he knows who is to be bound, and who is to be loosed."

In contrast with this view Taylor adduces the passage of S. Ambrose previously quoted: " He (S. Ambrose) adds one advantage more as consequent to the Priest's absolving of penitents; 'Men give their ministry in the remission of sins, but they exercise not the right of any power; neither are sins remitted by them in their own, but in the Name of the FATHER, SON, and HOLY SPIRIT. Men pray, but it is GOD Who forgives: it is man's obsequiousness, but the bountiful gift is from GOD.' "[1]   S. Ambrose's " one advantage more" will be better understood from another passage, where, speaking of Absolution, he says: " This is no work of man, but of GOD

---

[1] Jeremy Taylor, Dissuasive from Popery, sec. xi., vol. xi. p. 25. Heber's edit.

(namely, the imparting of the HOLY GHOST). The SPIRIT is indeed invoked by the Priest, but He is given by GOD."[1] Marshall quotes this passage, grounding upon it his statement, that forgiveness is equivalent to the renewal of the SPIRIT; "Pardon, or as S. Ambrose will be found speaking, 'impart the HOLY SPIRIT,' Who is evermore supposed to enter where the sin is pardoned."[2] S. Augustine, again, speaks of Absolution under the figure of Lazarus being loosed: "Attend to Lazarus himself; whereas he comes forth in his bonds, he already was alive in confessing; but as yet he walked not free, being trammelled in bonds. What then does the Church, to which was said, 'What things ye shall loose, they shall be loosed,' but that which the LORD says to the disciples, Loose him and let him go."[3] The type of the Levitical Priest cleansing the leper, represents the declaratory view of absolution; that of loosing Lazarus implies an effectual act in the renewal of life, while S. Ambrose's words explain the grace given to be a direct gift of the HOLY GHOST renewing the soul.

These different sides of truth are not necessarily in opposition. A writer may select one aspect of a complex whole, without thereby denying other aspects of it; or the context of a passage may require one portion of the truth to be put forth in the particular connection. Thus, e.g., the definition of Absolution would necessarily vary according to the view taken of the remission of sins. If remission of sins be regarded

---

[1] De Spir. Sanct. lib. i. c. 8, (p. 619, Ed. Bened. vi.)

[2] Penitential discipline, pp. 70, 71.

[3] Serm. viii., on S. Matt., vol. x. p. 19, fol. edit.

simply as a judicial act, a pardon of the offence, then absolution is but declaratory. Pardon, under this view, is but an external fact, which the Priest attests, his sentence coinciding with the sentence of GOD. If however remission of sins be viewed internally, as more than mere pardon, as a communication of fresh life, then Absolution becomes a channel of quickening grace.

Again, among those who take the higher view of Absolution, as more than declaratory, some regard it as having power only to remove a spiritual barrier hindering the reception of grace afterwards to be imparted, and thus far furthering its return; others as itself a means of imparting grace, an actual increase of spiritual life of which the Priest's ministry is the outward form and sign.

To attribute to Absolution more than a mere declaration of forgiveness, may seem to derogate from the supremacy of GOD. But the ministry of the means of grace is not the same with the gift of grace; the channel of the current not identical with the stream. To assert for the Church's ministry a delegated instrumental power, through which GOD vouchsafes to act by covenanted promise, is not to claim any Divine power. "Who can forgive sins," asks S. Ambrose, "except GOD alone?" but adds, "Who also forgives through those to whom He gives the power of remission."[1] And again more fully: "But they (the Novatians) say that they do honour to GOD, to Whom alone they reserve the power of remitting sins. Nay, rather none do a greater injury than they who desire to rescind His command, to reject the charge committed to

[1] S. Ambrose on S. Luke v. 19.

them. For when our LORD Himself in His Gospel has said, ' Receive the HOLY GHOST : whose sins ye remit, they are remitted, and whose sins ye retain, they are retained ;'—which gives most honour, he who obeys the command, or he who resists it ?"[1]

Moreover both earlier and later theologians have grounded the virtue of sacerdotal absolution on the passage in which our LORD claims to Himself, under the character of the " SON of Man," power to forgive sins on earth,[2] as specially intended by Him to show forth the commission which, first exercised by Himself in His Manhood, was after His Ascension in the descent of the HOLY GHOST to be perpetuated through sub-ordinate human instruments in the ministry of His Church. In claiming this power to Himself specially under this title, He connects it with His Humanity ; for the title is always understood to denote His human nature and attributes, which were to be communicated from Himself to His elect according to certain laws, of His own ordaining, and among others His attribute of Priesthood, of which the ministry of the forgiveness of sins forms a material part. He exhibited in Himself under this aspect the primary instance of the Divine prerogative operating through human means, that His people might be prepared for the continued operation of the same great gift, to be bestowed "on earth," (special emphasis being laid on this idea in the context,) —to be still indeed exercised by Himself, though me-diated through others, through a line of subordinate

[1] S. Ambrose, De Pœnitentia, lib. i. c. 2, 6. Both passages are quoted by Dr. Wordsworth. Theoph. Anglic., c. xiv., Absolution.
[2] S. Matt. ix. 2—8.

O 3

agency, His own commissioned ministers, deriving from Himself in an unbroken continuity of living grace. His words were so understood by the bystanders; for "they marvelled and glorified God, Which had given such power unto men." Their instincts, however dimly, discerned the momentous truth, that not Himself alone individually, but a plurality of persons to be viewed as in and of Him, and one with Him, were to be commissioned from among men for perpetuating the exercise of this same healing power.[1]

The maintainers of what may be called the higher view of absolution are to be found among those who are not commonly reckoned High Churchmen. E.g., Bishop Hall, after commenting on the sacerdotal commission of remitting sins, says; "Neither is this only by way of a bare verbal declaration, which might proceed from any lips, but in the way of an operative and effectual application, by virtue of that delegate or commissionary authority which is by CHRIST entrusted with them (His ministers). For certainly our SAVIOUR meant

[1] Mr. Freeman has expressed a valuable thought on this transmission of the power of healing from our LORD to His ministers. "The Levitical Priests received their consecrations in order to powers of binding and loosing, by eating of a sin-offering, and ever after discharged this part of their office by the same means, in eating of the sin-offering of the people. The Apostles received the like powers for themselves and others by our LORD's *breathing* upon them: and they exercise them by the analogous power of *speech*, made effective, by that one Breathing, to the loosing of sins. Nor can we fail to mark the gracious care of God for His wandering sheep, in thus making the re-admission of the fallen or the timorous a *personal* work: a work leaving an opening, if desired, for personal communication, reassurance, counsel, comfort." Theory of Eucharistic Worship, ch. i. sec. 18.

in these words to confer somewhat upon His ministers, more than the rest of the world should be capable to receive or perform."[1]

Even Chillingworth speaks of the glorious commission, which before He (our LORD) had "given to Peter, sustaining, as it were, the person of the whole Church, whereby He delegated to them (His disciples) an authority of binding and loosing sins upon earth, with a promise that the proceedings in the court of heaven should be directed and regulated by theirs on earth."[2]

Divines, whom all acknowledge to be standards of orthodoxy, have taken the highest view. Thus Isaac Barrow, closely following the track of S. Ambrose, and connecting the grace of Absolution with that of Baptism, says; "They (Priests) remit sins *dispensativè* by consigning pardon in administration of sacraments, especially in conferring Baptism, whereby duly administered and undertaken, all sins are washed away; and absolving of penitents, wherein grace is exhibited and ratified by imposition of hands, the which S. Paul calls χαρίζεσθαι, to bestow grace or favour on the penitent."[3]

But it is more important to observe, that the Church of England herself has expressed her mind, though in simple and general statements, yet in words and under circumstances which seem reconcileable only with the highest view of this ministry. Thus, to recall expressions of her mind already quoted, the doctrine of the Homily, that "Absolution hath the promise of for-

---

[1] Resolutions and Decisions, &c. Works, Hall's edit., vol. vii. p. 452, 5.
[2] Serm. vii. p. 83.
[3] The Power of the Keys. Works, vol. vi. p. 56.

giveness of sins," implying not merely a declaration, but also an application of the promised grace; Parker's assertion, when he, as the first Primate after the Reformation, was regulating the formularies of the English Church, that it is heterodoxy to deny, that " sins are remissible by penance," implying it to be an ordinary means of remission : the refusal of the Savoy Commissioners to substitute, " I pronounce thee absolved," for " I absolve thee," thus refusing the mere declaratory notion, and expressing a view of the ministry consistent only with the idea of spiritual inward grace being its proper result;—all alike involve a belief in the supernatural efficacy of the ordinance. There are moreover significant indications in our Offices, of the faith of our Church, that remission of sins is not a mere judicial process, terminating in a sentence of pardon, but an actual internal change from evil to good. Our Offices uniformly associate the idea of the remission of sins with this deeper view. Thus the Baptismal Office speaks of the " remission of sins by spiritual regeneration,"[1] a real effect therefore of renewed life. Similarly our general forms of Absolution, specifying the grace given and sealed to the worthy recipient of the sacramental act, express the same idea : " Almighty GOD . . . pardon and deliver you from all your sins, confirm and strengthen you in all goodness,"—words

[1] The term "remission of sins," may seem inappropriate in Infant Baptism, when there can be no actual " sins," only original sin, to be remitted. But the expression is here evidently taken in a wide sense as embracing generally all the blessings of redemption. The expression in the original collect which we thus translate, is "æternam consequi gratiam spirituali regeneratione." See Palmer's Antiq. of Eng. Rit. vol. ii. p. 174.

clearly implying that the remission of sin involves the removal of its power, as well as of its guilt.

That the terms of Absolution involve some positive change of state, is so strongly felt, that divines opposed to the idea of any inward spiritual grace, have suggested the explanation of a remission of ecclesiastical censures. An ordinance expressed in such high terms must, they assume, have some substantial effect on the penitent. They admit a reality and positiveness of result in the very endeavour to evade the arguments in favour of a spiritual benefit. They reject the idea of a mere declaration, and suggest a real effect in the remission of " censures." If their interpretation of " sins" to mean " ecclesiastical censures" be not allowed, these disputants may then be claimed as authorities in favour of the view of a real bestowal of grace; for what other result of a positive kind can be surmised?

Nor does it follow, even although through the force of contrition the forgiveness of sins has been obtained before Absolution be given, that therefore the Absolution is vain. God will surely honour His own ordinances, if used in dependence upon His promises, and the sealing of His gifts by a sacramental ministry is part of the Divine purpose. There may still be a true relation between the outward form, and the inward spiritual grace. The Absolution may be a continuance, or an increase of the grace already bestowed; it may still be necessary for the abiding effects of the spiritual healing. In the case of the " woman who had an issue of blood twelve years," who touched " the hem" of our Lord's garment, and at whose touch " virtue went out of Him," and " straightway the fountain of her blood was dried up, and she felt in her body that she was healed of that plague,"—our Lord spoke the healing words after her restoration to health, as though the miracle had yet to be wrought; "Daughter, thy faith hath made thee whole; go in peace, and be whole of thy plague." He recognises the fact of her healing already accomplished, —"hath made thee whole,"—and yet at the same time renews the assurance of the miracle, "go in peace and be whole of thy plague."[1]

A yet further and most important part of the doctrine of Absolution relates to the modes of its administration. A distinction has always been observed between the general and special, or speaking according to modern usage, the public and private forms, the latter being regarded as the more complete application of the ministry. This special or individual form has in all ages been confined to the special ministry of Penance. Though at the beginning administered in public, it was individually appropriated by imposition of hands, and given only after special confession. Our Church in her expositions has been careful to preserve the distinctive character, and so the peculiar virtues, of this individual Absolution. She speaks, e.g., to regular Church goers, i.e., persons in the habit of receiving general absolutions, of "the benefit of absolution," as something in addition, to be obtained only by special confession. She desires her Priests to "absolve" the sick after special confession, though they may be just about to receive the holy Eucharist in which a general absolution is administered. Again, the Homily, which affirms

1 S. Mark v. 25—34.

"ecclesiastical discipline" to be a "note of the true Church," contrasts absolution with excommunication. It speaks of "the authority of the keys to excommunicate notorious sinners, and to absolve them which are truly penitent," Absolution being here evidently viewed in its relation to formal excommunication, which cannot belong to it in the ordinary services, and therefore implying a distinctive use. Again, the Homily which describes Absolution as having "the promise of forgiveness of sins," speaks of "the imposition of hands," as its "visible sign," a characteristic which can attach only to its special individual form.

Another distinction which, because of the misapprehensions attached to the term, deserves a full consideration, and which is of the essence of the special ministry, has been carefully preserved by the Church's rule, viz., its judicial character. Private Absolution is appointed to be given only after special secret confession, and on the Priest's responsibility as to its rightful application, i.e., after he has had the fullest opportunity of testing the condition of the penitent, in order to form a judgment as to the fitness of exercising so solemn a trust in the particular case. The term, "judicial," in our use, does not mean that the Priest judges of the value of the sin, so as to apportion the due amount of punishment, nor under the forensic idea, as though forgiveness were limited to his sentence,—positions combated, as we have seen, of old by the mediæval, as in later years by our own, Reformers,—but that he is constituted the judge of the worth of the repentance in order to exercise his ministry only when satisfied on this point.

Our divines frequently dwell on this distinction.

Usher quotes S. Gregory as showing the nature of this power; "The causes ought to be weighed, and then the power of binding and loosing exercised. It is to be seen what the fault is, and what the repentance is that hath followed after the fault; that such as Almighty GOD doth visit with the grace of compunction, those the sentence of the pastor may absolve. For the absolution of the prelate is then true, when it followeth the arbitrement of the Eternal Judge."[1]

Bishop Hall says to the same effect; "Doubtless every true minister of CHRIST hath, by virtue of this first and everlasting commission, two keys delivered into his hand :—the key of knowledge, and the key of spiritual power; the one whereby he is enabled to enter and search into, not only the revealed mysteries of salvation, but also in some sort into the heart of the penitent; there discovering upon an ingenuous revelation of the offender, both the nature, quality, and degree of the sin; and the truth, validity, and measure of his repentance; the other, whereby he may, in some sort, either lock up the soul under sin, or free it from sin."[2]

Thus again Jeremy Taylor, in his Rules of holy dying, uses the term, "ordinary judge," as synonymous with a confessor.[3]

And thus again, Bishop Patrick; "Absolution of penitents as a thing of great moment which may alone be sufficient to convince you both of the dignity and the difficulty of your holy function. For what an high

---

[1] Answer to a Jesuit, of the Priest's power to forgive sin.
[2] Resolutions and Decisions of divers practical cases of conscience, case ix. Works, Hall's edition, vol. vii., p. 1852.
[3] Holy Dying, c. 5, §§ 2, 4.

honour is it to be made a judge of the state of men's immortal souls, and to pronounce a sentence upon them, according as you find them upon examination? But how industriously then ought you to labour to understand the Gospel of Christ, whereby you are to judge, that you may not pass a wrong sentence, through ignorance of the conditions of salvation by Christ."[1]

And lastly, Bishop Wilson; "As under the law of Moses God made His Priests the judges of leprosy, and gave them rules by which they were to determine who was clean and fit to enter into the congregation (which was a type of heaven), and who were not clean; even so under the Gospel He has given His Priests authority to judge sin, which is the leprosy of the soul. He hath given them rules to judge by, with authority to pronounce their pardon, if they find them qualified; for this is their commission from Christ's own mouth; 'Whosesoever sins ye remit, they are remitted unto them.' "[2]

To the foregoing proofs of the mind of our Church on this subject may be added the comments of our ritualists on the meaning of the language of our Offices. They vary in their expositions, but it is observable that the ritualists of the seventeenth century,—the period which we have taken as the truest standard for ascertaining the mind of our Reformation, because the nearest to its source,—agree in ascribing to the act of Absolution a real effect of grace upon the soul of the penitent, while the earliest ritualist of all makes a clear distinction between the general and special absolutions,

[1] The Work of the Ministry.   [2] Parochialia. Works, vol. i. 46.

representing the former as properly applicable to daily and lesser, the latter to more grave or deadly, sins.

Bishop Cosin,—whose notes on the Book of Common Prayer were written during a period ranging from 1619 to 1640,[1] one of the Commissioners at the Savoy Conference, thus explains the force of the general absolution of our daily Office; " In which confession we remember our daily offences in general, and there is no means so powerful to obtain pardon for them, as the daily prayers of the Church to that purpose; so that the course which our Church here prescribeth for the pardon of our daily offences, being put in practice, what can be more just, more due, than to declare that forgiveness and absolution, which those that are (as they pretend to be) penitent for those sins, do obtain? What more comfortable, than to hear the news of it from his mouth, by whom the Church ministereth these offices? What more seasonable, than to do this before we come to give GOD His solemn praise and honour in our public service, that we may be assured He accepts of the same at our hands."[2]

Of the special or private absolution, on the other hand, he says; " Venial sins, that separate not from the grace of GOD, need not so much to trouble a man's conscience: if he hath committed any mortal sin, then we require confession of it to a priest, who may give him, upon his true contrition and repentance, the benefit of absolution; which takes effect according to his disposition that is absolved . . . . . The truth is, that in

[1] See Preface to his Notes in the Library of Anglo-Catholic Theology. Cosin's Works, vol. v., p. xviii.
[2] Notes. Third Series, vol. v., p. 443.

the Priest's absolution there is the true power and virtue of forgiveness, which will most certainly take effect, nisi ponitur obex, as in baptism."[1]

Bp. Sparrow, in his Rationale, published in 1657, takes the same high view, but does not distinguish between the different forms. After quoting S. John xx. 23, he says, "Which power of remitting sins was not to end with the Apostles, but is a part of the ministry of reconciliation, as necessary now as it was then, and therefore to continue as long as the ministry of reconciliation, that is, to the end of the world. When therefore the Priest absolves, God absolves, if we be truly penitent."[2]

Bishop Sparrow seems to have varied in his opinion, though alway preserving a high view of the effects of the ordinance. In the passage referred to, he attributes an equal virtue to all our three forms; "All these several forms in sense and virtue are the same. All these are but several expressions of the same thing: and are effectual to the penitent by virtue of that Commission mentioned in S. John xx."

But in his sermon before the University of Cam-

[1] Cosin's Works, vol. v., p. 62, additional notes. Office for Visitation of the Sick.

This same belief prevails generally, as far as I am aware, among Churchmen of the present day: One whom public approval recognises among us as a faithful exponent of our Church's faith, privately expressed his belief on this point in these brief words. "I have looked on the Absolution in the Daily Service as the substitute for the Absolutio at Prime, and so, dealing as that professes to do with persons in a state of grace, refer it to venial sins. The second (the private and special form) I have regarded as authoritative, in view of the place which the precatory form holds in the Greek Church."

[2] The Absolution, pp. 17, 20. Oxford edition. 1859.

bridge in 1637, Sparrow speaks of a special Absolution to be obtained only through sacramental Confession, thus implying the same distinction between the individual and the general form, which his predecessor had preserved. "To put all out of doubt, let's search the Scriptures : look into S. John xx. 23 ; here is plainly a power of remitting sins granted to the Priest . . . . as the Fathers interpret the place, a peculiar power of pronouncing, as GOD's deputed judges, pardon and remission to the penitent, a power of absolving from sins in the Name of GOD, all such as patiently confess unto them : a form of which absolution our holy Mother the Church hath prescribed in the Visitation of the Sick. . . . . . Now the only means to obtain this absolution, is our confession to him.   The Priest may not and cannot absolve any but the penitent, nor can he know their penitence, but by their outward expression : it is GOD's prerogative to know the thoughts of the heart, the priest's eye cannot pierce so far, he only reads the sorrows of our hearts by our outward confession, without the which we cannot receive, nor he give, the benefit of absolution."[1]   He here evidently implies a special grace in this particular form.

Comber, in his "Companion to the Temple," A.D. 1685, hands on the tradition as to the distinction between the three forms, attributing to the private form a personal assurance not attached to the others. " The judgment," he says, " of the Church of England concerning absolution may best be gathered from the Liturgy, in which are three forms of absolving set down.   The

---

[1] Sermon on the " Confession of Sins and the power of Absolution," pp. 16, 19.

first, *declaratory*," (here he is speaking of the general
absolution at Matins and Evensong) "which is a solemn
promulgation of pardon by a commissionated person,
repeated every day when the whole congregation confess their sins, wherein they are assured of forgiveness,
if they repent and believe, so that to those who truly
repent, it is present remission, to those who do not, it
is a monitor that they may repent . . . . . and this
being pronounced to all the people, every one is to
take his portion . . . . . The second is *petitionary*, in
the Communion Service, where the minister lays down
the promise, and on that ground, by virtue of his own
office, begs of GOD to make that promise good . . . . .
The third is *judiciary*, in the Office for the Sick, wherein
the priest having declared there is pardon, and prayed
for the sick person, doth by GOD's authority, and as
His substitute, declare him (whom he believes truly
penitent) loosed from the guilt of his sins by CHRIST's
merits."[1] Yet Comber's words mark a state of transition, a token of the approaching decline of faith, when
sacramental grace was being less appreciated; for his
view of private absolution, though held to be judicial,
and so fuller of assurance to the penitent, is yet explained to be only the declaration of the fact of forgiveness, not an instrumental cause.

It is instructive to observe how later ritualists de-
viate from this traditionary interpretation, which during the first century following the Reformation ruled
the teaching of our Church. We have already seen the
difference, as to the use of Confession, between the last

[1] Oxford edition, vol. i. p. 99.

and the preceding century. It is but consistent with this change of practice, that the importance previously attached to special absolution should be less felt. The disuse of private Confession would necessarily involve the disparagement of private Absolution. But the instinct of a Church life tends so strongly to rest on the ministry of Absolution, that the result of depreciating the private, was to exalt the public, form. What was lost in the disuse of the one, was sought in the other still in constant use. What had been regarded as the peculiar prerogative of the now neglected form in the Visitation of the Sick, was transferred to those in the daily prayer and Communion Office.

Dr. Nicholls, who died in 1712, was the first to deny the characteristic grace previously thought to be connected with special Absolution. Speaking of the form in the Visitation of the Sick, he says; "It is not absolutely necessary for the forgiveness of sins," which is true, but he proceeds to add, "it is not judicial and authoritative."[1]

Wheatley, whose Commentary was published in 1720, was the first to raise the general public Absolution above the private form, attributing to the former a full release from sin, and, though with evident misgiving, reducing the latter to a mere relaxation of Church censures. "It looks," he says, "as if the Church did only intend the remission of Ecclesiastical censures and bonds;" and again; "It is only designed to remit to the Penitent the censures that may be due from the Church to his sins." But the daily general absolution he explains to be, "an actual conveyance of pardon at

[1] Nicholl's Commentary on the Book of Common Prayer. In loc.

the very instant of pronouncing it to all that come within the terms proposed."[1]

Mr. Warner, in his Commentary published in 1754, adopts without any variation Wheatley's explanation of private absolution.[2]

Mr. Shepperd, though differing from Wheatley, yet considers this form of Absolution to be the "mere declaration of the terms of pardon to a repentant sinner."[3]

Lastly, Bishop Mant quotes Dean Comber and Archbishop Secker, as authorities to determine the question, leaving it to the reader to select which of the two he prefers, while Secker himself is doubtful whether to follow Wheatley's or Shepperd's interpretation, though inclining to the former. His words referring to special Absolution, are as follows; "All writers on the subject have agreed, that this Absolution was intended, which indeed is most probable, only to set persons free from any Ecclesiastical censures which they might have incurred; an indulgence granted in every age of the Church to such as were dangerously ill, on their humble request, but which is no more intended to make a change in their eternal state, than a pardon from the king is; or if it means also to declare them restored to the favour of GOD, means it only on supposition of a sincere and thorough repentance." What authority there is for saying "all writers on the subject have agreed" on this interpretation, may be judged from what has been stated in these pages. Secker closes his remarks by saying; "As this (the form of Absolution

---

[1] Wheatley's Commentary, in loc.

[2] Warner's Illustrations of the Book of Common Prayer.

[3] Shepperd's Elucidations of the Book of Common Prayer.

in the Visitation of the Sick) is but seldom requested, and consequently the Absolution seldom pronounced over any one, so whenever it is, it may and ought to be accompanied with such explanations as will prevent any wrong constructions."[1]

It can be no wonder if this Absolution is "seldom requested," if understood to be no more than "a pardon from the king," or as a release from Ecclesiastical censures, when such censures have ceased to be imposed. But surely the very acknowledgment, that what the Church of all ages and many reformed communities separate from her, have deemed to be a vital ordinance of the Gospel, is sunk so low, as to be "seldom requested, and seldom pronounced over any one," would seem enough to prove that some grave error has of late years entered into the teaching, not of our Church, for this cannot change with changing times, or the fluctuations of belief or knowledge among her children, but of those who are of note and authority among her divines, and that a return to the earlier, and therefore truer, traditions of our Reformation has become urgently necessary.

NOTE.

THE INDICATIVE FORM OF ABSOLUTION.

The Form of Absolution used in the Church for 1200 years was simply precatory. This custom still prevails in the East, where the following form of prayer is in use at the present day in the exercise of this ministry:—

"GOD, Who by Nathan the prophet pardoned David on confession of his sins, and Peter for his denial when he wept bitterly, and the

---

[1] Mant's Book of Common Prayer, in loc.

harlot who shed tears at His feet, and the prodigal, may the same GOD, by me a sinner, pardon thee for all thy sins in this world, and in that which is to come, and place thee uncondemned before His awful judgment seat, and, having no more even one care for the offence thou hast confessed, go in peace."[1]

It has been already observed, that the prayer now following the Absolution in our Office of the Visitation of the Sick, with the variations noted, was the instrument of conveying the promised grace, employed from the earliest times throughout the West.

Afterwards the custom grew of adding to this deprecatory prayer the form, "Absolvo te." The object of this addition was apparently to express the positive effect of the ordinance, as an authoritative declaration to assure the penitent, that he was in truth justified according to the full meaning of the petition.[2]

In course of time the two forms were combined, and used together, acting and re-acting on each other, the prayer imploring the desired

---

[1] Offices of the Eastern Church. Dr. Littledale's Translations.

[2] Morinus supposes that the indicative form arose from the theory, according to which it was believed, that remission of sins followed instantly upon Confession made in a state of contrition, the Absolution in such case being simply an authoritative or judicial declaration of what GOD had done; and that, the old tradition of forgiveness depending on the prayer of the Priest still continuing to hold its ground, the precatory form was still retained; the two thus coalescing, as expressions of two schools of opinion, or two different views of the Divine operation.

It should be added that the imposition of hands which accompanied the act of Absolution was also considered to be an outward expression and seal of prayer. "Quid est aliud manus impositio, nisi oratio super hominem?" says S. Augustine, (lib. 3, de baptismo contra Donatistas, c. 16.) And again, S. Leo, Epis. 92, "manus impositionem et orationem velut unum et idem permutat, eo quod orationi manus impositio sit semper conjuncta. . . . . . . Illi (i.e., sacerdoti) manum imponere et orare idem sunt," (lib. viii., c. viii., sec. vii.) Morinus observes that both were retained,—" priorem (the precatory form) ut oratione sacerdotis auxilium a Deo impetraretur poenitenti, ut sufficienter ad absolutionem suscipiendam contereretur; posteriorem, ut jam contritus vere posset a sacerdote absolvi, et quod erat in coelo solutum, in terra quoque solveretur."

P

grace, the declaration sealing its assured possession. The opinion then grew, that the virtue of the ordinance depended on this authoritative declaration. This arose probably from the increasing prevalence of the theory, which regarded the relation of the Priest and penitent under the forensic idea; the Priest being supposed to be a judge according to the analogy of the forms of a court of law. In this view Absolution was understood to be the absolute sentence of the Priest, to be reversed only by an extraordinary interposition of superior power, and the indicative form would consequently be viewed as its essence.

The Council of Trent sealed the use of this indicative form, as the only legitimate expression of the absolving power, on the ground of its strictly judicial character. It was ruled that the words, "Ego te absolvo, &c." constitute the essence of the form of Absolution, and that prayers are not necessary to the administration of the sacrament, though suitably added as its accompaniment.[1]

It is difficult to reconcile this decree of the Council with the earlier Roman theory, which clearly taught, that the absolving power depended on the force of the sacerdotal prayer, accompanied as it ordinarily was with the imposition of hands, as the sign marking its personal application. Thus S. Leo uses the term, "supplicatio," as synonymous with "absolutio," and concludes from S. James that sins are remitted through sacramental prayer.[2] Again, in his letter, already quoted, to the

---

[1] " Docet praeterea Sancta Synodus sacramenti Poenitentiae formam, in qua praecipue ipsius vis sita est, in illis ministri verbis positam esse; Ego te absolvo, &c., quibus quidem de Ecclesiae sanctae more preces quaedam laudabiliter adjunguntur; ad ipsius tamen formae essentiam nequaquam spectant, neque ad ipsius sacramenti administrationem sunt necessariae." Sess. xv., xiv., cap. iii.

[2] Morinus says of S. Leo; "Dicit Deum praesidia suae bonitatis ordinasse, 'ut indulgentia Dei nisi supplicationibus sacerdotum nequeat obtineri.'" (Epist. 91, ad Theodorum.) Again he quotes S. Leo: "Multum utile et necessarium est, ut peccatorum reatus ante ultimum diem sacerdotali supplicatione solvatur." And again, "Oratione igitur sacramentali peccata remittuntur." The original passage of the letter alluded to in the text as previously quoted, is as follows: "Sufficit illa confessio quae primum Deo offertur, tunc etiam sacerdoti qui pro delictis poenitentium precator accedit." Lib. viii., cap. xii., sec. 11.

Morinus concludes after arguing the question; "Oratione igitur sacramentali peccata remittuntur et principaliter." Lib. viii., cap. xix., p. xxi.

Bishops of Campania, he speaks of the Priest being appointed to intercede with GOD on behalf of the penitent.

It is, however, carefully to be noted, that the virtue of the sacramental
ordinance is independent of the precise form used in its administration,
and therefore the definition of the Western Council implies no real variance between it, and either the present Eastern use, or its own earlier
practice. Our LORD was wont, in His miracles of healing, and in bestowing the grace of remission of sins, to use indifferently the indicative,
the declaratory, or precatory form. Thus, e.g., in absolving the paralytic,
He uses the declaratory form, "Son, be of good cheer, thy sins be forgiven thee ;"[1] in the case of the leper, the healing virtue is conveyed in
the indicative form, "I will, be thou clean ;"[2] while in raising Lazarus
from the dead He employed prayer; "And JESUS lifted up His eyes
and said, FATHER, I thank Thee that Thou hast heard Me."[3] The form
therefore is evidently unessential. The power employed by our LORD
was in each case the same. And this applies equally to the acts of His
Ministers. In every case the grace flows from our LORD through
their agency, whether they employ their intercessions in obtaining it,
and so use the precatory form; or seal it as His gift by an authoritative declaration, and so use the declaratory form; or attest its conveyance while employing the means which He has promised to bless,
and so employ the indicative form.

The intimate connexion between Baptism and Absolution has already
been noticed, the one being the initiatory sacrament in bestowing the
graces of the Covenant, the other the means of restoring grace, when
lost, or renewing it, when decayed. And it is remarkable that a similar
variety has obtained in the form of administration in the one case, as in
the other. The form of administering Baptism was originally precatory, and this usage still obtains in the East, while the Western use
has become indicative. There is no greater claim implied in the "Ego
absolvo te," than in the "Ego baptizo te." In both cases alike the
idea involved is not the power of bestowing grace, but only the exercise
of the instrumental agency through which it is imparted by GOD according to the terms of the Covenant. The "absolvo te," according to
Morinus, means, "impendo tibi sacramentum absolutionis."

Morinus, moreover, further states his opinion, grounded on the say-
ings of the Fathers, that the real force of the indicative form depends
on the invocation of the Name of the Blessed Trinity, Which accompanies

[1] S. Matt. ix. 2.　　　[2] S. Luke v. 15.　　　[3] S. John xi. 41.

it, and that therefore it is still essentially precatory. He is speaking
specially of Baptism, but applies the same principle to Absolution.
"Antiqui Patres, et Græci et Latini, baptismi effectum invocationi
Sanctæ Trinitatis semper attribuunt, sacerdotemque aiunt per precem
et invocationem S. Trinitatis baptizare, nec aliter de ea formula lo-
quuntur quam velut deprecativa." Lib. viii. 16, § 18.

It has been already shown that our form of administering Absolution,
following with certain minor variations the old Latin use, includes both
special prayer and also the indicative application. First the Priest
prays, "of His great mercy forgive thee thine offences," and then adds,
" I absolve thee," &c.

CHAPTER XVII.

IT is not the object of this treatise to offer directions for the use of Confession; to guide either the confessor, or the penitent. All that has been attempted is the tracing the progress of opinion on the various questions involved in Confession, together with the changes in its practice, and to show how the Church of England has been guided in forming her own view, and determining the rule to be followed within her Communion. Counsels and suggestions properly belonging to pastoral theology, have not been here intended. That sacramental Confession has a legitimate place in the practical system of the Church of England,—that it has assumed among us a distinctive form, bearing a close affinity to the systems prevailing in other branches of the Catholic Church, and yet preserving a character of its own, suited to our habits of thought and the great principles for which amid the controversies of these latter days we contend,—that the English view is grounded on the highest authorities, sustained by both scriptural and patristic testimony,—that to restore it from its state of abeyance, is to be loyally faithful to the truest traditions of the English Reformation equally as to the far higher judgment of the undivided Church, —these important positions the author trusts have been established with sufficient proof.

The question which has been argued has a momentous bearing beyond its own immediate purpose, as to the character of the Church of England herself. It is often urged that our system is cramped, unelastic, incapable of adapting itself to changing circumstances and varied phases of spiritual life;—that our Church is a stunted growth, its progress hopelessly checked, itself living on mere barren theories of the past, and having no powers of onward movement, but rather ever tending to decay without the possibility of putting forth fresh germinal shoots, which are the only true signs of inherent vitality.

Now if the foregoing argument be sound and conclusive, we have a decisive instance in contradiction of such a charge, at least in respect to the intention of our Reformation, or rather to the indications of GOD's merciful purpose overruling its course. For the present use of Confession is manifestly a development, taking the word in its true theological sense of adaptation of original principles to a new order of circumstances. The Church of England, acting freely, and asserting a power of judgment on the questions at issue,—practical questions legitimately left by Catholic use to the judgment of the separate Churches—when it was clearly open to her to have made a different choice, deliberately and with a succession of repeated decisions, chose to abide by the later use of Confession, i.e., to accept and perpetuate a development or practical adaptation of its principles, to meet the needs of the Church's altered circumstances. A momentous issue was determined in the case, as characteristic of the English Reformation movement,—that while firmly holding to ancient traditionary truths, its purpose was to shape and mould them so as best to satisfy real spiritual needs under new phases of life.

We have exercised our discretion, where a discretion was strictly lawful. Having the history of the past and modern experience before us, we have made our choice, not fearing to change what is proved to be hurtful, notwithstanding its antiquity, nor scrupling to adopt and apply what is shown to be good and serviceable, although bearing on it the stamp of novelty. Such at least was the principle acted upon in the case we have been considering. And it is an instance of such an eventful kind, as to mark a purpose, a mind, intended we can hardly doubt to be applied more widely, however the Church of England's course of action has been marred and hampered by the force of adverse circumstances, or from failure within itself, through division, or misapprehension, or lack of faith, incapacitating her for a living earnest correspondence with the movements of the Spirit of GOD in His gracious purposes towards us, and through us to Christianity, and to the world.

Although, as already observed, the design of this treatise does not embrace practical directions for the use of Confession, there are yet certain principles involved in the general consideration of the subject, to which it seems needful, however briefly, to advert. It has been shown that Confession is a sacramental ordinance, and from this it necessarily follows, that special care should be observed in its administration. If the Divine cha-

racter of the act be duly borne in mind, it would naturally regulate the outward forms of the ordinance, as
well as the inward feelings of those engaged in it.
That the Priest should wear the habit of his order;
that he should sit as one invested with authority to
judge of the state of another's soul; that he should use
the solemn form of Absolution appointed by the Church,
as one commissioned in the Name of GOD to apply the
Divine Promise,—that thus in this, as in other high
functions of his office, the sacerdotal character should be
preserved, would follow from the principles involved in
it.   On the other hand, it would likewise follow, that
the penitent should kneel, not indeed as confessing to
the Priest, but to GOD before him; that he should
make his confession, as one realizing the awful issues
of the last sentence in the presence of the Almighty
Judge, and receive as from GOD what His minister is
commissioned in His Name to impart.   Such precau-
tions for the formal exercise of such a transaction are
important to note, if it were only in order to prevent
the lapsing of so solemn an act into mere ordinary
familiarity of intercourse.   Still more vitally important
do they appear, if it be considered how much the
mind is influenced by outward circumstance, and how
liable to forget the very meaning and purport, and
especially the sacramental virtue, of the act, if divested
of what is calculated to represent it to the senses as a
Divinely ordained ministration.

At the same time, while it is of importance ordinarily to preserve the outward ritual of this ministry,
it would be unreal, not to regard a contrite expression
of sin acknowledged in the least formal way, the out-

gushing of a burdened heart under any, the simplest, circumstances, as a true and acceptable confession. The real utterance of the heart's secret guilt is the essence of the act; the circumstances under which it is made but the accidents. The outward mode may vary, as in extreme sickness, or sudden pressure, or other peculiarities of the individual case; the essential act may be the same. A discretion and freedom of use must be left, to be determined by the special circumstances, and secret guidings of the Spirit. There is an instinct which He inspires, to which such questions may be trustfully committed, while yet His guidance has led His Church to clothe her ministries with whatever of outward form most conduces to express their inner spiritual efficacy.

Again, putting aside the question of confession of deadly or more grievous sin hindering Communion, of which sufficient has been said, and confining our attention to the confession of lesser sins made with a view rather to the increase of grace and advancement of spiritual life, it seems important to remark, that it is as possible to over estimate the benefit of Confession in such cases, as it is to undervalue it. The· Church could not have left it an open question, if it were certainly and to all persons such a means of grace, that it could not be rightly omitted. Yet the rule of our first Prayer Book is clear, that none should judge or disparage another, whether he use Confession, or not, in such cases.[1] This order is grounded on the belief, that although

[1] See the Exhortation in the Communion Office of the 1st Book of Edward VI., already quoted in an early chapter.

Confession is a means of grace which may be greatly blessed in the discipline and advancement of the spiritual life, yet not in such a sense that the same grace may not be supplied through other means by which GOD may be equally pleased to work His perfect work. If the primitive Church had deemed such a use of the ordinance necessary and in all cases preferable for this end, it would unquestionably have appointed it for all alike. It did not do so, and our Church has followed this high example.

That Confession and spiritual guidance may be very influential in the advancement of the inner life, can hardly be questioned by any one who has considered the histories of many whose praise is in all the Churches of the Saints. But experience also proves, that it is not necessarily so; that there are limitations arising from circumstance and character which, according to a wise discretion, would modify or restrain its use.[1]

[1] This opinion is expressed in deference to what the author believes to be the judgment of the Church in this land, to which our allegiance is rightfully due, and also in the conviction that such judgment is sustained by a wise and sober experience.

It has been already remarked, that the Church of Rome does not consider the confession of venial sins to be a necessary means of advancing the spiritual life. The Council of Trent varies from the view here expressed only in making no limitation or condition to its assertion that such Confession is "right and profitable;" "Venialia, quibus a gratiâ Dei non excludimur, et in quæ frequentius labimur, quamquam recte et utiliter, citraque omnem præsumptionem in confessione dicantur, quod piorum hominum usus demonstrat, taceri tamen citra culpam, multisque aliis remediis expiari possunt." (Sess. xiv. cap. v.) It should be remarked moreover, that a great difference exists between our own and the Roman use of Confession, arising from the artificial classifications of sin by which in the Roman system life is ruled. The Canonists make deadly sins by

Moreover, it should be borne in mind that the benefit of Confession depends on moral causes co-operating with it, on the reality and depth of faith, on true contrition and humility of heart, on earnest care in the previous preparation, as well as the after diligence to sustain the soul's higher purposes. The reception of grace and its proportionate amount bear a relation to the meetness and capacity of the soul. The effect of the administration must therefore always be considered in connection with these incidental circumstances of needful dispositions, or personal qualities. The case of those who use Confession can be rightly judged only with this larger estimate of their whole state and tendencies of life.

Similar considerations determine the question of frequency in its use. Confession may very profitably be used from time to time more or less frequently for an indefinite period, or for special reasons during a definite period, or simply on occasions according to circumstances. No rule, generally applicable, can be laid down, each separate case having its own specialty.

On the other hand the view to be taken of such as

a formal rule, even irrespective of the ordinary catalogue of deadly sins. A breach of the Church's law is counted deadly. A need of Confession is thus established where yet there is no grievous sin on the conscience in its relation to the Divine law. It may be simply venial in itself, made deadly only by the Church's rule. Sin against the Church's system is viewed as sin against GOD. In our case on the contrary, sin is viewed in itself and its proportions only according to its aspect in the judgment of GOD, and its own real bearings on the inner life. A breach of the Church's law would of course in our case be an aggravated fault, because of its disobedience to a sacred authority, but its character would not otherwise be altered. Confession therefore in our case necessarily becomes more subjective..

do not use Confession, while living in communion with
the life of the Church, must depend on the causes
which determine their course in this matter.   If their
not using Confession, while yet conscious of its blessing,
and moved towards it, arises from an unwillingness to
part from sin, or lack of humility or earnestness of
desire, there must be a serious moral wrong in their
condition, quite independent of the question of the
advisableness or profit of this ministry.   If, however,
the cause lie in the conscientious conviction of the unfitness of Confession for their particular state, or the
honest scrupulous fear of disturbing the soul's rest in
GOD, or any single-hearted motive, or from consideration for others to whom obedience and respect are justly
due, persons thus influenced may assuredly receive
through the faithful use of the general ministries of the
Church that fulness of grace which they earnestly and
constantly seek.   The soul is free in such cases, neither
is the grace of GOD restrained.   Varieties of mind and
circumstance, and therefore of spiritual need, are manifold, and consequently there must be varieties of treat-
ment.   The elasticity of a practical system, its capa-
bility of adjustment to the idiosyncrasies of our complex
inner nature, is one necessary mark of its Divine
character, essential to the idea of Catholicity.   Sacramental Confession, as a means of aiding and advancing
the spiritual life of the faithful, was adopted in the later
ages of the Church; and it must remain, as it began,
one means of grace among others, which the Church
developes out of its treasures, to be used, or not, according to the dictates of the conscience, and the laws
of spiritual expedience.

It is often urged against the revival of this ministry, that it is, to say the least, inexpedient and unsafe, in consequence of the want of experience in the great majority of our Priesthood. That an experienced and cautious judgment is needed to decide aright, to whom and to what extent Confession is,to be recommended, as well as in applying it to the soul's necessities, is evident. But it is also clear, that the defect complained of only presents a temporary difficulty; and if the revived use of Confession be in itself advisable, it is surely better that the inconvenience be borne and the risk run, which is but for a season, rather than forego the certain benefit, which will be lasting. Moreover, if the Church enjoin her Priesthood to be ready to receive Confession, and in certain cases even to urge it, and the people are desirous of seeking it according to her express appointments, it is not a question of preference, but of duty and of principle. The call is too clear, and the issue too important, that we should shrink from some possible danger, in order to obtain so great a good, and to be faithful to the plain injunctions of the Church. And it is surely a case for trust, that He Who has awakened the desire for the restoration of so clearly ordained a ministry in His Church, will enable His ministers, if they diligently seek to prepare themselves, to fulfil it with His blessing; will supply their defects, and will not suffer His people to lose the benefit they seek, through any lack or imperfections of service. There is special grace promised to the Priesthood for the fulfilment of their office, to aid their efforts in preparing themselves for its due discharge, to guide them on the special occasions of its exercise, and to work through them (themselves, it may be, wholly unconscious of what is secretly passing through their instrumentality) what He wills for His own glory to impart to His elect.

That the habit of receiving confessions, would be an incalculable advantage to the parish priest, re-acting on himself in the deepening of his own life, ensuring a truer, more intimate and more affectionate knowledge of the souls of his people, and of the working of the grace of GOD in them, infusing greater reality and power into his teaching, and generally making his cure of souls a more personal and individualising, and therefore a more real and profitable, work,—can hardly be questioned. Nor can it fail to be a matter of anxiety and regret, that so much of pastoral intercourse among us is simply external, confined merely to kindly offices of charity, and periodical instructions sown broadcast, without the means of knowing, at least comparatively speaking, the special needs or aims of those who hear them.

For Priests themselves who may be called on, perhaps suddenly and unexpectedly, to discharge this most critical function of their office, there cannot but be continual anxious searchings of heart, only finding repose, through the boundless and tender mercies of GOD, in earnest prayer, that He may avert any evil which might, through their fault, light upon those whom He purposed to bless. The consciousness of such unfitness will lead every true heart to desire unceasingly before GOD, that our Church fail not to cherish whatever may tend the better to furnish and prepare her Priesthood, so as to meet a need which manifestly is being felt among us more and more, and which as certainly she is bound, as a main part of her solemn charge from GOD, to supply; and that her clergy may of themselves be stirred to the diligent study of spiritual theology, and more especially of the Word of GOD in its personal application to the workings of their own inmost life, that each may, having kept well his own vineyard, learn the better to be the keeper of another's. Their support and encouragement is to be found in the glory, wherewith they are girt about, as commissioned ministers of the Most High GOD, endued for this special end by His Spirit, Which from our LORD's own lips was breathed first upon the Apostles, the pulsations of Whose creative and inspiring Breath still thrill through each one, on whom the Shadow of His Hand, sealing them in their ministry, has rested. For with the momentous charge there is surely grace given, ever sufficient to aid and co-operate with their own efforts, even as it prevented their earliest thoughts of self-devotion. GOD ever gives strength according to the needs of His faithful ones, and special strength and guidance for the special ends to which He calls and sends forth individual members of the mystical Body of His SON; how much more will He fulfil this promise, when it concerns not only the individual possessors of His gifts, but others, even all to whom they are sent, and His own glory above all in the building up of His Church to be the recompense of His Passion, the price of His own Blood. That our Church, in common with the whole Catholic Communion, has trusted to this special grace, as the ground of its hope for the fulfilment of the ministry committed to it, is not to be questioned. It breathes throughout the forms in which the gift of holy Orders is conveyed. In this assurance alone could one " compassed about with infir-

mity," and "of like passions with" his brethren, dare to
step within the sanctuary, and bear the weight of the
sins of others, ever responsible before GOD, not only for
the saving of his own soul, but of theirs also.

Dean Comber's encouraging words should be im-
printed on the heart of the Priest. "Let the pastor
firmly believe, that so much of the HOLY GHOST and
His gifts are now (when the words are said at the laying on of hands, 'Receive the HOLY GHOST,' &c.) imparted to him, as are necessary for the discharge of the
office to which the Spirit hath called him, so much as
will qualify him to judge so rightly concerning remitting and retaining sins, that GOD may ratify his sentence in heaven, forgiving those he declares penitent,
and condemning such as he pronounces impenitent;
and this will make him careful in his managing of
sinners, and bring a great and deserved veneration upon
all his solemn acts of ecclesiastical discipline, as well as
an incredible benefit to his people's souls."[1]

Hooker, while solemnly reminding us of the momentous charge committed, speaks with his wonted richness
of the preternatural powers given to sustain it. "Besides that the power and authority delivered with those
words is itself χάρισμα, a gracious donation which the
SPIRIT of GOD doth bestow, we may most assuredly
persuade ourselves that the hand which imposeth on us
the function of our ministry doth under the same form
of words so tie itself thereunto, that he which receiveth
the burden is thereby for ever warranted to have the
SPIRIT with him and in him for his assistance, aid,
countenance, and support, in whatsoever he faithfully

[1] On the Office for making Priests, p. 363. Companion to the Temple.

doth to discharge duty. Knowing therefore that when we take ordination we also receive the presence of the HOLY GHOST, partly to guide, direct, and strengthen us in all our ways, and partly to assume unto itself for the more authority those actions that appertain to our place and calling, can our ears admit such a speech uttered in the reverend performance of that solemnity, or can we at any time renew the memory and enter into serious cogitations thereof, but with much admiration and joy? . . . . . We have for the least and meanest duties performed by virtue of ministerial power, that to dignify, grace and authorize them, which no other offices on earth can challenge. Whether we preach, pray, baptize, communicate, condemn, give absolution, or whatsoever, as disposers of GOD's mysteries, our ends, judgments, acts and deeds, are not ours, but the HOLY GHOST's."[1]

[1] Eccl. Pol., Lib. v. c. lxxvii. 8.

JOSEPH MASTERS AND SON, PRINTERS, ALDERSGATE STREET, LONDON.

www.ingramcontent.com/pod-product-compliance
Lightning Source LLC
Chambersburg PA
CBHW020859020726
47497CB00005B/1481

* 9 7 8 3 3 3 7 2 6 2 0 2 0 *